About the Chesapeake Bay Foundation

The Chesapeake Bay Foundation (CBF) is the largest nonprofit conservation organization working to save the bay. Founded in 1967, CBF is supported by contributions from philanthropic foundations, corporations, and 80,000 members nationwide. CBF has a staff of 120 and hundreds of active volunteers. With headquarters and a state office in Annapolis, Maryland, the foundation also has state offices in Harrisburg, Pennsylvania, and Richmond and Norfolk, Virginia.

The three major programs of the Chesapeake Bay Foundation are Environmental Education, Environmental Defense, and Land Management.

Each year, the Environmental Education Program takes over 33,000 students and teachers from the bay watershed out on the water in canoes, workboats, and historic skipjacks that serve as floating classrooms. These experiences begin at any one of the seventeen education centers around the bay—in Pennsylvania, Maryland, Virginia, and Washington, D.C.

The lawyers and scientists of the Environmental Defense Program have made restoration of the bay their careers by defending the bay in public forums, in the legislatures, and in the courts. They advise decision makers and offer specific recommendations to protect water quality. CBF does not hesitate to take direct legal action to bring major polluters into compliance with the law.

Protection of wildlife habitat, forests, and agricultural lands in the watershed is the goal of the Foundation's Lands Program. Staff conservationists also advance effective land-use planning and growth management strategies to help stem the tide of pollution to the bay from shoreline and inland sources. These land-use initiatives are conservation models both in the region and nationwide.

About Island Press

Island Press, a nonprofit organization, publishes, markets, and distributes the most advanced thinking on the conservation of our natural resources—books about soil, land, water, forests, wildlife, and hazardous and toxic wastes. These books are practical tools used by public officials, business and industry leaders, natural resource managers, and concerned citizens working to solve both local and global resource problems.

Founded in 1978, Island Press reorganized in 1984 to meet the increasing demand for substantive books on all resource-related issues. Island Press publishes and distributes under its own imprint and offers these services to other nonprofit organizations.

Support for Island Press is provided by Apple Computer, Inc., Mary Reynolds Babcock Foundation, Geraldine R. Dodge Foundation, The Energy Foundation, The Charles Engelhard Foundation, The Ford Foundation, Glen Eagles Foundation, The George Gund Foundation, William and Flora Hewlett Foundation, The Joyce Foundation, The John D. and Catherine T. MacArthur Foundation, The Andrew W. Mellon Foundation, The Joyce Mertz-Gilmore Foundation, The New-Land Foundation, the J. N. Pew, Jr. Charitable Trust, Alida Rockefeller, The Rockefeller Brothers Fund, The Florence and John Schumann Foundation, The Tides Foundation, and individual donors.

TURNING
THE TIDE

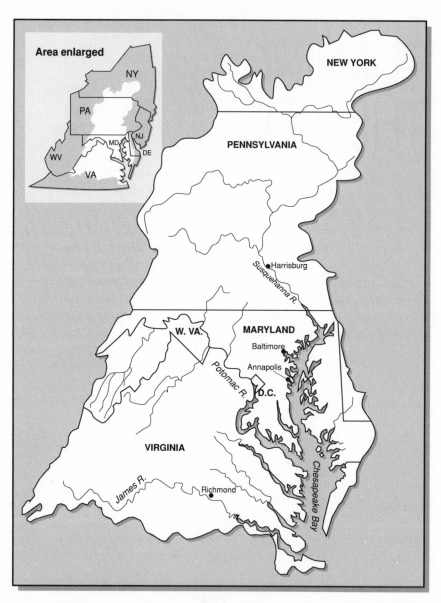

THE CHESAPEAKE BAY WATERSHED. [Adapted from EPA, *Chesapeake Bay: A Profile of Environmental Change*]

TURNING THE TIDE

Saving the Chesapeake Bay

TOM HORTON

AND WILLIAM M. EICHBAUM

CHESAPEAKE BAY FOUNDATION

ISLAND PRESS

Washington, D.C. □ *Covelo, California*

Figures on the following pages created by Joseph Hutchinson: iv, 5, 13, 16, 18, 32, 63, 68, 100, 102, 113, 115, 143, 144, 150, 151, 170, 172, 173, 182, 287.

Library of Congress Cataloging-in-Publication Data

Horton, Tom, 1945–
     Turning the tide : saving the Chesapeake Bay / by Tom Horton and
William M. Eichbaum.
          p.   cm.
     Includes bibliographical references and index.
     ISBN 1-55963-101-5 (alk. paper) — ISBN 1-55963-100-7
(pbk. : alk. paper)
     1. Water quality management—Government policy—Chesapeake Bay
Watershed (Md. and Va.)   2. Land use—Government policy—Chesapeake
Bay Watershed (Md. and Va.)   3. Land use—Environmental aspects—
Chesapeake Bay Watershed (Md. and Va.)   4. Estuarine area
conservation—Chesapeake Bay Watershed (Md. and Va.)   I. Eichbaum,
William M.   II. Title.
HC107.A123H67   1991
363.73'94'0916347—dc20   91-8586
                                                                   CIP

Printed on recycled, acid-free paper

Manufactured in the United States of America

10   9   8   7   6   5   4   3

To the 80,000 members of the Chesapeake Bay Foundation, whose support and dedication make possible our work to save the bay

Funded by
The Abell Foundation
Baltimore, Maryland

Contents

List of Figures

Foreword

In 1967 a handful of people identified the early signs of a deteriorating Chesapeake Bay that, if left unchecked, could destroy it. This group founded the Chesapeake Bay Foundation (CBF) with a single mission—to save the bay. There was a great deal worth saving. The Chesapeake Bay produced one-quarter of the nation's oysters, one-half of all hard crabs, and a staggering 95 percent of all soft crabs consumed in the United States. In addition, nine out of every ten striped bass caught from North Carolina to Maine were born in the Chesapeake Bay.

Ironically, the bay's tenacious productivity in the face of increasing pollution left the majority of residents complacent. The small group of CBF members kept pushing, however. Today, CBF claims over 80,000 individual and family members. These members still are determined to save the bay, an even more pressing agenda than when CBF was founded. The bay is now a far different place than in 1967. Overfished and stripped of much of its valuable habitat, its once-legendary bounty is now just that, legendary. The population of oysters is so scarce (only 1 percent of what existed 100 years ago) that CBF has determined that harvesting them must stop in order to give the species a chance to rebuild.

In short, as the human population has increased, the health of the bay has declined, all during a time of unprecedented national attention to environmental protection and an intense regional effort geared specifically to save the bay.

What is the current state of the bay? Is it getting better or worse? What are the primary sources of pollution? Why don't government agencies stop the pollution?

To answer these questions, and many more, CBF undertook a task that no individual or institution has ever attempted—a comprehensive assessment of the bay's condition, including recommendations to improve it. This was no easy task, for CBF defines the bay as the entire watershed—from the headwaters of the Susquehanna River in New York State, through Pennsylvania, most of Maryland, and a large part of Virginia, to the Atlantic Ocean—over 64,000 square miles. The watershed's total area comprises nearly one-sixth of the Atlantic seaboard.

Understanding how this system functions is the first order of business. Tom Horton, *Turning the Tide*'s principal author, brings to life complex scientific principles in a comprehensible and engaging style. He describes how the Chesapeake, once called the crown jewel of the world's estuaries, lost its ability to function the way nature intended. "Degraded," "abused," "polluted" all describe the current condition of the bay. But the bay is not "dead." At least not yet. For amidst the toxic waste, filled wetlands, and sediment-clogged creeks, there lies a body of water fighting for survival.

And live it will if we give it half a chance. A decade of intense private and public effort to save the bay has averted immediate disaster. But to really *turn the tide*, we will have to make fundamental changes in the way we conduct our lives. Simply "treating" our wastes before discharging them to the air and water, for example, will not be enough. We must alter the processes—both individually and collectively—to reduce the amount of pollution we create in the first place. *Turning the Tide* presents detailed recommendations on how to achieve such reductions, to stop the loss of valuable habitat, to improve fisheries management—in short, how to save the bay.

As any student of environmental protection knows, what works to protect the Chesapeake will help the Great Lakes, San Francisco Bay, or any other body of water. *Turning the Tide* will be valuable to people everywhere who want a better understanding of how nature works and how modern society works against her.

In fact, the Chesapeake Bay is a superb model of the planet as a whole. Not only does the bay encompass a large and diverse geographic region from which every possible environmental abuse is manifest, but it is a finite system in which most pollutants accumulate rather than simply pass on to a larger receiving body.

The Chesapeake Bay is a microcosm of the planet, and our efforts to save it constitute a living experiment for the management and protection of the earth as a whole. Valuable scientific and political experience can be gained as we grapple with some of the more subtle forms of pollution—those that flow not from an easily identifiable source, such as an industrial discharge pipe, but rather from all the little things that each of us does on a day-to-day basis: the toxics in car exhaust, the sediment released from a construction site, the manure that runs off a farm, the nontidal wetland filled to build a new house, the trees cut down for road construction. Multiply these routine impacts by the millions of people who live here (to say nothing of projected growth) and the tremendous stress on the system becomes apparent.

Achieving political solutions, however, is extraordinarily difficult. The "guilty party" is not always a faceless industrial giant, but is also each of us. Laws to abate such pollution, which may result in individual and community sacrifice, are extremely controversial and not easily accepted by society at large.

Turning the Tide reminds us that progress on the environmental front must not be measured solely by the number of new programs in place or the amount of funds appropriated. We must look to the very resources we are trying to protect—the bays, rivers, and the oceans; the forests and wetlands; the atmosphere we breathe—and measure improvement or decline. *Turning the Tide* expresses concern, even anger, over the bay's current condition. But there are signs that we may have seen the worst. *Turning the Tide* is full of hope that we will, in fact, succeed in saving the bay.

As we go to press, however, our optimism is tempered by an all-too-predictable reaction to a faltering economy. Even though there has been general agreement that a healthy environment and a robust economy are simply two sides of the same coin—one cannot exist without the other—lines are now being drawn in the sand as adversarial feelings reemerge to replace cooperation and coalition-building. The rhetoric is heating up as environmental programs are being fought, clean water regulations are targeted by industry lawsuits, and funds dedicated for conservation projects are diverted to balance the government's books. Even where there is agreement, such as on the need for an energy policy, the emphasis is misplaced. To lessen dependence on foreign oil, for example, we are being asked to accept massive new efforts to develop nuclear power and to drill for oil and gas in environmentally sensitive areas—like the Chesapeake Bay. A policy of energy conservation has all but disappeared from the nation's political and economic agenda.

Environmentalists, however, will not give up now any more than they did when President Reagan's Secretary of the Interior, James Watt, tried to reverse thirty years of bipartisan support for the environment in the early 1980s. Rather, our resolve will be strengthened.

At the Chesapeake Bay Foundation, we are determined to achieve environmental improvements during our second twenty-five years that are as dramatic as the declines of the first twenty-five. To launch this new era, we are proud to release *Turning the Tide: Saving the Chesapeake Bay*.

—William C. Baker
President, Chesapeake Bay Foundation

Preface

An excellent health examination for a human is more than a compilation of the body's vital signs; and so must assessing the health of Chesapeake Bay extend to more than examining water quality. Just as our physical well-being is tied to the world in which we work and play and love, so is the state of the bay intimately connected to a system extending from the ocean near its mouth to lands drained by its tributary rivers as far away as New York and West Virginia, lands populated by some 15 million people. Its health is equally inseparable from the quality of the air above it and the great, invisible seepages of groundwater from beneath it. What the growing human population does to transform the land and puts in the air is as important as what it discharges directly into the water.

It is the state of a host of interconnected environments—from mountain forests chittering with the bright life of songbirds to the silent black ooze of oxygen-starved deep channels; from forest clearing for development in the Shenandoah Valley to the dredging of new yacht basins on the Eastern Shore—that collectively communicate the state of the bay.

We may date our modern efforts to "save the bay" from 1968, when Governors Mills E. Godwin of Virginia and Spiro T. Agnew of Maryland jointly proclaimed the first annual Chesapeake Bay Week. It was a combined celebration of the bay and the start of attempts to understand its problems. Representing the public's awakening environmental interest was a fledgling organization called the Chesapeake Bay Foundation, founded in 1967. Two years later came a major turning point, both regionally and nationally, with the first Earth Day in April 1970. All the nation's islands of anxiety about the environment, from the redwood trees to pesticides and declines in fish and wildlife, coalesced into the framework of the modern environmental movement. In 1976 Congress, alarmed by suggestions of a broad and worsening trend of pollution in the Chesapeake, directed a several-year study of the problems there.

The climax of these efforts came in a historic gathering in December 1983 in Fairfax, Virginia, that included the U.S. Environmental Protection Agency (EPA), the District of Columbia, and the three states (Pennsylvania, Maryland, Virginia) that represent most of the lands and waters affecting the bay. For the first time, all these jurisdictions formally conceded that the bay was in decline and human activities were causing it. And jointly they committed themselves that day to halt and reverse the damage—a task they acknowledged would take years, even decades.

In the eight years since, undeniable strides toward that commitment have been made, many of them expanding significantly on programs under way since the 1970 Earth Day celebration. Better laws and regulations, more money, and millions of hours of dedicated citizen, corporate, and government energy have been expended on the bay cleanup. No one ever expected to be finished with the job by 1991; but the effort has been going on long enough now for a major assessment of how we, and the Chesapeake, are doing.

A question first posed on Earth Day 1970, in an extraordinary issue of *Fortune* magazine wholly dedicated to the environment, is still relevant: "What we still don't know is whether a high technology society can achieve a safe, durable, and improving relationship with its environment." Indeed we still don't know. But there is no more challenging arena, nor one at any more critical juncture for resolving that question, than our ongoing quest to restore Chesapeake Bay to health.

This book presents a new and better measure of what progress we have really made since becoming alarmed in the 1970s at unprecedented, system-wide declines in the bay's fisheries, its underwater grass beds, and its oxygen levels. It also tells us whether the current state of the bay is likely to be improved or worsened as human populations continue to grow without limit across the Chesapeake region. And it attempts to define what sort of bay we want: How clean is clean? What will we call success? Will we see it anytime soon?

This is above all a report card on the bay produced by laypersons for laypersons. It is based on the latest and best science available, but it recognizes that even the best science will not by itself save the bay. This is a task that calls for political and environmental leadership, a widespread sense of stewardship, and a clear vision of just what a "saved" bay would look like. We have drawn on the considerable expertise and experience of the Chesapeake Bay Foundation in Virginia, Maryland, and Pennsylvania, on the work of many state and federal agencies charged with managing the bay, and on our own experiences in this region—experiences ranging all the way from environmental regulation to hunting. We have also interviewed people from all walks of life in the bay region—farmers, foresters, environmentalists, businessmen, and legislators. The manuscript has been reviewed as it progressed by a board of respected university and private industry scientists, as well as the foundation's own technical experts.

The book is organized into seven chapters. Chapter 1, "Rethinking the Bay," lays the groundwork for a fundamental reconsideration of the Chesapeake as a living entity, an *ecosystem*, where rivers and the sea, people and trees, oysters and agriculture, all interact to shape the quality of life on land and in the water. It explores what makes the bay more productive of life than almost any other place on earth—but also terribly subject to environmental stresses. It develops the concept of *resilience*, the natural ability of the bay's plant and animal communities to respond and counteract these stresses. This chapter is also intended for use as a basic classroom primer on the bay.

Chapters 2 ("Pollution"), 3 ("Harvests"), and 4 ("Resilience"), the heart of the book, detail what we know about the state of the bay. They build on the ecosystem concept, extending our analysis from the forested mountain slopes and creeks, downriver and downslope through the Piedmont and Coastal Plain farms and cities, to the marshes at water's edge. They follow the land as it slips away into rich, shallow-water habitats of tidal mudflats and grass beds and, farther from shore, into oyster beds and finally the deep channels. These three chapters look at the many obvious and not-so-obvious ways in which we put pollutants into the bay. They also show how sometimes the real problems involve how much life we take *out* of the water. These chapters also reexamine our standards of "progress" in saving the bay.

Chapter 5 examines the need for changes in our individual habits—from the homes we demand to the cars we drive and the energy we use. This chapter also confronts perhaps the ultimate issue facing the bay: the question of limits to population.

Chapter 6 presents several case studies designed to dig deeper into the key issues raised in Chapter 1. For instance: If our biggest success story to date, on the Potomac River near Washington, is any example, can the bay, looking at life in the D.C. region, survive many more such successes? And how do our pollution control strategies translate from the optimism of the "big picture" to the farmer or county planner who is trying to make them work in the field?

Chapter 7, "Recommendations," presents a series of goals and recommendations for bay restoration. It uses a tough litmus test for each strategy: Can it work well enough so that even as millions more people move into the region, environmental damage is reduced?

While this book is principally a report card on the state of Chesapeake Bay, we are not alone. Nearly two-thirds of the nation's population now lives in the narrow margins of the continent near the coastlines (Atlantic, Pacific, Gulf of Mexico, and Great Lakes), a trend that promises only to increase. Worldwide, half the people on earth live on about 5 percent of the planet's surface; and much of that 5 percent is near the coasts.

The environmental struggles of the Chesapeake region are being joined from Puget Sound in Washington to Galveston Bay in Texas; from Pamlico Sound in North Carolina to Casco Bay in Maine. Moreover, environmental declines similar to the Chesapeake's are now reported in Australia, Mexico, Europe, South America, and Japan—and no doubt exist, undocumented as yet, in many other parts of the world.

While the Chesapeake is not the complete model for every problem of every coastal region, it nonetheless has much to recommend it as such. A world-class coastal resource in major decline, it has been launched for several years now on unprecedented efforts toward restoration, even as more people arrive every year to use its natural resources. Few other places afford such a combination.

The successes and failures recorded here are thus more than a barometer for one tiny indentation of the earth's coastline. They represent nothing less than a national and international test of the possibilities for reconciling growing human demands with the integrity of the natural environment.

Part I

THE CHESAPEAKE ECOSYSTEM

CHAPTER 1

Rethinking the Bay

The bay connects us. The bay reflects us.

The time has come to fundamentally rethink Chesapeake Bay. The bay is on our maps and in our minds as a large and dominant body of water, fringed on either side by tidewater Maryland and Virginia, ending at Norfolk on the south and at Havre de Grace on the north. Although it is commonly described as 195 miles long and from 4 to 30 miles wide, actually the bay is a system about twenty times that size. Nearly fifty significant rivers and thousands of streams, creeks, and ditches penetrate deep into the surrounding land. They extend the bay northward to Cooperstown, New York, site of the Baseball Hall of Fame; as far west as Pendleton County, West Virginia; southward in Virginia to Lynchburg and Virginia Beach; and eastward to Seaford, Delaware, and Scranton, Pennsylvania.

All of the land thus encompassed, sprawling 64,000 square miles between North Carolina and Vermont, slopes toward Chesapeake Bay. Every drop of rain that runs off these lands flows toward the bay. So does the discharge from every sewage pipe, industrial outfall, and uncontained oil spill, every styrofoam coffee cup casually tossed into a drainageway. When soil erodes from farmland, or from a forest bulldozed for development, the sediment can head only in one direction—bayward. This is what we mean by the drainage basin, or *watershed*, of Chesapeake Bay. And on such a map the bay appears neither dominant nor long and broad; just a smallish pool of water on the receiving end of all our activities, wise and foolish, across the vast lands of the watershed.

Even placing the bay in the context of its watershed may understate the degree to which the land can influence its waters. This is

3

because the bay's considerable length and breadth conceal the fact that there is hardly any water in it—for the Chesapeake is very, very shallow. Acre for acre across the lands of its watershed, it has less than *one-tenth* the volume of water of most of the world's coastal bays to absorb whatever pollutants wash from farms and cities around it. (See Figure 1.1.)

To understand how watersheds and their waters interact, start by visiting and comparing two kinds of small stream wherever you live in the Chesapeake basin—one in a mostly forested area, the other in an urban-suburban setting. Notice how when it rains in the wooded stream valley, the leaves and branches of the forest intercept and deflect the raindrops, softening the impact of those that reach the ground. The rain that falls is literally sponged up by the dense vegetation and the deep leaf duff of the forest floor. Only in very intense storms will the stream's channel receive enough runoff to go rampaging destructively down its course, cutting at its banks and scouring its bed.

By contrast, the paved areas, house roofs, and compacted soils of the second stream's more developed watershed will channel as much as 100 times the amount of water from the same rainfall into the stream course—and the runoff will occur several times more quickly, without the rough, spongy surfaces of the forest to slow its passage. Conversely, in dry periods the forested stream will continue to be fed by seepage through its banks and bottom from all the rain that soaked into the ground. On the developed stream, too much left the watershed too fast. Not enough soaked in. The same channel that raged with rainfall will lie nearly empty the rest of the time.

The upshot is that the forested stream has lower peak flows than the developed stream when it rains and has higher "base" flows when the weather is dry. It is, in a word, more stable. The natural vegetation creates this stability along with a host of other conditions—like the ability to filter pollution from runoff—that are most favorable to a diverse and healthy population of everything from aquatic insects to trout and bass.

We can extend this scenario to the bay. In pre-European times, its entire watershed was mostly forest (as opposed to around 60 percent of it in modern times). It has been estimated that peak flows of fresh water into the Chesapeake during storms—before development and agriculture removed millions of acres of forest—were lower by 25 to 30 percent. Base flows during droughts were 10 to 15 percent

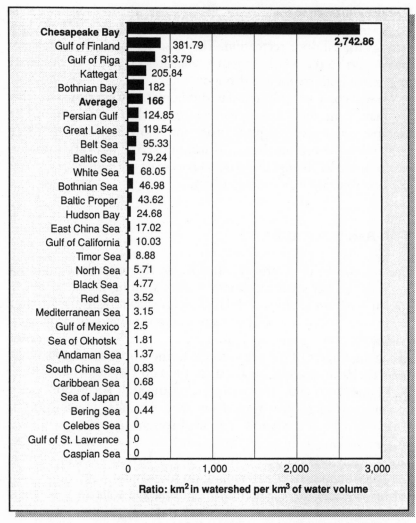

FIGURE 1.1. THE SHALLOW, VULNERABLE BAY   *Chesapeake Bay, compared to other coastal and inland bodies of water, has a huge drainage basin for
the amount of water it contains, a ratio of 2,742.86 square kilometers of land for
every cubic kilometer of water. The principal reason is the Chesapeake's extreme
shallowness—its average depth is less than 22 feet.* [R. Costanza, Chesapeake
Biological Laboratory, University of Maryland]

higher. Thus we see that forests, in relation to the bay, are more than homes for birds, sources of lumber, filters for pollution, and pleasant settings for outdoor recreation. They also wring order from chaos and impart to the whole system a *resilience*, a capacity to moderate impacts of both storm and drought.

We will come to understand in this book how other parts of what we may term the Chesapeake *ecosystem*—the bay's bottom, for example—also give the place order and allow it to rebound from tremendous natural and human disruptions. And we will see how, as we continue to change the original nature of the system's parts, we risk destabilizing it beyond recovery.

THE AMPUTATED BAY

The *tributaries*, or rivers and streams, of the watershed are much more to the bay than a collector system sending pollution downstream. They are highways and habitat for spawning fish, a vital link in the bay's fabled seafood production. For thousands of years, great schools of herring and shad glutted the bay each spring, extending like living fingers of the ocean to the farthest upstream limits of the drainage basin. Starting far at sea, they ran up Virginia's James River past Jamestown and Hopewell. Racing through Richmond, pushing ever upward, they turned into the Rivanna, pressing on to Charlottesville and beyond. The shad sought the rivers, while the smaller herring continued up streams no wider than a person's stride. Even larger numbers made for Pennsylvania's Susquehanna, the bay's biggest river, embarking on the longest migration of any fish in eastern North America, mounting the watershed as far as Binghamton and Elmira in New York state.

Fishes that run up rivers from the sea to spawn are called *anadromous*. The bay has several such species, of which the shad and herrings are perhaps the most ambitious voyagers. (See Figure 1.2.) Like the salmon of the West Coast, they appear to be drawn back to the exact waters where they were born by homing in on a sort of "organic bouquet" or scent that is unique for each river and stream in the vast drainage basin. In navigating from the open oceans the fish may also be guided by the angle of the sun, the earth's magnetic field, currents, temperature, the amount of salt in the water, or a

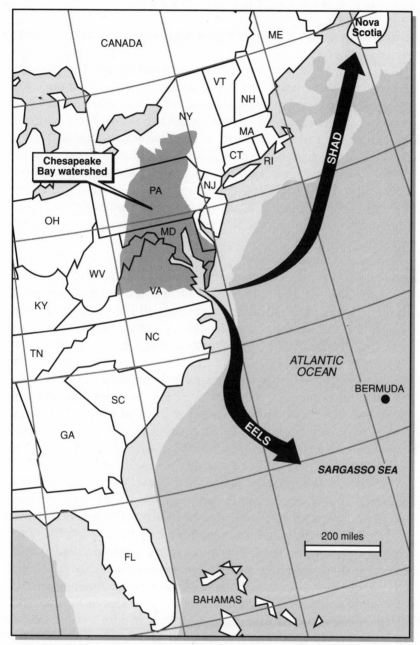

FIGURE 1.2. LIVING CONNECTIONS WITH THE OCEANS *Many species associated with the Chesapeake roam far and wide. Two prominent voyagers are eels, which spawn in the Sargasso Sea, and shad, which range as far north as the Bay of Fundy, returning to the Chesapeake to spawn.* [By Joseph Hutchinson]

combination of all these factors. Just how they find their way home remains a mystery.

Come autumn on the bay, usually on nights when the moon is dark and a storm has just passed, an even curiouser traffic stirs throughout the circulatory system that weaves together the bay and its basin. In the streams of lands as distant as the West Virginia mountains, the rolling farmland of Virginia's Shenandoah Valley, and the swampy river bottoms of Maryland's Eastern Shore, eels are stirring, undergoing physical changes to prepare them for the reverse of the shad's spawning trip. The eels will move downstream through the bay, homing in, along with eels from all over North America and Europe, on the Sargasso Sea, their universal spawning grounds.

Species that run down rivers to the sea to spawn are called *catadromous*, and eels are the bay's only full-fledged example of this behavior. Migrating eels may reach nearly 4 feet and more than 6 pounds (though this is unusual). The parent eels all die upon spawning, sinking into the depths of the Bermuda Triangle. Great, slow currents seize the helpless young, which at that stage of life resemble transparent willow leaves, and transport them months or even years later as tiny eel-like forms, or *elvers*, near the mouths of Chesapeake Bay and other inlets to the Atlantic coast. There is not even the possibility of a "bouquet" imprinted at birth to explain how they wriggle their way from there to every capillary of a watershed they have never experienced. We only know that what draws them back is a powerful force that has been working for millions of years.

During the last century and a half these living connections, anadromous and catadromous, between the oceans and the bay watershed have weakened considerably. Early settlers in Pennsylvania rejoiced as the shad runs saved them from winter's near-starvation in early spring. Today no living Pennsylvanian would remember those glad migrations. Overfishing during the spawning runs up the bay was intense. Shad were taken by the ton in huge nets that would sometimes block the entire river. George Washington used to employ such a fishing operation from Mount Vernon on the Potomac. But the death knell on the James and the Susquehanna was the erection of insurmountable dams, beginning in the 1800s.

Although the runs of shad and herring and other species continue to this day on some rivers and streams, it is well to remember, as we try to restore the former vitality of the bay, that its health is linked to the whole scope of the watershed. And with respect to fish migration, we are presently dealing with an *amputee*, several thousand miles of its circulatory system impaired.

AN UNRULY BEAST—THE ESTUARY

Just as the bay branches upstream throughout a sixth of the Atlantic Seaboard, downstream at its mouth it is open to the full scope of the ocean. The resulting collision of sweet and salt—fresh river water flowing seaward and ocean pushing inland—makes what we call an *estuary*. The Latin verb *aestuare*—to heave, boil, surge, be in commotion—gives fair warning that this place is no mere river running in only one direction for all time. Nor is it a lake, its waters turning over sedately once or twice a year as the surface layers cool and warm. Neither does it feature the predictable currents and constant, salty chemistry of the oceans. Estuaries in their behavior are among the liveliest natural systems of the planet. They are the aquatic world's three-ring circus of motion, productivity, and changeableness. There are about 850 such places in North America, from Long Island Sound to San Francisco Bay, but none among them so large and potentially bountiful as Chesapeake Bay.

We must say "potentially" because the modern-day Chesapeake, as this book explains, is a system in deep trouble and struggling for its very survival. In these pollution-conscious times, we are always asking: What is the quality of our waters? How are they doing? Do they and the life they hold seem to be coming back or going sour? If we were to observe and monitor the bay for a few days, or even a few years, to try and give it a grade, we might end up wanting to flunk it solely for unruliness. That is the essential nature of estuaries—neither ocean nor river nor land, but a transition zone, an edge where all three systems overlap and struggle to assert themselves. As we shall see, it makes for a complex and quirky system, one that is taxing both to creatures who would live in it and those who would understand it—a system that needs all the stabilizing mechanisms (such as its forested lands) it can get, but also a system capable of sustaining more life and more productivity for its size than virtually any other place on earth. To see the method in the bay's apparent madness—to develop a frame of reference for asking, "How's the bay doing?"—it helps to begin when the only history was written by wind, river, and rock.

In their very existence here on earth, estuaries demonstrate the extraordinary *variability*, or dynamism, that characterizes their every behavior. Our present Chesapeake Bay is just the latest in a long line of bays here. Indeed there may well have been at least ten bays here during the last 5 million years. Through the bulk of the last half million years, there has not even been an estuary at this point on the coast, just the narrow river valley carved by the mighty Susquehanna across the coastal plain and the continental shelf. A second channel was cut by the James, the two joining around Norfolk. The ancient channels today form the paths for big ships traversing the bay.

Intermittently throughout geological time, the earth's climate has been so cold that large portions of our present oceans have been bound up in the polar ice caps and in glaciers. Sea level then was as much as 325 feet below where it is today. Only in the relatively short (measured in tens of thousands of years) *interglacials*, the warmest periods between recurring ice ages, does the ice melt and the heave and surge of the seas fully flood the coastal river valleys and inlets. During those brief, geological summers, estuaries like the Chesapeake swell and blossom like rare flowers within the nooks and crannies along the continental fringes, only to wither away with the onset of the next ice age and the reabsorption of the seas into the polar ice.

Our Chesapeake began to fill about 10,000 years ago as rising sea level reached the present mouth and backed up the river flows from the Susquehanna and the James. The slope of the river channels was so slight that the flooding proceeded rapidly up their valleys. Around 9,000 years ago the head of the newborn bay had almost reached Baltimore, though it was much narrower and shallower than at present. Some 6,000 years ago, as Sumerians in Asia were inventing writing, the bay had widened and deepened, assuming something like its present form. By 3,000 years ago, as Rameses II ruled Egypt and Troy was sacked, the Chesapeake as we know it had formed.

Perhaps there were a few seconds of geological time when the estuary could be said to have been in equilibrium, neither coming nor going, but ever since then its channels have been filling in with the sediments that continually wash from its shores and from the lands of the watershed. As it fills, its waters eventually will be squeezed upward and outward, spreading in a wide, shallow film across much of today's Eastern Shore, also inundating the western shore's low-lying peninsulas from Aberdeen on down to the marshes of Guinea in Virginia. This process will take a few thousand years unless human influences—dredging, for example, or the sea level rise predicted to ensue from global warming—override expected climatic and geological events. Ten thousand years from now, perhaps only a marsh will commemorate where the Chesapeake dwelled.

The great estuary will be gone. Or will it? Water will still flow from the watershed, still seek its level in the sea, slowly carving new channels into the sediments left behind, setting the stage for the next coming. And even a quarter million years hence, as the glaciers lie heaviest on the land and the seas have shrunk back off the continental shelves, who can say that November's eels and April's shad will not continue to come and go in a few, remnant tributaries of the coastline, safekeeping in their genes and instincts the annual rituals of once and future bays?

SLOSH AND BURP—THE WIND'S WILL

The bay's variability with the epochs is mirrored on time scales short as the everyday circulation of water. Tides send a charge of water rippling up and back the 195-mile basin's entire length twice in every 24-hour day. These tides, two highs and two lows every day, stretch as far up the bay's rivers as Washington on the Potomac and Richmond on the James. Many creatures of the estuary synchronize their lives to these periodic movements of water. The abundant periwinkles that scale the stalks of marsh grass to stay above the rising tide will continue their up-and-down migrations far from their native bay. (People taking them to Alabama have found them on the living room floor the next morning—as the tide rose back on the Chesapeake, the periwinkles scaled the walls of their aquarium in Birmingham.) Likewise, crabs taken from Tangier Island, Virginia, and put in a tank in, say, Harrisburg, Pennsylvania, will shed their shells in accordance with the tidal clockwork back on Tangier.

Nothing would seem more regular and predictable than the tides—and this is true as far as when each high and each low occurs. But *how* high and low they go is quite another matter. Because of the Chesapeake's long and shallow shape, movement of water in it is ruled to an unusual extent by the caprice of wind. A northwest blow may literally shove much of the water out the mouth of the estuary and hold it there for days. High tides come pretty much on schedule, but there is not much to them. The succeeding lows are memorable, however, exposing thousands of acres of normally submerged bottom—just one of the many stresses that life in the estuary must deal with. Similarly, a steady northeast wind may pile up water in sections of the bay several feet above normal, flooding low-lying shorelines with salty water, severely limiting the kinds of plants and animals that can survive there.

Certain winds, it appears, may also have potentially harmful effects by triggering *seiching*, or sloshing, motions within the bay's deeper waters, tilting them from eastern shore to western shore, much like the motion you can set up by wiggling your hips in a full bathtub. This in turn can cause the bay to "burp," heaving up oxygen-poor waters from its deep channels into shallower areas— another in the long series of unpredictable and stressful behavior encountered by life in estuaries. It appears that on the Chesapeake, local winds tinker as much as 90 percent of the time with the regular cosmic clockwork (such as the moon's gravitational pull) that drives the tides. An extreme wind, such as a hurricane, may temporarily increase the volume of water in the bay by more than 30 percent. Routinely winds play the bay like a concertina, pumping and squeezing its normal volume upward and downward by 10 to 20 percent.

Such phenomena are not just abstract physical quirks. The fortunes of seafood lovers from Harrisburg to Norfolk also ride the wind's caprice. It affects the yearly availability of the succulent blue crab. About half of the nation's entire harvest comes from the bay. As many as a quarter of a billion individual crabs may be taken in a good year; but like almost everything else in the estuary, the numbers of crabs can fluctuate wildly. In Maryland waters, the catch once went from 36 million pounds to 10 million, and back to 27 million, all in a four-year period.

All the bay's crabs are hatched near its mouth, in sight of the bridge-tunnel between Cape Charles and Virginia Beach. Here tides and currents conspire to flush most of the helpless larvae, or *zoea*, right out into the ocean. Here, dozens of miles out on the continental shelf, is the other boundary of the system that begins in the forested mountains of West Virginia and New York. And the baby crabs drifting toward the point of no return from the Atlantic are highly dependent on winds blowing from just the right direction at just the right time to get back into the Chesapeake. Thus part of the answer to the annual comings and goings of crabs may literally be "blowin' in the wind."

THE ONLY CONSTANT IS CHANGE

As if it were not enough that the bay is shoved around at the wind's will, consider that it also flows two ways at once (Figure 1.3). Since the fresh water from its rivers is lighter than the salty water pushing

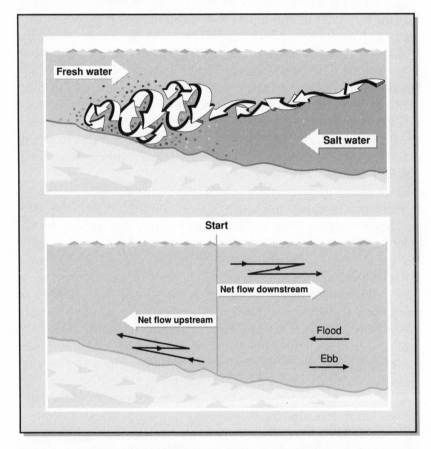

FIGURE 1.3. MIXING AND FLOWS OF WATER IN THE ESTUARY   *The bay not only flows two ways* (top), *out on top and in on the bottom, but it mixes. The tides* (bottom) *also flow in and out with two highs and two lows every day, but the net movement of water is usually downstream on top and upstream on the bottom.* [Adapted from White, *Chesapeake Bay: A Field Guide*]

up from the ocean, the fresh spilling off the watershed runs atop the salt. So the bay on its surface is usually heading toward Norfolk, while on its bottom it is Baltimore-bound. The tides, of course, still move up and down the bay, reversing at times the effect of the two-layered flow. But for a particle of water near the surface, the *net* movement, tides notwithstanding, is downstream; while a particle near the bottom will likewise work its way up-bay.

A lot of life in the bay has evolved to hitch free rides on this two-way circulatory train. The feeble-swimming larvae, or early life stages, of many fish and crabs are able to sink or rise in the water to ride the flows of salt and fresh up or down the bay from where they are born to areas with better food or growing conditions. But what is fine for these travelers presents a major problem for the many other bay creatures who survive best by staying put. These include larval oysters and many other species of plankton, the tiny floating plant and animal communities that flourish in the estuary. They cope by intermittently rising toward the surface and then sinking toward the bottom, performing a roughly circular movement that lets them maintain stability in a system that is constantly trying to wash them either to Baltimore or out to sea.

It all seems quite neatly worked out: fresh on top, salty on the bottom, one layer flowing south, the other north—this is the "classic" bay circulation. But the bay hardly ever seems to play by the rules for long. The willful wind is one reason; another major one is the great bursts of water issuing from the mighty Susquehanna River at the bay's head. Carver of the bay's channel in geological time and source of half its fresh water, the Susquehanna dominates circulation and water quality for nearly half the estuary's length. When Mother Susquehanna clears her throat, delivering billions of tons of new rainfall throughout the estuary, it can set the lesser river mouths of her children to chattering—flip-flopping their flows up and down both shores of the Chesapeake.

So it was that one of the first long-term measurements of the bay's circulation found that the estuary was flowing in classic pattern—out (seaward) on top and in on the bottom—less than half the time. The rest of the year the flows went any of the following ways, always returning to the classic pattern within ten days:

In on top, out on the bottom
In on top, out in the middle, and in on the bottom

Out on top, in in the middle, and out on the bottom
Out on the top, middle, and bottom
In on the top, middle, and bottom

The classic two-layered flow does occur more often than any other pattern; but for plankton, larval fish and crabs, or environmental managers attempting to track the movements of pollutants through the estuarine system, there are never firm guarantees of where things will end up in Chesapeake Bay.

INVISIBLE FENCES

As much as any single factor, the bay's layered flows define the patterns of life within the estuary. They call the tune to which everything there must dance; they zone the bay and its rivers into biological regions as distinct as mountain and plain on the land—all because of a very simple thing that happens among the layers. They mix. Not totally, or we would no longer have layered flows, but they mix enough. And suddenly we have a system that is not only fresh as a lake (in its upper reaches), and salty as an ocean (at its mouth), but also everything in between—an almost infinite range of habitats for aquatic life, depending on each species' level of tolerance for salt.

The amount of salt in water is expressed in parts of salt per thousand parts of water (by weight). Fresh water has a salinity of zero parts per thousand, while the ocean is around 35 parts. The salt gradations also extend in the water from top to bottom. An exquisite ability to differentiate among these salinity variations is how the oyster larvae maintain position in the bay, rising and sinking peri- odically to stay in about the same place. Salt also sets the boundaries of spawning and nursery areas for crabs and fish and dictates the kinds of vegetation that grows in marshlands and underwater grass beds. It limits and unleashes diseases and parasites, enhances the reproduction of oysters, and determines where the blue crabs shed their shells.

If we go out and measure salinity up and down the bay on any given day, we will get a picture of neat compartmentalization, lines of salinity, or *isohalines*, grading from saltier to fresher as we move up-bay. But like almost every other "snapshot" of the ever-shifting estuary, this picture can be misleading. In fact the isohalines routinely are sent scuttling down and up the bay like fallen leaves before the gusts of autumn. The reason is that some times of the year—and some years—are wetter or drier than others. (See Figure 1.4.)

In some years nearly three times as much river water flows into the bay as in others. Even whole decades can vary tremendously: nearly every year of the 1970s was wet, for example, well above the average annual flow, while almost all of the 1960s were bone dry. The estuary, after extended wet periods, can resemble a freshwater lake as far south as the Potomac. A year later, if the rains are scant across the watershed, salinities as far north as the Maryland Bay Bridge can reach as high as 22 parts per thousand (25 is average at the bay's mouth).

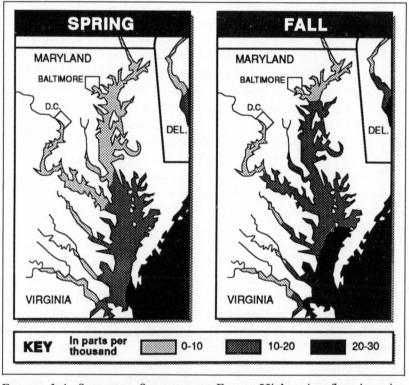

FIGURE 1.4. SALINITY: SPRING AND FALL *Higher river flows in spring* (left) *push back the ocean's saltier influence; in autumn* (right), *drier weather diminishes river flow and the ocean marches up the estuary.* [Adapted from Cronin, *The Biology of the Estuary,* and White, *Chesapeake Bay: A Field Guide*]

Most species of aquatic life on earth have a narrow range of tolerance for salinity—either they can't stand it, or they need the full strength of the ocean's salt. Such dramatic alterations in this basic parameter of life in the water add considerably to the stresses on life in the estuary.

IF YOU FARM THE BAY, PRAY FOR DROUGHT

The up and down swings in the water moving off the watershed can also have major pollution consequences. Consider the quantities of nitrogen and phosphorus and soil that wash from the land and are delivered to the bay by its rivers. Up to a point, all of these substances are a good thing. Nitrogen and phosphorus, both of which occur naturally in soil, are the nutrients that fertilize much of the bay's growth of phytoplankton (floating, tiny plants). They also nourish the bay's submerged grass beds, which in turn support a host of higher life forms. Similarly, sediment flowing into the estuary acts as a sort of "fertilizer" to its marshes. It is filtered and trapped by the thick vegetation of the marshes, which build more plant matter atop it to keep from being drowned by a sea level that has been rising ever since the end of the last ice age.

In the last several decades, principally through large increases in discharges of human sewage, farm fertilizers, and animal wastes, and through deforestation and land development, we have dramatically increased the watershed's contributions of essential ingredients like nitrogen, phosphorus, and sediment to the point where they have become major pollutants of the Chesapeake, an issue we will discuss in more detail in Chapter 2.

The difference between a wet year and a dry year across the bay's basin can double the amounts of nutrients that are washed off the land—a difference of more than 100 million pounds a year (Figure 1.5). For sediment the difference between wet and dry can be billions of pounds. Wet years, or more specifically wet springs, can also cause so much fresh water to flow down the bay that it does not mix normally with the salty, heavier, bottom layers. This condition, known as *stratification*, amounts to something like clamping a lid over the bottom waters. With the normal mixing processes thwarted, sometimes for months, bacteria in the bottom layers consume most of the oxygen, and no more can descend from the surface.

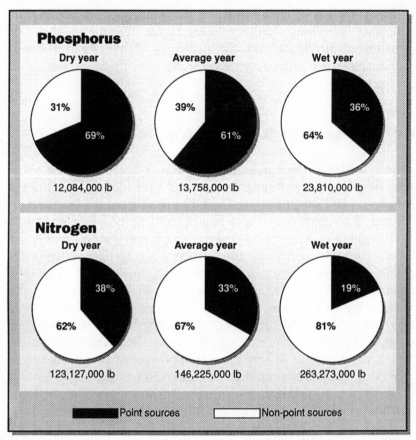

Phosphorus

Dry year	Average year	Wet year
31% / 69%	39% / 61%	36% / 64%
12,084,000 lb	13,758,000 lb	23,810,000 lb

Nitrogen

Dry year	Average year	Wet year
38% / 62%	33% / 67%	19% / 81%
123,127,000 lb	146,225,000 lb	263,273,000 lb

▬ Point sources   ☐ Non-point sources

FIGURE 1.5. WET AND DRY YEARS AFFECT BAY POLLUTION *Polluting inputs of "nonpoint sources" of phosphorus and nitrogen, in stormwater runoff from farms and development, become dramatically more influential in wet years, less so in dry years. "Point sources," mainly sewage, are relatively constant in absolute terms but tend to shrink or grow in influence relative to runoff.* [From EPA, *Chesapeake Bay: A Profile of Environmental Change*]

This phenomenon, discussed in more detail in Chapter 2, seems to have been worsened by pollution. The bottom line is that massive regions of the bay may become as devoid of oxygen as the surface of the moon. Large portions of the bay, which still look clean and vital to the eye of a boater sailing across them, may in fact be as hostile to fish and crabs as a sandy desert.

While those who farm the land often pray for rain across the watershed, the watermen who "farm" the bay would, on the whole, prefer it dry—the less runoff, the less water pollution. It is often tempting, following a couple of dry years, to attribute the improvements that may occur in the bay's water to our many and expensive efforts to restore the estuary's health. The real test, however, is to wait until after a few wet years, or even a wet decade, as happened during the 1970s, and see what things look like. Conversely, one might mistakenly seize on conditions during an extremely wet year to paint an overly pessimistic scenario of the estuary's future. Though human pollution may be the bay's bad actor, it is still Nature, with wet and dry years, who sets the stage. (See Figure 1.6.)

This is why the unglamorous task of monitoring environmental conditions in the bay for long periods of time is so critical and so frustrating. It can take years, even decades, given the great natural variability of the estuary, for patterns or trends to emerge that will give us a clear understanding of the way the bay is headed. Day to day, year to year, the only thing we can be sure of is that the bay won't be the same as it was the day or year before.

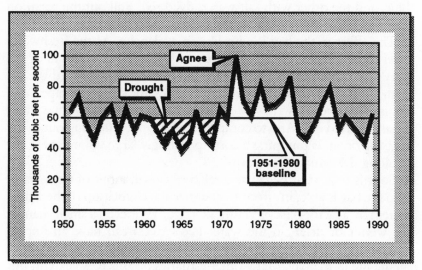

FIGURE 1.6. HISTORIC VARIATIONS IN THE BAY'S FRESHWATER STREAMFLOW *Differences in rainfall and subsequent runoff of polluted stormwater (Figure 1.5) not only influence the bay annually, but can color whole decades. The 1960s were drier than average, with relatively little runoff, while the 1970s were much wetter than average, with high runoff. Tropical Storm Agnes in 1972 made that year one of the wettest ever recorded.* [Adapted from USGS data by Joseph Hutchinson]

A Bit of River Goes a Long Way

Thus far we have talked a good deal about how the water flowing from the bay's watershed influences it. So it may come as a surprise to learn that the daily freshwater flow to the bay is only a tiny fraction of the 18 trillion or so gallons that is the volume of the bay and its tidal tributaries. If the bay were to be drained, and dammed to keep the ocean out, the rivers would have to run for half a year to refill its basin, assuming average rainfall.

But think of that freshwater input as something like a catalyst—those two or three dollops of chemical you add to a big glop of epoxy glue to make it a powerful cement. Or think of leverage—using a long pry-stick to multiply your muscle power in moving a large rock. So it is that the movement of fresh water, as it proceeds down the bay, encourages more and more of the heavier ocean water to slide up the bay underneath it. You can observe this effect by partitioning an aquarium, filling one half with fresh water, dyed blue, and the other with salt water, dyed red. Pull out the partition and watch the salt run under the fresh.

The effect in the bay is a bit like an avalanche. As the freshwater layer moves ever seaward, it mixes with increasing volumes of the salty, lower layers and pulls them upward and back toward the sea with it. By the time this process reaches the Virginia capes, the volume of river flow has been *amplified* from three to nine times what it started out. And to compensate for what is flowing out of the bay, the ocean is pumping a correspondingly large volume of water in along the estuary's bottom.

So it is that what began as a relatively small input of fresh water into the bay is able, in effect, to energize the circulation of the whole system by a factor of several times its size. Thus even a small change, for wetter or drier, in the watershed's rivers can have an impact several times that on the circulation of the estuary and, by extension, all the life in the bay. Many other estuaries do this to an extent, but few so forcefully as the Chesapeake. This circulation, in turn, underlies the bay's world-standard capacity for productivity, as we shall see in the next section. It also demonstrates how changes in the land, such as our continuing destruction of the watershed's forests, can cause changes in the bay. Forest loss causes rivers to run higher during storms, lower during droughts—and the consequences of this instability may be magnified further in the bay.

And so the bay goes—and comes—and goes. Here and gone with the ice ages, up and down with the tides, in and out with the salt and fresh (also out and in, in-out-in, out-in-out, and more); the wind blows, the bay burps, a zillion crabs are lost at sea; it rains in Pennsylvania, and in Virginia salinity retreats, fish nurseries shrink, the bay bottom gasps for oxygen. . . . How is one to make sense of such a place, where land and water mingle and the seas and the rivers make such an infernal commotion?

Some scientists think powerful computer graphics might be the only way to visualize what is going on out there. In fact, they're already working on simple programs that digest several years of data on, say, changes in the oxygen content and then animate it. We are already, on a very limited basis, tracking and counting the migrations of fish with photoelectric cells in the banks of spawning rivers. Satellites give us increasingly accurate and lovely color pictures of plankton densities, sediment concentrations, and more. Perhaps the day is not far off when we can portray all this coming and going à la Disney—and then what a shifting, shimmering, quixotic creature the old Chesapeake will appear.

This notion may be fanciful, but the extremely variable character of the estuary is not. And it raises a very real question: Why, with all the uncertainty and stress associated with its behavior, are estuaries like the Chesapeake so incredibly rich with life?

PRODUCTIVITY—THE BAY'S BOTTOM LINE

By any measure but its own historical bounty, the modern bay is still richly productive. To value its natural systems against the economics of dredging, sewage treatment, or other human projects with environmental harm, we often invoke the bay's production in commercial terms: more than 100 million pounds of seafood landed annually with a dockside value of tens of millions (close to a billion pounds annually if we include the coastwide catches of menhaden rendered into oil and fertilizer at Reedville, Virginia); more than half the nation's blue crab catch; 90 percent of its soft crabs; 15 percent of its oysters; spawning grounds, until their recent decline, for 90 percent of the East Coast's striped bass—all this from a mere pinprick on the North American coastline that contains a few billionths of the planet's water.

A study performed in 1989 for Maryland's Department of Economic and Employment Development added up all the economic activities that could not take place in Maryland and Virginia without the bay, along with the value added to lands along the bay's shoreline by being on the waterfront. The "conservative" estimate of the Chesapeake's economic value to the two states' economies was $678 billion. Yet these dollar and pound measures only hint at the true biological worth of the estuary. Scientists who compare the richness of life among earth's different regions of land and water prefer to look at their *primary production*. This is the overall production of plant life—the basis everywhere for the food webs that ultimately sustain the higher predators like rockfish, bald eagles, and humans. Primary production can range from cactus in a desert region, to agriculture's corn and soybeans, to lichens in the Arctic and plankton and seaweeds in the water.

The land/water edges, where estuaries lie, excel at "crop" production, towering over all the earth's other land and waterscapes, natural and managed. The only systems of human invention that come close to estuaries are intensive rice culture in flooded river plains and year-round cropping of sugarcane in the tropics; but even these efforts require large inputs of human time and petroleum-based chemicals such as fertilizers and pesticides. An estuary does its job for free. All we have to do is not impair (or, these days, to *repair*) its natural functioning.

To begin understanding the secrets of the bay's enormous capacity for life one needs no Ph.D.—only a pole several feet in length and a canoe, although you can make do in many places with old sneakers and the willingness to wade out from one of the marshes or beaches along the estuary's shoreline. Probing the bay's waters this way (or "progging" as the watermen say), you will quickly discover a profound truth. You can touch bottom easily almost everywhere. If you know people who boat on the bay, ask if they have ever run aground. If they say not, they most likely never leave the dock (or they are lying).

Chesapeake Bay is quite *shallow*. Nearly 200 miles long and up to 30 miles wide, it looks like a lot of water out there; but that water is spread *thin*. The average depth of this huge bay is around 21 feet (27 feet if we don't include its tidal rivers)—less than halfway from home plate to first base at any rate. It has been estimated that 10 percent of the bay is less than 3 feet in depth and that 20 percent of it is less than 6 feet, 6 inches. In this simple fact—that its bottom lies very near its top—lies much of the bay's uniqueness . . . and also its vulnerability to modern pollution.

Its shallowness means that sunlight, the first essential for plant growth, can penetrate a large part of the bay's waters. This light and warmth, combined with the continuous flow of nutrients, minerals, and dissolved gases from the estuary's dozens of rivers, support vast stocks of phytoplankton. Similarly, excellent potential growing conditions extend to at least 600,000 acres of shallow bottom. Here is the bay's second engine of primary production: huge underwater meadows of grasses. More than a dozen varieties of this vegetation occur throughout the bay, ranging from grasses near the head of the estuary that can barely tolerate salt to grasses near its mouth that thrive in oceanic salinities. Collectively they are referred to as *submerged aquatic vegetation* (SAV). They are not only food for waterfowl but are high-quality habitats—nurseries, hiding places, breeding grounds—for shrimp, crabs, fishes, seahorses, and a host of less familiar life forms in the food web. Finally, the sunlit shallows also foster rich bottom-dwelling growths of the plant form known as algae.

The same gentle slope of its basin that forms the bay's broad submerged shallows continues at marginally higher elevations around its shorelines. Half a million acres of tidal marshes, or wetlands, flourish there. These marshes extend food and habitat as lush as anything the grass beds offer for up to thousands of feet inland. In effect, with its floating plants, its rooted grasses and tidal marsh, and its algae, the bay's primary production is running on four cylinders, while most other natural regions of the planet run mostly on one (plankton in the oceans, forests on the land, for example).

DOING MORE WITH LESS

Now, a mystery arises. Although the bay's big watershed and many rivers deliver it a goodly supply of nutrients, this supply seemed not to be nearly enough, when scientists measured it several years ago, to sustain more than a small fraction of the life that is there. (It takes, for example, at least a few tons of phytoplankton—eaten by larger creatures, which in turn are eaten by larger ones, and so forth—to produce a single pound of striped bass, or rockfish. For many years the bay was yielding 5 to 8 million pounds of striped bass every year, and that is only one of several varieties of fish abounding in the estuary.)

The other part of the mystery is that the watershed's rivers don't deliver the goods in anything like a constant or predictable manner. (Remember wet and dry years, as well as the dynamic and variable nature of estuaries.) Generally there is a relative glut of nutrients each spring, when river runoff is high, and a famine during the winters and some summers when the rivers run low. But plants and animals in the estuary have to live year-round and need a fairly steady supply of food. How are they to get three squares a day from such an unpredictable host as the bay?

The bay, it turns out, is a system elegantly adapted to do more with less—to recycle—something we humans are just beginning to realize makes a lot of sense in our own lives. (Conversely, the bay is not at all well adapted to handle the excessive levels of nutrients flushing from our farms and sewers in recent decades, but more on that later.) Recycling works like this. The phytoplankton absorb nutrients from the water and grow. As they die, or get eaten and passed through a larger creature's digestive tract, their remains fall to the bay bottom—a never-ending, baywide shower of nutrients. Then the many kinds of bacteria that are abundant in shallow estuaries rapidly decompose the remains, freeing the remaining nutrients for reinjection back into the water to fuel new plankton growth.

This recycling is further aided by the bay's two-layered flow and the mixing between its top and bottom layers. These unique circulatory patterns mean that nutrients don't just shoot down the rivers and out into the oceans—not by a long shot. On average, a particle of water (and its nutrients) takes around *half a year* to pass from the Susquehanna to the ocean. All this gives the recycling processes plenty of time to work. Think of it like swishing a gulp of a tasty drink around in your mouth for a long time, getting all the goodness out of it, before letting it pass down your gullet. (Another important side of the bay's long retention time is that for pollutants like sediment and toxic chemicals that bind to sediment, the bay is an almost perfect *sink*—that is, what flows in stays there instead of just flushing out to the oceans.)

All bodies of water—oceans, rivers, lakes—recycle nutrients to an extent. The bay just happens to perform better and faster than just about any of them. In addition to the way its circulation retains materials washing into the bay, the estuary is so efficient at recycling because of its extraordinary shallowness. Nutrients that fall to the bottom are never far from the top. Tidal currents and wind churn the bottom back into the water, where sunlight and phytoplankton begin the cycle of growth all over again.

Another way nutrients get quickly back into action in the bay is through uptake by the worms, clams, and other bottom-dwellers, or *benthos*, that eat them and are in turn eaten, passing their food energy up through the food web. Again, it all works so well here because the bottom is so very close to the top. The ocean's average depth, by contrast, is 12,000 feet, nearly 500 times the bay's. Nutrients there fall to such depths that they never get back into the action on any meaningful time scale. Thus the oceans, except for their shallows, are virtual deserts of primary production.

These days, there is a downside to the bay's tremendously efficient recycling. The bay was suitably adapted to make the most of nutrients when the watershed was mostly forested, as relatively few nutrients flowed in from such lands. But currently we are overloading the estuary with nutrients from human sewage and from fertilizers washed off lawns and farms. The effect, given the bay's ability to maximize use of nutrients, is a bit like pouring kerosene on a hot fire. The bay is producing too much phytoplankton. And too much of this floating plant life, in turn, is consuming oxygen from the water and clouding the water, cutting off vital light from the underwater grasses.

You might sum it up by saying that the estuary has a higher metabolism than most other regions of the earth. Such terms, usually applied to higher life forms, make it sound as if the bay were a living organism. And indeed, the more we discover about the sophisticated interaction of its parts—from ocean to oyster to watershed—the less certain the line gets between living and nonliving.

ORDERING THE BAY'S HOUSE

Scientists have begun to speculate upon how the estuary may handle the big variations in delivery of food via its rivers, which fluctuate with rainfall across the watershed. The underwater grass meadows, which in their prime may have carpeted half a million acres or more of bay bottom, play a role here that goes far beyond their better-known values as habitat for crabs and fish and food for water birds.

Their time of maximum growth occurs in the spring—about the same time that the bay in most years gets its maximum freshwater runoff, a time when much of the nutrient supply it will see for the whole year is circulating through in a matter of weeks. The grasses as they grow can absorb large quantities of phosphorus and nitrogen. The grassy bottom may, in effect, be functioning as a bank or warehouse—the bay's means of smoothing its peaks of food energy. As an added benefit, the grass beds clear the water by trapping and filtering tremendous loads of sediment that enter the bay as runoff.

From late summer through early winter, when river and nutrient flows are low, the grasses die back and decompose—thus providing, scientists think, a timed release of nutrients, allowing the recycling machinery to sustain the estuary's improbably large production. It is ironic that just when we need such natural regulation the most, with our current nutrient pollution of the bay, the excess nutrients have helped to kill off great acreages of the grass beds.

There is a term scientists apply to individual creatures—and increasingly to whole natural systems—to describe mechanisms that work like the bay's grasses to maintain order and stability and to limit departures from the conditions best for survival. It is called *homeostasis* ("staying the same"). A familiar example of homeostasis is the way we sweat when we're hot, to let evaporative cooling bring our body temperature back toward a normal 98.6. A lovely example in a big, natural system is the life cycle of certain Pacific salmon, which return, fat and sleek, after years of roaming the oceans, to spawn and die in the streams and rivers where they were born. These waters, which must nourish the newly hatched salmon, are nutrient poor because of the barren soils of their watersheds. But by dying and decomposing there, the adult salmon effectively fertilize the nursery with nutrients harvested thousands of miles out to sea.

Estuaries, as we have discussed, are among the most dynamic, variable, potentially chaotic natural regions of the earth, with all the stresses that implies for life there. Their functioning is characterized, on scales from daily plankton production to their geological filling and draining, by rapid and severe swings of behavior. Scientists trying to chart trends in the bay's health often complain of its high level of background noise—the extreme natural variability makes it hard to sort out which way the environment really is headed, just as the static on a radio makes it tough to hear the announcer's message.

Such places would seem especially in need of mechanisms like the underwater grasses and the marshes to smooth out the peaks and valleys—all the more so since we continue to destroy another major ordering influence, the forest, throughout much of the watershed. And indeed, the bay and the creatures that dwell in it have evolved a number of ways to deal with the hassle of estuarine life. When all of these mechanisms are functioning well, we may say the system is *resilient*—that it can fluctuate with respect to river flows, salinity, sediment, nutrients, or whatever, but will always return fairly quickly to equilibrium. As we begin to understand how this power of recovery depends on the healthy condition of the bay's creatures, its plants, and the lands of its watershed, we may conclude the following: *Maintaining resilience is an overarching goal for the bay.*

OYSTERS ARE MUCH MORE THAN HORS D'OEUVRES

It is on the shallow bay bottom, along with the grass beds, that we find yet another regulatory system on the order of the forests, marshes, and grasses. You may know this elegant mechanism of homeostasis as the old, gray oyster (variously rendered as "aryster," "oistuh," "erster," and "arschture"). The oyster is a good example of how we sometimes underestimate the importance of bay creatures by considering them mainly as they relate to our bellies and our commerce. For more than a century, dating from the 1860s, our huge harvests of the tasty bivalve were synonymous with Chesapeake Bay's incredible bounty.

In retrospect, it is clear that the towering peaks of oyster production during the late nineteenth century were not sustainable. Rather, they simply represented a short-term mining of the wealth accrued on the bay's bottom. The edible oyster meat harvested in Maryland waters alone during the peak of that exploitation was equivalent to the yield from 160,000 head of prime steers. It is a testament to the resilience of the estuary and the oyster that harvests could remain at world-class levels (1 to 3 million bushels a year) almost until the last decade of the twentieth century. Overfishing, combined with diseases, mismanagement, and pollution, has now reduced the oysters in the bay to an estimated 1 percent of their numbers before heavy harvesting began after the Civil War.

One percent! Think of that. And think of what it would be like to live in your house if you had sold off 99 percent of the plumbing, or 99 percent of the heating and air conditioning system, or 99 percent of the roof. Because in taking too many of the bay's oysters, we have been losing much more than a plentiful supply of appetizers or a significant portion of our seafood economy. We have been destroying a vital filter, a recycler, a habitat for other creatures, and a banker of food energy like the underwater grasses.

After their free-floating larvae attach to other oyster shells and become *spat* in the first weeks of life, oysters never move. They have traditionally been superabundant in the bay because its vigorous circulation brings them plenty of food, and because their food is phytoplankton, which grows so well in the sunlit shallows. (The bulk of oysters grow in water 30 feet deep or less.) They are superb filterers, feeding by gaping their shells slightly and pumping bay water through their gills at rates up to 2 gallons per hour.

In addition to growing fat oysters, this process has at least two other important consequences for the estuary as a system. By sucking in sediment that clouds the bay's waters, and depositing it on the bay bottom as compacted fecal matter, the oyster clears the water, thereby helping sunlight penetrate and grow more plankton and more underwater grasses. It has been estimated that the pre-1870 stocks of oysters in the bay had the potential to filter a volume equal to that of the entire Chesapeake every few days—compared to a "filtration time" of nearly a year for today's diminished stocks. (Although there is no scientific evidence that oysters ever were filtering every bit of the bay's water—since even at peak abundance they never lived in every part of the bay—the point that they once made a major impact on water clarity seems indisputable. Similar filter feeders such as mussels and clams have caused dramatic increases in water clarity when introduced to the Great Lakes, San Francisco Bay, and sections of the Potomac River.)

Moreover the oyster, like the grasses, seems to have been a "banker" and recycler of the huge pulses of nutrients that surged off the watershed in the wet springtime. It filters the lush, nutrient-fertilized spring plankton bloom through its gills, using some of it for growth but also depositing nutrient-rich feces on the bay's bottom. On the bottom, which is never far from the top, these nutrient packages can be recycled into production again. But just as the bay's oysters no longer vacuum much sediment from the water, so has their capacity to bank and package food for recycling declined drastically. Estimates are that the pre-1870 oyster population could have removed 23 to 41 percent of the plankton blooms. Now they are thought to remove about 0.4 percent—a drop of fiftyfold or more. Where does the unfiltered plankton go nowadays? It appears that it goes to the bottom, where its decomposition can intensify problems with low oxygen.

In addition to these regulatory functions, a healthy oyster bed was also the bay's equivalent of the tropical coral reef, its hard surfaces and millions of crevices providing habitat for a whole host of other creatures. These in turn attracted feeding fish in warmer months and sea ducks and possibly loons in the winters. Young crabs also seem to prefer oystery bottoms as wintertime habitat over almost any other part of the bay. In times (pre-Civil War) before intensive dredging broke them apart, oysters literally did grow so thickly as to form true reefs, posing hazards to colonial navigation and probably begetting the term watermen still use for an oyster bed: oyster "rock."

THE CHESAPEAKE ECOSYSTEM

We may never know precisely the extent to which the bay's shallow bottom—its grasses and its oysters—regulated their own environment. But the concept is not far-fetched. The Amazonian rain forest, for example, is well documented as maintaining a microclimate of the very moist conditions ideal for its own perpetuation. (And cutting it down destroys those conditions, making regrowth of the original jungle impossible.) Similarly, the Swiss Alps once were forested, but after clearcutting by the Romans they never recovered—the climate without the trees was too dry; and the mountain soils, without a protective cover of forest, lost their fertility to erosion. The climate protected the trees, which protected the climate, which . . .

It is all a circle, an *ecosystem* of plants and animals and people, air, water, and soil. And these parts are no more important than the patterns by which they connect and influence one another. This is how we must learn to understand Chesapeake Bay—not just as water, or watershed, or in terms of seafood and sport; but also as an interrelated system of buffers and banks, of filters and traps and sinks, all working together to keep the bay's house in order, to maintain resilience.

Clear the forests and you disrupt the quantity and quality of the rivers. Kill the underwater grasses and you lose more than duck food and ducks (and duck hunting with its rich tradition and history). Overharvest oysters and more is removed than can be measured in pounds or bushels or dollars, or even by the thrill of graceful and historic skipjacks dredging shellfish under sail. Fill the marshes and the loss of their rippling green and golden beauty is only the most obvious change for the worse, because you have also lost a vital filter and buffer between water and watershed. Damage parts and you damage patterns. The ecosystem we call the estuary will in each case lose part of its ability to rebound from the fierce natural and man-made forces that constantly are buffeting it. Resilience will be lost.

WHAT THE ANIMALS ARE SAYING

The damage humans have done to the bay and its watershed is nothing short of staggering. And with more millions of people moving into the region, the odds may seem long against a major turnaround. Indeed, this book details many alarming trends. But reading all the reports in the world cannot give one a full sense of this marvelous, 64,000-square-mile creature called Chesapeake. The best way to start saving the bay is through contact with parts of its system, whether it be made with a fishing rod or binoculars, from a duck hunting blind or the ooze of its bottom squishing up through the bare toes. Sometimes it is best to quit analyzing the bay and just listen to what its creatures have to tell us.

It may seem surprising, given the reputation of estuaries for producing and attracting huge quantities of species, that not many *kinds* of creatures live in the bay. To be sure, many visit at times of the year, either descending from their upstream, freshwater habitats or moving in from the oceans to feed or spawn. But in terms of full-time residents, both freshwater systems and the oceans, though far less productive than estuaries, support many, many times more varieties of life.

This seeming paradox simply reflects the estuary's basic nature—lots of food production on the one hand, but also tremendous variability in environmental conditions: salinity that can swing from oceanic to lakelike and back; temperatures in the shallows that may freeze to the bottom mud in winter and soar above 90° in summer; water quality in the rivers that can change with an overnight rainfall. As a bay scientist once summed it up: "The chow's great if you can stand the hassle."

And that is just the point, and maybe the bay's best hope for survival into the next century—much of what has survived there is able to stand a lot of hassle, is adaptable, tough, resilient to its core. So it is that blue crabs, while they find salinities highly suitable around the middle of the bay, near Tangier and Smith islands, also flourish in the freshwater reaches of the bay's tributaries and the near-ocean of its mouth—and do better than one might expect in grossly polluted sections like Baltimore's harbor and Norfolk's Elizabeth River.

Oysters, though they can't move away from pollution, are able to survive days, even weeks, of depressed oxygen in the water by clamping their shells shut and switching their entire metabolic process. If overharvesting of big oysters, which are mostly females, creates problems for reproduction, male oysters are able to change their sex as needed to compensate. Even in their current, depleted state, they are still capable in some years of excellent reproduction.

Rockfish, harvested down to only a few percent of their previous numbers in the bay, were capable of rebounding with a spectacularly successful spawn of young in 1989, even in moderately polluted spawning areas, after a moratorium on fishing gave them just a few years of breathing room. (Several more years will be needed to see whether their spawning success, coming after a decade of poor reproduction, is a clear upward trend.)

Great blue herons, one of the few birds found year-round on the bay and in every county of its five-state watershed, prefer to dine on soft crabs, small fish, toads, and snakes—but when food is scarce they have been observed eating baby kittens and even a full-grown muskrat. Canvasback ducks, after pollution killed most of their normal food, the underwater grasses, changed their diet almost completely to small clams. Wild geese turned to feeding in grain fields, with great success.

In sum, although the bay we are trying to restore is, on the one hand, a crippled version of the original, healthy system (see Figure 1.7), its primary inhabitants are anything but fragile and nothing if not adaptable to change. They are the opportunists, the plants and animals that are best able to rush in and colonize new habitats during the intervals—brief in evolutionary time—when fertile estuaries like the Chesapeake occur during the short warming spells between the long ice ages. If you have ever hooked a rockfish or a shad on a line and felt it tug for its freedom, or tried to pry apart an oyster's shells, or attempted to pick up a big feisty jimmy (male) crab, then you know—the bay vigorously, vitally, desperately wants to live. Given half a chance to survive, its inhabitants will not be shy grabbing it.

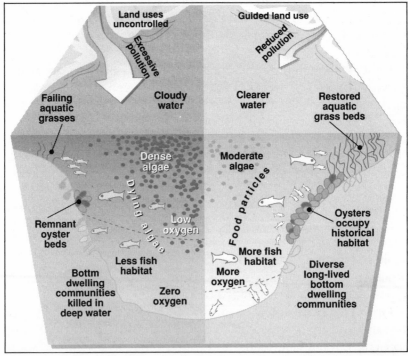

FIGURE 1.7. THE BAY WE HAVE (*left*) AND THE BAY WE WANT (*right*). [Adapted from Mountford and others, EPA Chesapeake Bay Liaison Office]

Assessing the State of the Bay

Are we likely to create and maintain such conditions across the bay and its watershed? There is no doubt that in each of the last few decades the intensity and scope of efforts to preserve the Chesapeake ecosystem have increased. But at the same time so has the offsetting magnitude of human impacts on the environment. This section and the chapters that follow attempt to balance the bay's books for these forces of preservation and damage—to see whether we are just generating an impressive cash flow or really showing a profit.

The health of Chesapeake Bay depends largely on three factors:

- The pollution factor: what we put into the bay that harms the water, plants, and animals there
- The harvest factor: what we take out of the bay, that is, how many fish and crabs and oysters we catch
- The resilience factor: how well we maintain the natural features of the bay ecosystem that help it cope with the first two factors

Many parts of the bay ecosystem, of course, are all the more important for overlapping these three categories. Oysters, whose enormous capacity to filter and cleanse pollution from the water is part of the bay's resilience, also provide a seafood harvest.

The next three chapters examine our progress in eliminating pollution, managing harvests, and maintaining resilience. First, however, let's define what we mean by progress. If we measure it, as we often do, by the money and effort expended on bay restoration, and by the increasing sophistication of our environmental regulations and scientific knowledge, then we have been making progress fairly steadily since the first Earth Day in 1970. But if we measure it by the responses we see to date in the bay's water quality, in its fisheries, and in its resilience, or ability to rebound from environmental insult, then progress is more muddled.

In many cases we must go further still and measure progress by whether it is enough to offset impacts not only from our current pollution but that which is to come from millions more people who will be living and working around the bay in just a few more decades. The examples that follow—summarized here and detailed in succeeding chapters—measure progress by these tougher yardsticks.

Pollution

ITEM: Real progress has been made in reducing some, but not all, important pollutants from sewage and industrial discharges. There is corresponding improvement in the aquatic environment of the upper tidal Potomac and Patuxent rivers.

ITEM: Concentrations of toxic chemicals in the bay and its creatures do not appear to be increasing, and severely polluted Baltimore Harbor is showing modest improvement. Although toxics do not seem to be the primary cause of any baywide problems, we have failed to learn enough about their possible long-term impact to really say what role toxics may be playing in the bay's decline.

ITEM: Control of pollution from agriculture, a major source of the bay's water quality problems, is proving much more difficult and less effective than we had hoped.

ITEM: Air pollution is turning out to be a larger source of contamination to the bay than was thought just a few years ago. The federal Clean Air Act of 1990 will improve this situation, but it is not focused in comprehensive or timely fashion on the water quality impacts of air pollutants. Nor is it keyed to offset the impacts of continuing population growth.

ITEM: Sediment and stormwater control devices are proving inadequate compensation for removing the natural filtering and buffering qualities of vegetation during land development. About a quarter of ninety sites surveyed across the watershed were doing a good job of controlling sediment; only about 10 percent were removing pollutants from stormwater runoff.

ITEM: In the bulk of the bay and its main river, the Susquehanna, there have been no strong trends of improvement or further decline in water quality during the last decade. There are encouraging indications that one pollutant, phosphorus, is just beginning to decline. But nitrogen, another pollutant, has increased slightly.

Harvest

ITEM: While we may never fully sort out the relative influences of pollution, disease, and simple overharvesting, it is amply clear that overfishing, both sport and commercial, has been a major culprit in the bay's widespread fishery declines.

ITEM: Populations of striped bass, or rockfish, have rebounded sharply after more than a decade of generally poor reproduction in most of their bay spawning areas.

ITEM: Other species whose populations have dropped severely have not yet shown much rebound. And harvest pressure on virtually every other major commercial and recreational species, including crabs and oysters, ranges from extremely heavy fishing to serious overfishing.

ITEM: With the exception of rockfish, neither Maryland nor Virginia has yet demonstrated an ability to manage fishing for any bay species on a sustainable basis. And to a large extent the success with rockfish was forced by federal legislation—a special case not likely to recur with other bay species.

Resilience

The concept of resilience is not as commonly understood as pollution and fishery harvests. But it is just as vital to the bay's health as good sewage treatment and proper conservation of seafood resources. It lies in the bay watershed's forests and wetlands, which filter and cleanse stormwater running off the land and stabilize the environment of the bay's rivers and streams by absorbing water in storms and releasing it during droughts. Resilience includes the bay's submerged grasses and its oyster beds, which perform similar cleansing and filtering and stabilizing functions in the water. It springs from the rich and extensive habitats that offer extraordinary spawning and nursery and feeding areas to support its fish and fowl. When we say of any natural system, "leave it alone and it'll come back," we are talking about resilience. Almost without exception, the bay's resilience is down and continuing to decline.

ITEM: We continue to lose forests and wetlands. Historically, the watershed has lost about 40 percent of its forests and more than half its wetlands. Yet policies to maintain present levels range from inadequate to nonexistent.

ITEM: The *distribution* of forests is as important as total acreage.

Losses along the edges of waterways, where they have maximum effect in filtering pollutants, probably are more extreme and damaging to water quality than total forest change.

ITEM: Oysters, long afflicted by overfishing and more recently by disease and pollution, have been reduced to 1 percent of historic levels. The major question in the short term will be simply one of survival.

ITEM: The decline in submerged grass beds, whose health is perhaps the best single indicator of baywide water quality, seems to have bottomed out in 1984 and reversed slightly in the last few years. Acreage remains far below levels of two decades ago.

ITEM: Our ability to contain the suburban sprawl that is converting huge quantities of open space to developed land across the bay's watershed remains grossly inadequate.

ITEM: The bay we would restore is an amputee in terms of potential fish production—thousands of miles of prime spawning and nursery waters have been severed from use by hydro dams, highway culverts, and other obstructions.

Paradise Lost?

In sum, then, the picture is one of encouraging improvement on portions of a few rivers; evidence that a species or two are capable of rebounding from depressed levels; continued declines in resilience; and the lukewarm satisfaction that conditions would have been much worse had we done nothing to offset the polluting effects of rapid growth in both human and farm animal populations.

Nearly eight years after the historic agreement to restore the bay's health made by Maryland, Virginia, Pennsylvania, the EPA, and the District of Columbia in December 1983, there still is no discernible trend toward a system-wide comeback. Progress too often is still of the variety that has been characterized as rowing ahead at four knots when the current is moving against us at five.

A recent example of this situation was the editorial in a Baltimore newspaper that reflected as well the views of local governments in the metropolitan area. "Victory at Fort Meade," it proclaimed. A compromise had been reached on 9,000 acres of field and forest. It was surplus military land proposed by the U.S. Army for development, but championed by local governments and the state for a wildlife refuge. The army, the editorial said, had agreed to the refuge and would only develop 1,400 acres.

Was that a victory? Or was it a decline of nearly 3 square miles in open space in an already congested part of the bay's watershed where—surely as humans drive cars and flush toilets and build houses—pollution would increase? "Compromise, when it comes to the bay, is the halfway house to surrender," said Rogers C. B. Morton, the late U.S. Secretary of the Interior. He was speaking at a conference on the health of the bay. The date was 1968.

The point is that in assessing real progress we must subtract any increases in impacts on the environment from a human population that continues to grow across the bay region without any talk of limits. In these pages we will frequently refer to the huge portions of the bay's wetlands, forests, oysters, and submerged grasses that have been destroyed during the history of European settlement. The point is not to rub our collective noses in a "paradise lost" that can never be restored. Rather, it is to make it clear that every time we compromise these aspects of the bay's resilience, we are dealing with systems that have already been hugely compromised.

The peril of forgetting this point was demonstrated during a recent heated discussion at a conference on San Francisco Bay about the technical pros and cons of filling several acres of tidal wetlands. The participants were brought up short by a speaker who reminded them that, historically, nearly 97 percent of the bay's wetlands had already been destroyed—and yet there they sat haggling fiercely over how much of the last 3 percent should be saved.

So when we lose an acre of tidal wetlands from the bay, we are not just losing an acre. We are losing an acre of the fraction that still remains (27 percent in Maryland, 58 percent in Virginia). Similarly, we are dealing not with protecting forest but protecting the last half of our forest. The same holds true for the last 10 percent of our underwater grasses; for the last 1 percent of our oysters.

To restore and maintain Chesapeake Bay in the long term we are going to need, at a minimum, to keep its remaining natural systems intact—and to enhance them. There are obvious limits to regaining the watershed's historical forests, and there is evidence that natural, uncontrollable losses of wetlands to rising sea level are increasing.

Therefore we must be all the more zealous in controlling pollution to "help out" an ecosystem that cannot help itself as well as it once could.

We must not only reduce the present level of human impacts enough to restore the bay; we must also reduce those impacts enough to offset another 2.6 million people (a very conservative figure) who are projected to move into the watershed by the year 2020.

Are we on track to make that kind of progress? What does it mean for the bay? Let's examine where we stand and where we are headed in the three key categories of pollution, harvests, and resilience.

Part II
STATE OF THE BAY

CHAPTER 2

Pollution

The Chesapeake Bay across large portions of its rivers and main stem is not as clear nor as fishable as it was even a few decades ago. In a few areas, isolated incidents so far, it is hazardous to one's health to swim in it or to eat from it.

Many positive and ambitious actions have been taken in the last decade to protect water quality; but, in general, they have only been able to hold the line on pollution or slow the decline. Too often we have let the burden of proof fall on the bay to tell us it is sick, rather than acting conservatively with the wastes we allow to enter it. The danger is that environmental decline does not necessarily follow a gradual and predictable downward slope on a graph. Rather, it may follow a stair-step pattern, approaching an unseen threshold with little apparent change, and then plummet abruptly to some lower level.

Pollution routinely follows four paths to the bay:

- The runoff of rainwater from the land—washing with it everything from agricultural fertilizers and soil to dog and cat feces from urban pavements, not to mention pesticides from suburban lawns and complex hydrocarbons in the oily residue from highways

- Pipes that discharge wastes from sewage treatment plants and industrial facilities directly to the water
- The air—as contaminated particles settle out over the bay or over land where rain then washes them into the water
- Groundwater—the subsurface flows that may pick up contaminants that soak into the ground, as from septic tanks and heavily fertilized cropland

In addition the bay is at risk from occasional but potentially disastrous pollution from illegal dumping of chemicals, oil spills, and ruptured underground storage tanks. Small spills from such sources already occur frequently. And the bay must also absorb the discharges from marine toilets on tens of thousands of boats on peak recreation weekends. The following sections examine the major sources of pollution to the bay and apply the measures set out in Chapter 1 to determine our progress in reversing it.

AGRICULTURE

Agriculture intimately involves us directly with the soil, water and other living creatures of God's creation. . . . The nature of that relationship—whether it is in harmony with the Creator's plan or in opposition to it—determines whether we are either responsible stewards . . . or irresponsible destroyers.

—GREGORY CUSAK,
Iowa Department of Agriculture

We may think of the bay as a great tree which is rooted by its river systems in every nook and cranny of watershed lands covering fifteen times the area of the waters to which they drain. And since it is so very shallow—average depth about 21 feet—there is very little water beneath the bay's broad surface to absorb and dilute pollutants from the land. What we do on the watershed thus greatly influences the quality of the water.

Agriculture, involving more than a quarter of the bay's watershed, an area nearly twice as large as Maryland, is one of the most important sources of pollution from the land to the water. Even as farm acreage shrank by 30 percent in recent decades, the tonnage of "nutrients"—nitrogen and phosphorus in commercial fertilizers and animal manure—doubled and even tripled per acre of cropland in many parts of the bay's watershed. In addition, modern animal agriculture during the same period was concentrating cows, hogs, and poultry in densities 5 to 100 times greater than in the 1950s (Figure 2.1). Spread evenly across the watershed, all the manure

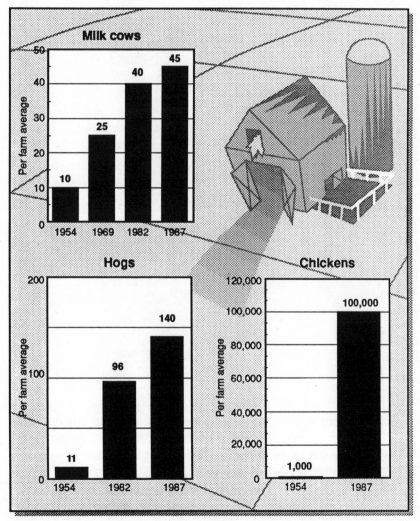

FIGURE 2.1. THE CONCENTRATION OF ANIMALS ON PENNSYLVANIA FARMS. [Adapted from USDA Census of Agriculture by Joseph Hutchinson]

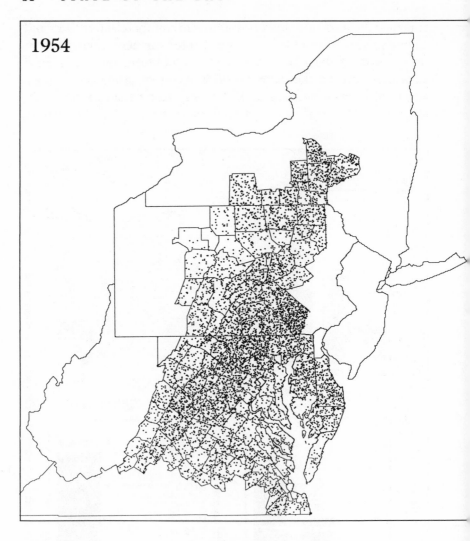

1954

generated there would amount to less than a pound per acre per year. But in fact some counties have more than 8 tons per acre, which is disposed of by spreading it on the land, often in addition to commercial fertilizer. (See Figure 2.2.) The result of all this is that large acreages of soils in the watershed have become "polluted" in the sense that they are saturated with more nutrients than can be sopped up by crops as they grow. The nutrients move into waterways by trickling underground or in surface runoff during storms.

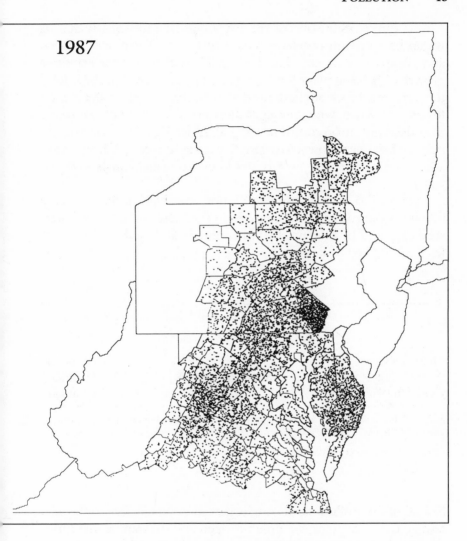

FIGURE 2.2. NITROGEN CONTENT OF MANURE IN THE CHESAPEAKE
WATERSHED: 1954–1987 *Charting farm manure trends, as measured by
nitrogen, a nutrient in manure that is polluting the bay, reveals that the
patterns of manure distribution are what have changed most dramatically,
rather than the absolute amount of manure, which has grown about 10 percent.
Growing concentrations of farm animals in areas like Pennsylvania's Lancaster
County, Maryland's Eastern Shore, and Virginia's Rockingham County have
made it difficult to control manure from running off into waterways. Note: Each
dot = 25 tons* [By S. Tennenbaum and R. Costanza, Chesapeake Biological
Laboratory, University of Maryland]

As a direct result, one of the bay's biggest problems is that its waters have become overfertilized, or eutrophic. Too much nitrogen and phosphorus are entering the bay. There they fuel the explosive growth of floating plant life, or algae, so extensively that they cloud the water and block out light needed by the bay's underwater grasses for growth. Then, when the algae die, they sink to the bottom where their decomposition consumes oxygen. Indeed, the bay's deep channels can become so low in oxygen they are as hostile to fish and crabs and other aquatic life as a desert. Polluted land equals polluted water.

A rough idea of agriculture's pollution potential is indicated in the following table comparing nutrients generated in the bay's watershed each year by humans, by farm animals, and by the commercial fertilizer applied to farm crops:

Source	Nitrogen (lb/yr)	Phosphorus (lb/yr)
Human wastes	142 million	22 million
Animal wastes[a]	350–365 million	92–115 million
Commercial fertilizers[a]	330 million	200 million

Sources: Pennsylvania Manure Manual (Harrisburg: Pennsylvania Department of Agriculture, 1987); USDA 1987 Census of Agriculture (Washington, D.C.: Bureau of the Census, 1987).

[a] Best estimates; sources of data vary, and there are data discrepancies.

Not all of this pollution, of course, gets into the bay. Not only does sewage treatment remove some nitrogen and substantial quantities of phosphorus from human wastes, but plants and crops remove large quantities of nutrients.

More than 60 percent of the nitrogen and 40 percent of the phosphorus that does reach the bay and tributaries comes from land runoff in an average rainfall year. In dry years, land runoff represents less of the total; in wet years it is more. This overall bay percentage varies widely among rivers. The James in Virginia, for example, is overwhelmingly dominated by nutrients from sewage treatment plants. Of all land runoff that is related to human activities (what comes from forests, for example, is not), agriculture baywide accounts for seven to twenty-five times the nitrogen of the next leading source (urban and suburban runoff) and ten to fifteen times the phosphorus. (Septic tanks are a potentially large but unquantified source of nitrogen.)

The Cleanup Effort

A primary goal of the Chesapeake Bay cleanup effort since 1987 has been to reduce the amount of agricultural nutrients that get into the water (as well as nutrients from other sources like sewage) by 40 percent of 1985 pollution levels (or an average rainfall year). The reductions are supposed to be permanent. In effect, they are meant to "cap" any further growth of nutrients polluting the bay, even as their sources, such as human and farm animal populations, continue to grow.

Such reductions from agriculture are achievable, but they are highly unlikely without substantial redirection of current approaches. Unlike the straightforward technology used to treat sewage, the ways of cleaning up land runoff are as varied as the ways in which farmers grow crops and husband animals. Even so, they all fall into two categories: keeping nutrients from entering the water or putting less nutrient on the land in the first place.

Known generally as *best management practices* (BMPs), the techniques range from farming with less fertilizer to planting seeds directly into existing vegetation, a practice that avoids plowing and disrupting the soil and also reduces runoff. Other BMPs involve storing manure in concrete or steel pits, altering farm slopes to retard runoff, fencing cattle from streams so they don't pollute the water and cause stream bank erosion, and planting winter cover crops to take up excess fertilizer left in the soil after the main harvest.

EPA estimates that BMPs installed between 1985 and 1990 have reduced phosphorus by 10.5 percent and nitrogen by 9.5 percent. However, a recent study by the Metropolitan Washington Council of Governments estimates that nutrient reductions from agriculture in the Maryland and Virginia counties of the Potomac River watershed are ten times less than reductions projected by using current federal and state accounting methods. These methods often just assume that a certain amount of soil is retained by a given BMP and then multiply that amount times a standard amount of nutrients in each ton of soil. In reality, however, it appears that controlling the movement of soil does not always control equally the runoff of nutrients placed on the soil in the form of manure or commercial fertilizer. In some cases, particularly with water-soluble nitrogen, retarding runoff only redirects the nutrient problem—concentrating pollution in groundwater where it eventually makes its way into streams, rivers, and the bay. Worse yet, drain systems incorporated with some of these BMPs actually hasten the passage of nutrients toward waterways.

Groundwater seeping into waterways is in dry weather the source of virtually all the water flowing to the bay. This flow has been roughly calculated to amount to an "invisible river" on the order of the James—the bay's third largest tributary. Studies of groundwater done in agricultural areas of Maryland, Virginia, and Pennsylvania have found substantial nitrogen contamination; indeed, the amounts are frequently dozens of times higher than natural background levels. Phosphorus, the other agricultural fertilizer that is polluting the bay, is not nearly as soluble in water as nitrogen fertilizer and therefore does not readily end up in groundwater.

Another BMP being called into question concerns the storage of animal manure. Currently EPA takes credit for keeping virtually all of the nitrogen and phosphorus in the stored manure out of the water. A few hundred of these storage facilities have been built, and many more are planned. But nutrient experts at Penn State University and local conservation agents (see the Centre County case study in Chapter 6) note that farmers spread their manure on their fields whether they store it or not—the difference is that a storage facility allows them to spread it perhaps a couple of times a year, rather than daily. This is theoretically a plus for pollution control, since farmers can avoid spreading manure when weather and field conditions would just cause it to wash off into nearby waterways. But critics say it is doubtful the difference in pollution is as great as the near-total reductions that states and EPA are claiming.

Another flaw is that manure often is spread on the basis of how much nitrogen the soil can use. This practice can result in overloading soils with phosphorus contained in the manure. A study prepared by Lancaster County's solid waste management authority says that many areas could absorb more manure, but only if soil needs are calculated on the basis of nitrogen: "If nutrient needs were based on phosphorus ... a significantly smaller amount of manure would balance the [soil needs]. ... There would be a definite excess of manure in the county if it were applied according to phosphorus needs." Manure pits are another example of how pollution control efforts remain heavily biased toward capital-intensive solutions. Roughly 80 percent of the $9.4 million dollars spent by government and farmers in Pennsylvania in recent years under a bay pollution control program went to manure pits—an amount of money disproportionate to the amount of nutrients kept out of the bay by such installations.

The need to take extreme caution in taking pollution reductions for granted with traditional BMPs is underscored by one of the few areas in the watershed where actual, in-the-field monitoring of agricultural pollution control has been done since 1983—a grain and livestock farm in Lancaster County. The farmer applied numerous techniques to hold soil on his farm, dramatically reducing erosion eightfold. Then he put in a manure storage facility. At the same time, he cut in half the nitrogen he was applying through commercial fertilizer, after an analysis showed the crops could get enough additional nutrients from the manure his animals were producing.

The results? According to EPA, despite all these efforts nitrogen flowing in surface runoff to a nearby stream fell by just 9 percent—and meanwhile had gone up by 9 percent in groundwater, which eventually would flow into the stream. More surprising was the tiny reduction in phosphorus runoff. Since that nutrient supposedly clings to soil, and soil movement off the farm was reduced by 88 percent, one might expect a dramatic reduction. Yet phosphorus runoff fell by less than 7 percent.

A single farm is not necessarily representative of a whole watershed, and experts warn not to draw major conclusions from this example. The results may mean that the land and underlying groundwater, insulted for so many years by excessive nutrient applications, will in effect take several years to lose all traces of this pollution. In other words, even if we stop overfertilizing the lands of the watershed today it may take several years before the sins of the past stop oozing out of the saturated earth and groundwater toward the bay. It is also worth noting that while the foregoing examples have concentrated on Pennsylvania, where agriculture is the major focus of bay restoration programs, many of the same concerns extend also to Virginia and Maryland.

The Outlook

All of this is not to say the picture for controlling agricultural pollution is bleak. There are tools, BMPs, that show great promise for controlling the nutrients and soil contributed by agriculture. Research and field tests at the University of Maryland's Wye Experiment Station, for example, show potential for controlling nitrogen by sowing fields in winter cover crops like rye. On many soils the largest pulses of nitrogen leaving fields, it turns out, are not in the spring, when fertilizer is applied, but in the winter, as the leftover residues of crops decay or manure is spread when no plants are growing to take it up. Cover crops can absorb the bulk of this runoff. And plowed back into the soil in the spring, they can substitute for part of a farmer's purchases of commercial fertilizer.

Establishing forests—or retaining them where they exist between farms and waterways—appears to do a remarkable job of improving polluted runoff, including the elusive subsurface flows of nitrogen in groundwater. According to research by the Smithsonian Institution's Rhode River Laboratory in Maryland, it appears that the majority of nitrogen removal is not done by trees, per se, but by the bacteria whose growth is fostered in the rich leaf litter of the forest floor. As early an authority as Captain John Smith recommended forested buffer strips (as protection against bad weather) in his *Theory and Practice of Colonization*: "Leave every [field] environed with so many rows of well grown trees as you will. . . . [It is] as easy as carelessly and ignorantly cutting down all before you."

"Nutrient management," which means knowing precisely how much fertilizer you need to grow your crop, and using that amount and no more, holds huge potential. For example, if farmers in the Potomac River watershed of the bay, whose lands feed 20 percent of the bay's riverflow, used all the nutrients in their manure to grow crops, they could virtually eliminate the 70 million pounds of nitrogen and 15 million pounds of phosphorus they apply to the land each year in commercial fertilizers, according to the Council of Governments study. Pennsylvania, which has some of the severest nutrient pollution in the watershed, probably is in the forefront of the states in pushing nutrient management.

Some of these practices are beginning to happen. Penn State recently reduced its recommendations for how much nitrogen farmers should apply by 20 percent. Virginia and Maryland are starting to include cover cropping as a BMP they will pay farmers to use. Almost weekly somewhere in the watershed, articles appear in farm publications like "Using Manure Can Cut Fertilizer Bills: For years people have looked at chicken manure as something of little value that had to be disposed of on the land, but now . . ." (*Salisbury Daily Times*, Farm and Home Section, July 1990). In addition, most of the many thousands of BMPs installed since 1985 are producing *some* reductions in the runoff of phosphorus and, to a far lesser extent, nitrogen. Even if a BMP reduces only the runoff of soil, that is a plus for water quality. For sediment entering the bay is also a killer. It smothers the eggs of spawning fish, damages the gills of young fish, and combines with nutrient-induced growth of algae to cloud the bay's waters, reducing the growth of underwater grasses.

But major obstacles to meeting our goals for agricultural pollution remain. There is no systematic framework for true nutrient control and nutrient management among the watershed governments and their agencies. What exists is rather a hodgepodge of attempts at nutrient control that have been piggybacked hopefully onto an existing agricultural bureaucracy that is set up for maintaining farm productivity through soil erosion control.

The two goals—clean water and soil productivity—do overlap, but not nearly enough. For example, the federal Soil Conservation Service sets the goal for reducing soil washed from farm fields at a level of 3 to 5 tons per acre per year. (Five tons is a loss of soil whose depth, spread over an acre, is equivalent to the thickness of a dime.) But this is a goal based solely on maintaining long-term soil productivity, not on achieving clearer and cleaner water. Excellent soil conservation can achieve much better results—as low as a ton per acre.

Agriculture is notable for having exempted itself from many environmental regulations throughout the years. (See the accompanying box.) Pennsylvania, for example, recently exempted livestock wallowing in streams from its water pollution control regulations to make sure farmers didn't have to erect fences. (At the same time the state has implemented a nonmandatory program to encourage stream fencing.) In other words, much of what farmers do is voluntary. This approach can seriously warp the effectiveness and direction of pollution control programs. (See the case study of Centre County in Chapter 6.) It has led to difficulties in spending all the money available for agricultural pollution control. It also handicaps

AGRICULTURAL EXEMPTIONS FROM ENVIRONMENTAL LAWS

- Virginia's Chesapeake Bay Preservation Act stipulates a mandatory 100-foot buffer next to waterways—but only 25 feet for farmers with an approved water quality conservation plan.
- Federal and Maryland nontidal wetlands regulations allow farmers to develop any nontidal wetland that has been farmed since 1985. All ongoing agricultural activities are essentially exempt from normal permit requirements in wetlands.
- Maryland's Critical Area Act declares agriculture to be a "protective" use of the shoreline, the same as forests. It requires only a 25-foot buffer (versus 100 feet for other uses) and allows variances to restrictive shorefront zoning for development.
- Pennsylvania's Clean Streams Law exempts farmers from keeping livestock out of streams.
- State sediment control laws exempt all agricultural activities, such as plowing, from getting permits.

cleanup programs in targeting funds on the most effective pollution controls and the worst-polluting farms.

Even where there is water quality regulatory authority, as in Pennsylvania, the evidence is that farms make up a disproportionately tiny fraction of enforcement activities. Similarly, when the federal government recently required all farms benefiting from federal programs to have erosion control plans implemented by 1994, they also permitted farms to follow "alternative" plans that would allow about twice as much erosion.

CONCLUSIONS

□ While there is a great deal of activity across the bay's watershed to control agricultural pollution, it is neither as well focused nor as cost-effective as it must be to have any hope of meeting our goals of a 40 percent reduction in nutrients.

□ Programs are based too heavily on trying to keep pollution out of the water and not enough on reducing its sources. Until the lands of the watershed are essentially "in balance"—with no more nutrients being put on than plants can take up—the waters to which these lands drain will continue to have contamination problems.

□ Too much of our very limited money is being directed toward capital-intensive structural solutions such as manure pits (although these cannot be ruled out as one of many tools to be used in reducing pollution).

□ Programs are based too heavily on farmers' voluntarism and on soil conservation programs that were originated to maintain productivity, not to prevent water pollution—and which have not achieved even their soil conservation goals satisfactorily after decades of effort.

□ There is still a tendency to think that agricultural runoff—even though it rivals or surpasses sewage discharges to the bay as the source of a major water quality problem (eutrophication)—can be resolved on the cheap. Compare, for example, the expenditure of about $9.5 million to date of bay cleanup money (including farmers' shares) to control nutrients on millions of acres of farmland in Pennsylvania versus the more than $1 billion the states estimate will have to be spent to control nutrients at sewage treatment plants in the 1990s.

□ Forested buffers next to ditches and streams on farms, a particularly promising tool for pollution control, may need to be 100 feet wide or more. Although some government subsidies are available, farmers in many cases may not be able to recoup their losses for taking so much land permanently out of production. A farmer who sells grain, for example, cannot charge more than the national norm simply because his growing techniques are "less polluting."

While farmers can, to an extent, benefit economically by controlling pollution (example: substituting manure for purchased fertilizer), they may have to go further to meet the bay's water quality needs. For example, a recent Penn State study explored what would happen if a typical dairy farm managed its operations solely for the maximum benefit of water quality in Chesapeake Bay. That scenario produced a drop of more than 20 percent in income. The author suggests that it currently is difficult for farmers, who must sell their milk in a national arena, to get a premium for producing milk regionally in an environmentally superior (that is, less polluting) way. The alternative might be society's decision to help subsidize his production.

◻ The bay's pollution load from agriculture, in sharp distinction to pollution from an ever-expanding human population, does not seem likely to get much worse. After dramatic growth through the early 1980s, commercial fertilizers across the watershed have declined by about a fifth, and use seems to be leveling off or decreasing slightly. An exception is the continuing trends toward concentration and growth in animal agriculture—with all the problems that scenario presents for handling and distributing the manure produced. In parts of the watershed, continued concentration of farm animals may negate any gains in nutrient control.

◻ Finally, current accounting procedures are almost certainly over-stating progress in keeping agricultural nutrients out of the water. The very process of counting BMPs or calculating tons of soil theoretically saved is flawed. Many experts appear to be leaning toward a "mass balance" approach. Essentially this involves account-ing for all the nutrients entering a farm—in feed, in fertilizer, in manure, and so forth—and then accounting for all the nutrients leaving—in harvested crops, in livestock sold off, and so on. What is left is what you must reduce in order to leave the land, and ultimately the water, unpolluted. The approach is rather more complex than this in practice, but it deserves much more consideration than it has gotten so far.

SUSQUEHANNA—THE RIVER THAT *IS* THE BAY

I drain a thousand streams, yet still I seek
To lose myself within the Chesapeake . . .

—from "WE HEARD THE RIVER SINGING,"
  a Susquehanna sonnet

If we want to find out whether our efforts at controlling pollution from agriculture are winning or losing, there's no better place to start than the Susquehanna River. Its drainage basin contains 40 percent of the cropland in the bay's watershed and perhaps the world's most concentrated populations of farm animals. More than any other of the bay's rivers, it is there that agriculture influences water quality. And the Susquehanna in turn determines the water quality of the upper Chesapeake—in fact, it *is* the upper bay. From the river's entry to the bay's main stem around Havre de Grace, Maryland, to the Patuxent River nearly 90 miles south, about 90 percent of the bay's fresh water comes from the Susquehanna. For the nearly 200-mile length of the bay, it constitutes about 45 percent of all the bay's fresh water. (See Figure 2.3.)

The influence of this Susquehanna water can extend far down the bay's main stem, playing a role in low oxygen levels in all the western shore rivers down to Virginia's Rappahannock. In some cases, the Susquehanna also extends its influence far upstream from the other rivers' mouths. For example, a recent study of severe water pollution in Rock Creek, in Anne Arundel County, Maryland, found that most of the problem was the poor quality of water entering the creek from the bay, not the water running from the smallish drainage basin or watershed of the creek. And the quality of that bay water was in turn dictated by the Susquehanna.

Extent of the Damage

The Susquehanna is one of the few places in the bay system where we have more than a decade of measurement of actual levels of polluting nitrogen and phosphorus flowing to the Chesapeake (Figure 2.4). Nitrogen levels in the river as it flows into the bay actually increased between the 1970s and the 1980s. This reflects the difficulty of controlling nitrogen from farmland. Nor have most of Pennsylvania's sewage treatment plants, which account for about 10 percent of all nitrogen and 23 percent of all phosphorus entering the river, done anything to control nitrogen. The fact that phosphorus levels appear to have decreased slightly may reflect improved sewage treatment or Pennsylvania's recent efforts in agricultural pollution control.

It is not only Chesapeake Bay that is degraded by these nutrients. In Pennsylvania's latest statewide water quality assessment, 13 of 53 major lakes surveyed (out of a state total of 125) were "eutrophic," which means they are suffering from too many nutrients. Programs to help the bay will also help these lakes. The federally mandated assessment also looked at about half of the state's 50,000 miles of streams, finding that nearly a fifth of these, or 4,500 stream miles,

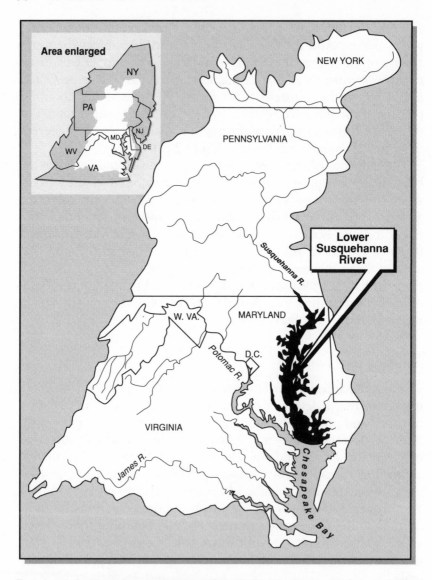

FIGURE 2.3. THE SUSQUEHANNA RIVER IS THE BAY   *The upper half of the Chesapeake is in fact the broad, lower tidal portion of the Susquehanna, comparable to the widening portions of the Potomac River below Washington, D.C. Cleaning up the Susquehanna is critical to cleaning up the bay. [Adapted from EPA,* Chesapeake Bay: A Profile of Environmental Change, *by Joseph Hutchinson]*

did not fully support state and federal water quality goals. More than a thousand miles of these streams were degraded by the same pollution sources that bay cleanup programs are trying to control. Acid mine drainage from past coal mining practices is degrading the largest stream mileage in Pennsylvania. While this pollution does not directly affect the bay, it does mean that efforts currently under way to restore fish migrations from the bay throughout the Susquehanna drainage will be less successful.

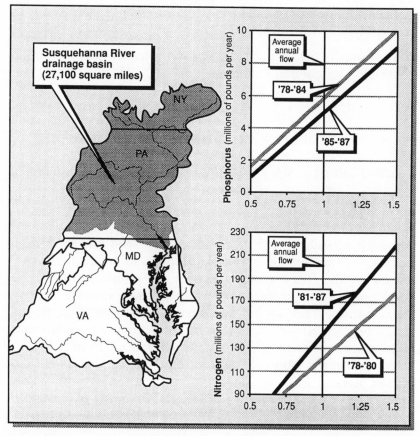

FIGURE 2.4. POLLUTION TRENDS IN THE BAY'S MAIN RIVER: THE SUS-QUEHANNA   *In the last decade, phosphorus loads in the Susquehanna, whose huge portion of the Chesapeake drainage is critical to water quality in the bay, have fallen slightly, but nitrogen loads have risen.* [Adapted from EPA and Susquehanna River Basin Commission reports by Joseph Hutchinson]

CONCLUSIONS

☐ It is one of the greatest political challenges to restoration of the bay that the water quality of Maryland's bay, and to a lesser extent Virginia's portion, is greatly affected by a principal river of Pennsylvania, which borders not a square foot of the Chesapeake.

☐ Large sections of the bay's waters are not likely to respond adequately to cleanup efforts in Maryland or Virginia without help from Pennsylvania. And water quality trends to date in the Susquehanna range from quite modest improvement (phosphorus) to worsening (nitrogen).

☐ The future of the Susquehanna cleanup is heavily tied to success in controlling agricultural pollution.

RUNOFF—SEDIMENT AND STORMWATER POLLUTION

In the 1980s, the acreage of lawns in Maryland surpassed the acreage in corn, the largest agricultural crop.

—MARYLAND TURFGRASS SURVEY

Although agricultural use of the watershed—and pollutants from that use—represents the largest contribution to polluted land runoff, by far the fastest-growing part of the problem involves the development of open space for residences and commerce. During the next thirty years—in less than a tenth of the time since the bay region was settled—a third of all land development that has ever taken place will happen. The watershed will go from being 11 percent urban and suburban to about 15 percent, an alteration of 1.6 million acres of fields and forest. In Maryland, the most rapidly urbanizing of the three principal bay states, acreage of developed land will nearly double.

Sediment

Whenever it rains, an acre of land cleared for construction can flush a hundred times the soil into waterways as well-managed farmland—

and up to a thousand times as much as a forest. A certain amount of sediment is healthy for the bay. It is a source of nutrients and silica needed for the growth of plankton, which support the higher food web, and some of it is captured by marshes as a source of building material to keep ahead of rising sea level. Thus a sediment-free bay would be quite clear but less productive.

But in modern times these needs have been far exceeded. The abrupt inflows of thousands of tons of soil from construction, rapidly running into a stream, can be as deadly as a spill of oil or raw sewage—perhaps more so, since sediment never degrades but just keeps getting stirred up by tide and storms and wind to cloud the water. Sediment pollutes by smothering fish eggs, by tearing at the fragile gills of just-born fish, and by covering gravel bottoms that are prime habitats for fish spawning and for aquatic insects. Further downriver it may cover oyster beds, leaving no clean shell exposed for the spat and young to attach to and form their own shell. Sediment also clouds the water, cutting off sunlight needed to grow the submerged grass that is critical habitat in streams and the bay.

Although, baywide, the bulk of sediment comes from natural shoreline erosion, it is sediment from upland portions of the watershed that may do the most damage and where the bay's tributaries are most vulnerable to sediment's impacts. (See also the discussion of shoreline erosion in Chapter 4.) The bay's watershed contains more than 100,000 miles of streams and river above the influence of tide, and half of this either supports or has the potential to support trout, whose various species are quite vulnerable to sediment. According to a 1989 *Trout Magazine* article, seven of America's top ten trout streams are in the Chesapeake watershed. This part of the bay's drainage network also supports fishing for smallmouth and largemouth bass. Additionally, it was once a world-class spawning and nursery ground for shad and herring and, to some extent, rockfish, before dams blocked their traditional annual migrations. With a major goal of bay restoration to remove these blockages from thousands of miles of waterways (see Chapter 4), controlling the impacts of sediment even hundreds of miles from the main Chesapeake is critical to success.

No matter how much we relate to the bay, it is on the smaller streams, which are most vulnerable to sediment pollution, that most of us live. Virtually no one in the watershed lives more than half a mile, about a fifteen-minute walk, from a stream. The bay is our larger heritage, but the little waterways are our everyday connections to it.

During the 1970s all three bay states enacted laws designed to control sediment from developing lands. The techniques include erecting "filter fences"—the straw bales and black cloth that one sees staked into the ground around roadbuilding and other construction sites almost everywhere—as well as the building of settling ponds to catch and filter all water draining from the construction site. These controls cannot eliminate sediment pollution, but they have been demonstrated to reduce it by as much as 90 percent by weight. (Note, however, that the finer, lighter particles of sediment that escape stay suspended in the water the longest, so water clarity may be degraded despite efficient sediment trapping.)

How are the states doing? For this book, a study was commissioned in which ninety construction sites were sampled randomly during May and June 1990. The survey covered thirty-one counties and townships from Scranton to Norfolk. Sediment controls were compared to the regulations applicable in each state. The study is not presented as a statistically precise representation of the situation in the entire watershed. Nonetheless, it is probably the most detailed, independent check in recent years on what progress the state and local governments are making in controlling polluted runoff.

Overall about a quarter of the sites were judged adequate, the highest rating. This means that sediment control was in full accordance with all requirements. By state, Maryland had about 40 percent of its sites adequate, Virginia about 20 percent, and Pennsylvania slightly worse than Virginia. (Pennsylvania's specifications were somewhat tougher than those of the other two states. Pennsylvania would have scored slightly better than Virginia, but still a good deal worse than Maryland, if the same standards were applied to all three states.)

About two-thirds of all sites surveyed were rated inadequate, and a few of the sites, all in Pennsylvania, showed no sign of using required sediment controls. On an acreage basis the impact of poor controls was substantial. Of a total of 820 acres of exposed soil considered in the survey, the runoff from 517 acres was not being trapped. Similar performance across the watershed would mean largely uncontrolled sediment pollution from about 20,000 acres a year for the next thirty years, based on current estimates of development. The damage from that pollution would vary greatly, depending on weather, slopes, and stream sizes, but a rough calculation, projecting the survey results watershed-wide, shows that damage to more than 4,000 miles of streams a year would result. Even if sediment sources are all controlled, recovery from sediment pollution can take decades.

All three states are in the process of upgrading their sediment control programs, but if the results of this survey are at all typical, then some big improvements could be made simply by enforcing what is already in place. Beyond that, however, it appears that there simply are limits to what sediment control structures can contain. Some huge highway projects, for example, which were not part of this survey, have literally wiped out or jeopardized whole stream systems despite state-of-the-art attention to sediment control.

Stormwater

Although sediment loads drop dramatically once a site has been paved and landscaped, the damage to the environment doesn't end. Fertilizer and weed-killing chemicals are often applied to lawns. In Maryland, the acreage in lawns for homes, golf courses, cemeteries, median strips, and grounds of public and commercial buildings covers nearly 700,000 acres—more than 10 percent of the state's land surface. (Corn, the largest crop in the state, covers about 650,000 acres.) In Virginia, lawn covers more than a million acres, up from about 750,000 acres in 1972. Pennsylvanians had nearly a million acres in 1966 (the latest data available).

Very little attention has been paid to monitoring the runoff of chemicals from this substantial and rapidly growing acreage. University test results indicate that, in general, there is less runoff of nutrients and pesticides from turf grass than from croplands. But unlike in agriculture, the applications of fertilizers and other chemicals tend to be performed by huge numbers of amateurs without much supervision or education. Home lawns, for example, spread across more than half a million acres of the watershed, involving hundreds of thousands of potential fertilizer and pesticide appliers. Other turf-related uses include golf courses—whose plushy, manicured greens can require several times the fertilizer loads of agricultural croplands.

More is known about pollutants that come from paved or "impervious" surfaces. The quality of rainwater washing off urban pavement can be shockingly polluted—especially the "first flush," in which dry-weather accumulations of pollutants that have fallen from the air, from car exhausts, and from accumulations of oxygen-demanding organic matter like grass clippings all wash into storm drains and creeks. Pets are estimated to deposit more than 7 million pounds of feces annually on the streets of Washington, D.C., alone.

Rains in the greater Harrisburg area (both shores of the Susquehanna) annually flush to the river around 2 million pounds of nitrogen, a third of a million pounds of phosphorus, and 8.5 million pounds of organic matter from leaves, grass clippings, and garbage, all of which creates a demand on the water's oxygen when it decays. Similarly, in Baltimore, the same study estimated that in 1988 as much copper—a metal toxic to aquatic life—washed off in rainfall as came into the harbor from industrial discharges. In Washington, D.C., now that the Blue Plains sewage treatment plant has drastically reduced phosphorus pollution, runoff carries several times as much phosphorus annually to the Potomac as the giant plant. National surveys of urban stormwater have detected more than half of the EPA's list of 126 "priority pollutants" in runoff. These pollutants are either acutely toxic or known or suspected cancer-causers. About a dozen of these substances exceeded safe levels for aquatic life in some of the samples.

Stormwater that is channeled through sewage treatment plants in some urban areas may so exceed the plant's capacity that it releases raw or poorly treated sewage as well as the polluted runoff. This type of "combined sewer overflow" is a problem plaguing Richmond and Washington. Where it is not a problem, as in Baltimore, however, it may just mean that storm drains dump directly to waterways. The next time you are tempted to dump anything into a storm drain, remember that, as far as the bay is concerned, this is just like putting it in a natural stream or river.

Stormwater also causes severe physical degradation of smaller waterways. Most people think of paved or impervious surfaces as just roads and parking lots, but they also include roofs, driveways, sidewalks, patios, even car tops. It does not take extreme urbanization to "harden" as much as half of a developed piece of land. Once that has happened, rain that used to soak into the soil goes quickly and directly down gutters and drains and into streams. The stream is thus subject to fierce flooding for a few hours. Then, when it is dry, it no longer is fed by the slow seepage through its bed and

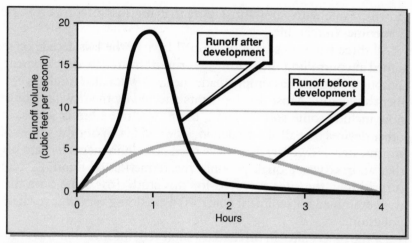

FIGURE 2.5. RUNOFF OF STORMWATER FROM A FORESTED WATER-SHED BEFORE AND AFTER DEVELOPMENT   *Clearing forest and rendering parts of the watershed impervious (streets, roofs, driveways, and such) dramatically changes the quantity and timing of runoff—with damaging impacts on streams.* [Adapted from Maryland Wildlife Administration, Integrated Watershed Plan]

banks—the water that used to seep underground, replenishing the water table, has all run off in the new, paved environment. (See Figure 2.5.)

This "feast or famine" flow wreaks havoc on the stream's habitat. It is easy to see if one compares an urban to a rural creek. In the urban setting, the channel will be widened and the banks eroded; after a rain, the creek will surge wildly with water, then run almost dry within hours or a day afterward. The country creek will be more stable, rising less in rainstorms, falling less in droughts. It will be, in short, a better place for a fish to live. Studies in various parts of the bay's watershed have found that as the amount of paving in a stream's watershed goes up, aquatic life in the stream declines—even if there are no specific pollution sources present. Such degradation can start by the time even 12 percent of a stream's watershed is paved, which is equivalent to putting it all in suburban homes on 2-acre lots. By the time imperviousness reaches 25 percent—equivalent to two homes per acre—degradation can be severe. Increased runoff from paved-over watersheds also causes flooding downstream, with substantial potential for loss of property and sometimes human life.

All three bay states have developed laws in the last decade or so aimed at controlling the stormwater runoff from new development, although Virginia has simply made the law optional at local government's pleasure. Most developments affected by the new laws must now include some sort of pond, basin, vegetated buffer strips, or other devices that all aim to detain, slow, and even out the surges of stormwater. However, there have been no requirements in state law that address water quality—only the reduction of flooding. Not surprisingly, the sites surveyed for this study (the same ones that were examined for sediment controls) were doing very little to check pollution.

Of the ninety sites in three states surveyed, information was available to assess seventy-eight for stormwater controls. A quarter of these were exempt from using controls because of their small size or because it seemed the controls themselves would do even more damage (a debatable decision in some cases). Nearly half of the seventy-eight sites will employ control measures that do little to protect bay tributaries beyond minimizing flooding. Less than 10 percent of the sites will rely on measures that address the wider range of pollution impacts associated with stormwater runoff. This means that for the ninety sites, about 15 percent of the nitrogen and 25 percent of the phosphorus and copper will be kept on site. The rest will be discharged to a bay tributary. Maryland led in efficiency of stormwater controls. An estimated 20 percent of the nitrogen and 40 percent of the phosphorus and copper will be controlled from its sites. In Pennsylvania and Virginia, it was estimated that controls would handle only about 10 percent of the nitrogen and about 20 percent of the phosphorus.

As with sediment control, all three states are upgrading their stormwater controls to address the quality as well as the quantity of runoff. The seventy-eight sites are calculated to be increasing stormwater pollution from two to five times, depending on how polluting the predevelopment land use was. If the bay watershed is to accommodate an anticipated 2.6 million more people by the year 2020 in conjunction with restoration of bay water quality, then new development must aim, at a minimum, for a *zero increase* in polluted runoff.

Urban Retrofit

A thorough study of stormwater and sediment controls by the metropolitan Council of Governments in the Washington area concluded that even the best controls might slow the growth of pollution but would not reduce it or even hold the line. The best hope, the study said, lay in trying to reduce the pollutants coming from existing development as well as new development. Such urban "retrofit" is being tried on an experimental basis in several parts of the watershed, most notably the Anacostia River in Washington and the Gwynns Falls, a tributary to Baltimore Harbor. Baltimore County, Maryland, has used it to stem the pollution of a reservoir, Loch Raven.

Urban retrofit may involve a range of techniques: frequent street sweeping and scooping up after pets, as required successfully in New York City; placement of gravel-filled "infiltration trenches" on the edges of developments to let the first flush of stormwater soak into the ground; or techniques to trap the superpolluted first flush and send only that amount of stormwater through sewage treatment plants. Reducing air pollutants, which would have many other benefits for human health, would also reduce the pollution in urban runoff, since much of the problem comes from the toxic metals and hydrocarbons and the oxygen-robbing nutrients that are deposited onto paved surfaces. There may be potential, too, for "porous paving"—asphalt made with coarser materials to let water run through it—as well as for modifications to individual homesites ranging from infiltration trenches to maintenance of vegetative ground cover.

Currently few of these techniques are required, and none is strictly enforced. Nor are there widespread educational efforts or much in the way of technical and financial assistance across the watershed.

CONCLUSIONS

□ After more than a decade of official commitment to controlling sediment from construction, less than half the sites surveyed in Maryland for this book were in full compliance with all standards. Virginia scored slightly less than half as well as Maryland, followed closely by Pennsylvania. (Pennsylvania, if rated by the standards used in the other states, would have scored slightly better than Virginia but still far worse than Maryland.) In all, ninety sites were surveyed.

☐ Stormwater management in all three states has scarcely begun to address the quality of water that runs from impervious areas like pavements and rooftops, still concentrating mostly on controlling flooding.

☐ Runoff from developed lands is largely uncontrolled and makes a significant impact on local waters.

☐ Our runoff control programs to date have relied heavily on structural solutions to halt pollution—such as concrete catch basins and filter fences—rather than reducing the sources of pollution by making less land impervious, disrupting less soil when developing land, and cleaning up the air pollutants that fall on urban areas.

☐ We have not even come close to being able to develop the bay's watershed without causing substantial and lasting degradation of adjacent waters. Development is accelerating, and there is no reason yet to believe losses of water quality are not going to accelerate along with it.

☐ The proportion of the watershed that is in turf, from home lawns to golf courses and cemeteries, is increasing rapidly. And applications of fertilizers and pesticides on this acreage are also growing, even as agricultural applications appear to have peaked and slightly declined.

SEWAGE

The pollution of sewage of our ever increasing population and the waste from our rapidly growing industries is affecting the entire fish and oyster industry in and around Hampton Roads.

—VIRGINIA COMMISSIONERS OF FISHERIES, 1919

In contrast to our attempts to control pollution from land runoff, which wasn't even on most lists of bay threats twenty years ago, programs regulating discharges from sewage treatment plants and industries have been maturing for nearly two decades. Not surprisingly, it is on the bay's rivers—where the majority of pollutants come from these specific or "point" sources of pollution—that the few clear-cut restorations of bay water quality have come. On bay rivers like the Potomac, Patuxent, and James, discharges of nitrogen and phosphorus from human wastes dominate water quality much as agriculture does on the Susquehanna.

Reducing Nitrogen and Phosphorus

We have invested sums of money on sewage treatment that dwarf our spending to date on controlling land runoff—more than a billion dollars on the Potomac alone and more than a hundred million in the last decade on Maryland's Patuxent. Virginia estimates its current annual spending on sewage treatment at more than $300 million. Significantly, however, one of the largest reductions in pollution from sewage pipes in recent years has come almost cost-free, with none of the engineering or chemistry associated with sewage treatment.

From 1985 to 1987 Maryland, Virginia, and Washington, D.C. (joined by Pennsylvania in 1989), banned the use of phosphate laundry detergents. This painless change in a single consumer prod-uct, multiplied by millions of homes whose wash water flowed to sewage treatment plants, reduced phosphorus discharges by 30 to 50 percent. Although the ban was bitterly opposed by a detergent industry scare campaign that said it would only cause disgruntled consumers to revolt, it is a major reason why the baywide goal of a 40 percent reduction in phosphorus from sewage plant dis-charges is likely to be reached years before the year 2000 target. (See Figure 2.6.)

In the freshwater and slightly salty parts of the bay, removing phosphorus is a key to improving overall water quality. Remarkable improvements in the Potomac have brought back fish and wildlife within sight of downtown Washington. (See the case study on the Potomac in Chapter 6 for more detail.) More recently the Patuxent, after a twenty-year decline, has begun to show a trend of improving water quality in its upper and middle portions. Virginia's historical monitoring of water quality has been insufficient to determine simi-lar trends on the James and other of its waters, but discharges of phosphorus there have declined markedly. As a result, according to EPA there is evidence that phosphorus levels in many sections of the main bay have declined modestly since 1984. Even 1989, which was

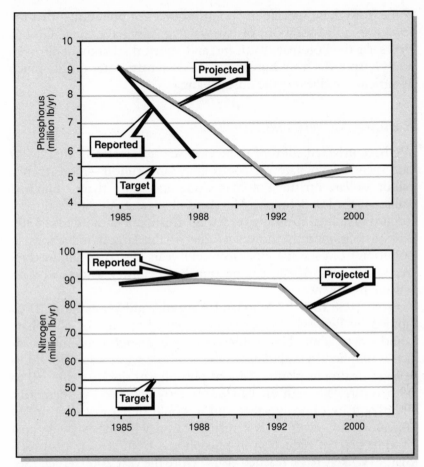

FIGURE 2.6. PROGRESS IN REDUCING SEWAGE POLLUTION OF THE BAY *Progress in reducing the nutrients in sewage discharges by 40 percent has been more rapid than expected with phosphorus, and slower than expected with nitrogen. Note that phosphorus levels begin turning up again around the end of the century, because of increasing population.* [EPA, Chesapeake Bay Liaison Office, State of the Bay Report, 1990]

a wet year, the kind expected to bring in additional nutrients from land runoff, continued this trend.

But for the other pollutant of baywide concern in sewage, nitrogen, the goal of a 40 percent reduction is not in sight. Only Maryland has made a serious start, committing to an ambitious nitrogen removal strategy on one river, the Patuxent, and at Back River, the Baltimore region's biggest treatment plant (a combined expenditure of more than $50 million). Virginia, which is undertaking some innovative pilot projects aimed at more cost-effective nitrogen removal, recently estimated that achieving the goals for nitrogen at its sewage treatment plants by traditional methods would cost $800 million. Although there is reason to think that newer, cheaper methods of nitrogen reduction may make that an overstatement, no one thinks that the bay's nitrogen goals can be reached cheaply. Estimates for Maryland's meeting the 40 percent nitrogen reduction goals for sewage treatment plants range from $243 to $319 million. Pennsylvania, which has planned to meet its nutrient reduction goals mostly by controlling land runoff (see the "Agriculture" section), has not made estimates for sewage treatment.

The bottom line is that sewage discharges of nitrogen in recent years have actually been rising slightly for the bay as a whole. That may be one reason why no significant improvement has occurred in the aquatic environment of the main bay in the last decade or in the large, tidal portions of the Potomac and Patuxent nearest the bay's main stem. It is in the saltier waters of the lower rivers and the middle-to-lower bay that nitrogen can become a factor in the growth of plankton that clouds the water and lowers oxygen levels.

On a jurisdictional basis, Virginia has the largest flows of sewage in the watershed (419 million gallons per day from its major plants). Next is Maryland (356 million gallons), the District of Columbia and its Maryland and Virginia suburbs (300 million gallons), and Pennsylvania (280 million gallons)—all 1988 figures.

If these sources are ranked by whose sewage flows have the least pollution per gallon, however, the order shifts somewhat. If we use the District of Columbia with state-of-the-art phosphorus removal at its Blue Plains plant as our benchmark, then Maryland averages thirty times as much phosphorus per gallon. Virginia averages thirty-six times as much, and Pennsylvania forty-three times. (Given the quality of the data, this means all three states are roughly equivalent.) For nitrogen, all jurisdictions are roughly equivalent, although Pennsylvania shows next best to Blue Plains, followed by Virginia and Maryland (whose new upgrades for nitrogen removal are not yet on line).

If the degree of sewage treatment on the Potomac is a generation ahead of most other places, then looking a generation ahead for that river raises some serious questions for long-range reliance on discharging wastes to the bay's waters as the preferred disposal option.

In calculating how it will reach an overall 40 percent phosphorus reduction for its sewage plants by the year 2000, Virginia actually shows phosphorus discharges to the Potomac going up by 15 percent. (Reductions on other rivers are forecast to offset that increase and achieve the overall goal.) The reason for the rise is that nearly 80 percent of the sewage on the Virginia side of the river is already being treated to the limits of technology; as population and sewage flows rise, very little more phosphorus can be feasibly removed. Maryland hints at a similar scenario developing on its Patuxent River.

The real impact of the 40 percent reductions for nutrients from both land runoff and sewage is that they are also supposed to be a "cap." In other words, even if population doubles and triples in the future, we will not let their nutrients degrade the bay. But as long as we pursue present policies of putting human wastes into the bay, it is difficult to see those caps meaning much in the long run unless much stronger growth management evolves soon.

Compliance

Like any technology, sewage treatment plants don't always run right, whether due to poor maintenance, waste flows that exceed their capacity, or inept operation. A major tool by which government tries to ensure that both municipal and industrial dischargers of nutrients and other wastes don't degrade water quality is by issuing each facility a federal/state permit limiting what can be discharged.

An EPA audit of how major dischargers in industry and municipal governments were complying with their permits characterized Pennsylvania, Maryland, and Virginia, as well as EPA's regional office that oversees them, as lax in enforcement of permits during the three-year period from 1985 to 1988. Since 1988, however, a Chesapeake Bay Foundation review of about 100 of the largest sewage treatment plants discharging to the bay in all three states has shown no serious noncompliance with permits. And as of July 1990, EPA said that of the 135 biggest industrial dischargers in the bay region only three, all in Pennsylvania, were out of compliance with their permits.

But remember that when you read a plant is meeting its permit, it does not necessarily mean that pollution is eliminated or even reduced as much as needed for first-rate water quality—only that it is meeting the legal limit that was negotiated between it and government regulators. Many permits still do not push anywhere near the limits of cleanup technology, or they simply don't address the full range of pollutants in the discharge. (See the next section on toxic chemicals.)

There is no guarantee how long today's relatively good rate of compliance will last, but pressure by the states to enforce permit limits is currently at a high level. A troubling exception to this encouraging trend is with facilities owned and operated by the federal government itself. Around 50 of 311 federal installations, including dozens of military bases, have had significant violations of environmental laws, including discharge permits, during 1989–1990, according to the EPA. (Although EPA is prohibited by law from taking action against other federal agencies, the states have somewhat more leeway. Yet traditionally they have found it difficult to pursue federal polluters or have been reluctant to do so.) The problems listed recently by EPA include violations of sewage treatment and air quality laws and buried hazardous chemicals. Part of the problem has been the federal government's denial of requests by its bay facilities for additional pollution control funds.

Sludge

Assuming that we are successful in removing pollutants from sewage discharges, we must then ask what is the ultimate fate of these pollutants. The short answer is they go into sewage sludge—the semisolid residue produced in mountainous quantities by advanced treatment plants. One of the lessons of all environmental cleanup, still not well learned, is that we have to be careful about taking a pollutant out of one medium, air or land or water, only to put it in another where it continues to cause problems. It is occasionally possible to partially destroy pollutants—as with high-temperature incineration of PCBs—but often we just shuffle them from one medium to another. An example is the way nitrogen appears to be moving into the atmosphere from farm manure stored in pits, returning shortly thereafter to the ground where it can again pollute the water.

By the time a sewage plant is removing the last few percent of nutrients like nitrogen and phosphorus, it is adding so much chemical to extract the pollution that its sludge consists of about 100 pounds of additive for every pound of pollution removed. Blue Plains creates more than 3 million pounds of sludge every day of the year. Something has to be done with the sludge. Rich in phosphorus and nitrogen—and declining somewhat in toxicity as industries "pretreat" the wastewater they send to sewage plants to remove its more noxious elements—sludge is gaining acceptance for spreading on farmland in many parts of the watershed.

There is pressure to find enough acreage on which to spread all this sludge. While it appears that all three states are attempting to spread sludge on the land in an environmentally safe manner, they all are spreading it on the basis of how much nitrogen the soil needs for growing crops. (The concentrations of toxics such as cadmium and lead may also limit spreading.) The trouble with spreading sludge on the basis of nitrogen requirements is that it may overload the soil with more phosphorus than it can possibly need. Then, if soil erodes from the farmland, it may carry phosphorus with it—returning to the water via land runoff the same pollutant that was removed from sewage discharges earlier.

This sort of overenrichment of soil has occurred in Lancaster County, Pennsylvania. The county contains many areas with far more manure than farmers in the immediate vicinity can spread on their fields in an environmentally sound manner. To make matters worse, it also imports sewage sludge from Philadelphia to the tune of about 6,000 tons annually. A report prepared for the local solid waste management district on manure spreading said that county-wide there were plenty of soils that could use extra nitrogen, which happens to be the basis for spreading both manure and sludge. But the report conceded that if phosphorus needs were used as the guide for spreading, there would then be considerably more nutrients to be spread than there were soils in need of them.

It is true that it's easier to keep excess phosphorus out of the water than nitrogen. Nitrogen is water soluble and escapes to waterways readily, while phosphorus tends to bind to soil. But most soil conservation programs do not keep all soil from eroding into the water; and even phosphorus, at high enough levels, appears able to dissolve and run off easily in surface and groundwater. Experience tells us that polluting the land with *anything* runs an unacceptably high risk of ultimately polluting the waters that drain that land.

Septic Tanks

Although a great majority of the bay watershed's population flushes its wastes to sewage treatment plants, a substantial number are hooked up to septic tanks—about 250,000 households in Maryland, more than a million in Pennsylvania, 656,000 in Virginia. Septic tanks usually serve one or a few households and discharge human wastes underground. They operate on the principle of allowing bacteria in the soil to break down sewage into components harmless to human health. Traditionally they have been regulated on a human health basis, as they can be a source of bacteria in soils and waterways that may lead to the closing of shellfish beds and swimming beaches.

The nitrogen compounds discharged into groundwater by septic tanks also can pollute wells and cause declines in underwater grasses and oxygen levels when they reach the bay. (Phosphorus, the other worrisome nutrient in human wastes, does not usually move through the soil with groundwater like nitrogen.) A properly working septic tank removes only 15 to 45 percent of the nitrogen in wastewater, according to EPA estimates. A study by University of Rhode Island researchers concluded that replacing heavily fertilized farmlands—a well-documented source of groundwater pollution—with residential development hooked up to septic tanks would do nothing to improve groundwater quality. (It should be noted that, to date, sewage treatment plants are not removing much nitrogen from the waste stream either, though unlike septic tanks they can be upgraded to do so.)

Estimates on the number of malfunctioning septic systems in the bay watershed are nonexistent. They are a common problem in older developments where soils are not adequate to support them or where maintenance (such as the pumping out of tanks) has not been performed for years. In addition, the sludge from pumping out septic tanks, like sewage sludge, has to go somewhere—either through a sewage plant, which in turn produces more sludge, or directly onto farmland in many cases. As with all our production of waste, the pollutants can never be totally eliminated. They can only be shuffled among air, water, and land.

Traditionally, local governments have used septic tank regulations as a check on explosive development—a rough substitute for good land use planning. Building lots must have adequate size and well-drained soils and minimal slopes for the septic tanks to work well enough to get approval from health authorities. But such health rules governing septic tanks have actually tended to steer development into low-density sprawl patterns that consume more open space and are economically inefficient (see Chapter 5). They also steer development to prime farm and forest soils that should be kept in food and timber production and in open space.

CONCLUSIONS

☐ In contrast to our struggle with controlling pollution running off farms and developed lands, pollution from pipes discharging sewage into the bay is undergoing significant reduction. The difference is that the latter effort has been backed by more money, supported by a mature legal and regulatory framework, and implemented with tried and true technology.

☐ The Potomac, the place where pollution reduction has most clearly translated into environmental improvement (see the case study in Chapter 6), is the easy victory and might not be repeatable across the watershed. On Lake Erie, on Scandinavian lakes, and elsewhere, just as on the Potomac, extreme phosphorus pollution from sewage plants discharging to fresh water has proved most susceptible to dramatic improvements in water quality. But the cost of the enterprise, paid mostly by the federal government to clean up "the nation's river," may not be easy to muster elsewhere.

☐ Despite some successes on sewage-dominated river systems of the bay, we have not yet improved water quality for any entire river system. The bay's main stem, affected heavily by both sewage and land runoff, as well as by the loss of natural filtering systems like oysters and submerged grasses (see Chapter 4), has shown no trend toward overall environmental comeback since conditions deteriorated in the 1970s.

☐ Projecting into the future our plans for continued discharge of ever more but ever cleaner sewage into the waters of the Chesapeake shows a time not so far away when population growth is going to bump against the limits of technology—with dire consequences for our goals of "capping" sewage nutrients forever at acceptable levels.

Although pollution from agriculture currently is roughly equal to sewage pollution of the bay, agricultural pollutants (with the exception in some areas of farm animals) appear to have peaked. But no limit on human population and its wastes is in sight.

□ The pollutants removed from sewage often end up being returned to the land as sludge spread on farms. Currently there appears to be a risk that this practice is overenriching soils in some areas with phosphorus that may leak back into the water.

□ Maryland is the only state making vigorous efforts to reduce nitrogen, the other pollutant of baywide concern in sewage, although Virginia has some pilot programs. Meeting goals for this reduction, baywide, consequently is behind schedule.

□ Properly sited, septic tanks can remain a useful and environmentally sound alternative for waste disposal. But considerations of their impact on water quality must go beyond whether they harm human health and address the impact of added nutrients on the bay system. Moreover, their widespread use is not conducive to environmentally and economically sound growth management wherever they perpetuate sprawl development on large lots that consume open space inefficiently.

□ Compliance with permits that limit what major sewage treatment plants and industries discharge to the water is better than it has been for many years. Yet these permits do not set uniformly tough restrictions and still do not address the full range of pollutants discharged.

□ The federal government, which has the ultimate responsibility to enforce water pollution laws, has itself set a bad example by dragging its feet in cleaning up violations at dozens of federal facilities in the watershed.

TOXICS AND BACTERIA

Nothing says you shouldn't eat these crabs . . . the levels [of toxic chemicals] are below federal action limits. But if you gave me a crab from the Elizabeth River, I would probably be reluctant to eat it.

—JOHN GREAVES, author of a recent study of crabs
in Virginia's most polluted river

The least understood—and potentially the most damaging—pollutants of Chesapeake Bay are the mind-boggling array of toxic chemicals discharged into the air and water of the region. The following pages look at what is known about their role in the health of both bay species and the human species who eat seafood from the bay. Also of concern, given the millions of oysters slurped raw from Chesapeake waters each year, is the level of bacteria from sewage and animals that is present. A bay that was thriving with a diversity of natural creatures would still only be half-a-loaf if it were hazardous to our health to sample its delicacies.

Toxics and Human Health

Toxic chemicals—which include both industrial metals like arsenic, cadmium, and mercury and organic compounds such as DDT, PCBs, and a range of pesticides—have been documented throughout the bay's waters and its sediments. Fish, shellfish, and crabs have been found to contain a range of toxics in Maryland and Virginia's bay and rivers during the last fifteen years. Although federal health guidelines usually are not exceeded, even in urbanized areas such as the Patapsco and Elizabeth rivers, the presence of chlordane, a termite extermination chemical, has caused Maryland to warn people not to eat a few species like catfish and carp from the Back River (Baltimore) area. Consumers are also advised to halt or limit consumption of fish from about 430 miles of rivers in the watershed, including upstream portions of the James, Potomac, and Shenandoah. Of that total, mercury is the culprit for 193 stream miles, PCBs for 44 miles, dioxin (from paper mills) for 90 miles, and kepone for 113 miles.

For the most part, there are few clear trends of either increasing or decreasing levels of toxics in seafood samples from the bay since the 1970s. Sampling techniques have by no means been adequate to give definitive answers to these questions, however. For some of the toxics, no federal standards or guidelines even exist.

Both Maryland and Virginia in recent years became concerned about the potential health impacts from consuming crabs that are caught on surprisingly large scales in the bay's most polluted areas around Baltimore and Norfolk. Consequently, these "industrial-strength crabs" were tested for a range of toxics. Results were similar for both areas. Crabs did not show levels that exceeded current human health standards, but they were generally more contaminated than crabs from cleaner parts of the bay. The creatures tended to concentrate very little of the surrounding contaminants in their meat, but they did concentrate higher levels in their "mustard," or hepatopancreas, a portion of the crab favored by some. Although a steady diet of crab mustard from the harbors is not officially unhealthy, few health officials would personally endorse such a regimen.

The results of the crab surveys may be more of a testament to the crab than to water quality. Crabs are extraordinarily able to rid their flesh of chemicals they ingest. Moreover, they migrate up and down the bay and don't stay in one place all their lives; neither do they live long enough (two to three years) to "bioaccumulate" toxics as much as they might if they were to inhabit the industrial areas for longer periods.

It is notable that many of the bay's best-known species do not make particularly good "indicators" of the estuary's toxicity: Oysters feed so low on the food chain, filtering plankton for a living, that they do not bioaccumulate much; rockfish live a long time and eat high on the food chain, but as they mature and begin migrating, they feed extensively from Labrador to North Carolina and thus are not representative of just the bay; ditto for American shad. Still there are marked differences between rockfish born in the Chesapeake and those native to the Hudson River. The Hudson River fish carry much higher levels of PCBs, a widespread industrial toxic, to the point that they often exceed federal health standards.

Two species that are good indicators of toxic problems—birds who live at the top of the food web and feed heavily on bay fish year after year—are looking up. Bald eagles and ospreys, whose numbers sank to historic lows throughout America as the pesticide DDT accumulated in their systems, have rebounded strongly around the bay in the last decade. But sometimes we may miss a mounting problem with environmental toxicity because we tend to monitor the status of species that we eat or hunt or somehow regard as special, like the bald eagle. Science is just beginning to put together evidence that significant declines have been occurring around the bay, and worldwide, among certain types of frogs, salamanders, and other amphibians. Their decline may be related to acid rain (see Chapter 3), which can degrade their breeding habitat.

Bacteria and Human Health

Is it safe to swim in the bay? Will eating its seafood make you sick? These questions are most often related to the threat of bacterial contamination, which around the bay may come from malfunctioning septic tanks or sewage plants, from animal waste runoff, runoff from urban streets, or the overboard discharge of boat toilets around marinas. Historically, it was concern in the oyster industry about contamination by Baltimore's raw sewage that forced the city in 1909 to open the first modern sewage treatment plant in the nation. (An alternative idea was to spray the sewage on the land in an area now known as Glen Burnie.) Since the federal Clean Water Act of 1972 made large grants available to build and upgrade sewage treatment plants, an action also followed by more stringent regulation of septic tanks, the number of bay beaches closed to swimming has changed dramatically. Today there are very few areas closed to swimming on the bay.

With regard to closures of shellfish areas due to bacterial contamination, however, the record is not so bright. Shellfish, particularly oysters, are used as the most sensitive indicators of such pollution because unlike most seafood in this country they traditionally are eaten uncooked. Extremely serious problems like hepatitis and parasitic infestations can result from eating contaminated oysters. Shellfish waters are graded along a spectrum from "approved" for harvesting to "prohibited" for any harvesting, with several levels of restriction in between. Along the mid-Atlantic coast between 1971 and 1985, some 64,000 acres of shellfish areas were moved from a less restrictive to a more restrictive category because of bacterial threats; 26,000 other acres were upgraded due to cleaner water, according to a recent Department of Commerce report.

On Chesapeake Bay, the acreage of shellfish beds closed by bacterial pollution has fluctuated between about 5 and 6 percent of the total, or 50,000 to 75,000 acres, during the last decade. As of 1988, Maryland had closed or partially restricted harvesting on about 110,000 acres of its total shellfish grounds of 1.1 million acres. Virginia between the 1970s and mid-1980s gained about 2,500 acres but lost about 35,000 other acres to contamination-related closings or restrictions, according to the Commerce Department. Between 1986 and 1988, some 6,000 acres were reopened under a special shoreline sanitation program. More than 80,000 acres of the state's total potential shellfish grounds are closed or restricted.

To some extent, the closures of recent years reflect increasingly tighter standards for bacterial levels, rather than an absolute increase in contamination. Both Maryland and Virginia are considered to maintain vigorous programs to keep contaminated shellfish from getting on the market.

Toxics and the Bay's Health

Human health threats from toxics and bacteria in the bay are compounded by concerns about the impacts on the species that live there. The bay continues to be plagued by downturns in reproduction of a number of its fish species. Low levels of the same toxics that pervade the bay are frequently found in their tissues and in their eggs. And exposing eggs and larvae to the waters of their spawning rivers can cause significant mortality.

"It seems clear that pH/aluminum toxicity [impacts of acid rainfall] may limit production of striped bass in some of the spawning grounds in the Chesapeake in some years. . . . It is not presently known how widespread this problem is," says a 1990 report on rockfish prepared for the Atlantic States Marine Fisheries Commission. Other bay species such as herring, shad, and white and yellow perch may be vulnerable to acid rain also, according to other reports. There is nothing conclusive, however. Such vagueness has underscored our floundering efforts to link parts per million, billion, trillion, and quadrillion of toxic chemicals to impacts on the bay's health during the last decade.

Scientists also have found higher than average rates of a specific tumor in brown bullheads, a bottom-feeding fish that inhabits bay rivers. The tumors seem related to levels of toxics, but not to the presence of cancer-causing compounds. Liver cancers, usually representative of extreme toxic levels as in Puget Sound and the Niagara River, have not been found in the bay, although growths that are precursors, or warning signs of such cancers, have been seen in fish in Maryland's Severn River (cause unknown).

Probably no species in the Chesapeake has been analyzed more than the striped bass, or rockfish, for links between its decline of recent years and toxic chemicals in the water. The links, however, remain elusive. In the spring of 1989, for example, rockfish larvae showed high mortality when exposed to the waters of one of the bay's major spawning rivers, the Choptank; but two weeks later, spawning in a slightly different section of the river, the rockfish had one of their most successful reproductive efforts since record keeping began in the 1950s.

"The pervasive, low level contamination occurring in the main stem of the bay has not been unequivocally linked to any biological deterioration," concluded an article by top Maryland and Virginia toxic scientists in 1987. Yet, for a number of reasons, we cannot discount the threat of toxic chemicals, which continue to be discharged into the bay from thousands of industries, from the air, and from illegal dumping and leaking landfills and old industrial sites. Toxics may persist for years and even centuries in the bay's sediments. They may *biomagnify*—that is, very low levels in the sediment or water can become increasingly concentrated as they are passed up the food web by higher and higher levels of consumers, ending with the more predatory fish and birds . . . and with us.

Toxics may also cause subtle, hard to observe changes in the bay's plants and animals that cause mutations or interfere with reproduction. DDT, for example, tended not to kill bald eagles and ospreys outright. It made their eggshells thin, cutting down on hatching success. Finally, toxic chemicals may exhibit what are called *synergistic* effects, which means that the impact of two or more chemicals on an organism together may add up to more than just the sum of the impacts of each chemical calculated in a laboratory.

Two areas of the bay heavily polluted with toxic chemicals are Baltimore Harbor and the Elizabeth River in Norfolk, where urban-industrial centers have engulfed the shorelines for more than a century. Concentrations of metals such as cadmium, lead, and arsenic, as well as organic chemicals like pesticides and PCBs, occur there at levels several times those in pristine environments. Fish samples from the Elizabeth show a high incidence of tumors, fin rot, and cataracts. Fish exposed in a laboratory to sediments from Baltimore Harbor and from an uncontaminated area died at concentrations of harbor sediment 100 times lower than concentrations of clean sediment.

The state of these two areas, contaminated for centuries, predates the bay's more widespread, modern-day decline. Indeed, the evidence is that the great bulk of the toxics entering the two locations has stayed there—the result of circulatory patterns that trap and settle out pollutants rather than flushing them vigorously into the main bay. So much poison has accumulated around Baltimore and Norfolk that they probably never will be high-quality environments. Because of that, and because the bulk of the threat appears trapped forever within the localities already polluted, there is often a tendency to write these areas off in terms of their fish and wildlife.

The other side of the equation, however, is that these are the areas where huge numbers of the bay region's people live and work and have the bulk of their opportunities to make frequent contact with the bay. Recreational crabbing, for example, draws people to Baltimore Harbor by the hundreds on summer days and is actually carried out on a commercial basis within the Elizabeth River. Similarly, city dwellers in both places catch and consume an unquantified but clearly substantial number of fish from both areas. In August 1990, a Maryland program to promote fishing interest in Baltimore Harbor was completely overwhelmed when more than a thousand youth showed up—three times the number expected—clamoring for their promised rods, reels, and plastic tubs of earthworms.

Regulating Toxics

The only toxics we currently even attempt to control from entering the bay are those from sewage and industrial discharge pipes. To the modest extent that we have begun to regulate these sources, it has been through industrial permits that set levels on some of the most common toxic metals. There has been significant progress here, most observers say, although no one has quantified it baywide.

The other aspect that has shown some progress is a federal/state program known as pretreatment. It requires sewage treatment plants that receive wastewater from industrial sources to make those sources remove certain toxic substances from the water before sending it to the plants, which are not designed to handle toxic wastes. A 1989 Chesapeake Bay Foundation survey of how pretreatment was working at ten large sewage treatment plants found serious flaws with the programs. But it also found that pretreatment programs, when adequately designed and enforced, could significantly reduce the quantities of many industrial toxics—lead, cadmium, chromium, nickel, copper, and mercury—that were flowing through the plants.

A combination of industrial shutdowns, cutbacks in steel production, and increasing regulation of toxic chemicals flowing from industries and sewage treatment plants has resulted in environmental improvements recently in Baltimore Harbor. The middle and outer harbor areas, for example, have experienced a modest comeback in bottom-dwelling organisms since the 1970s. Virginia's monitoring data for the Elizabeth River so far have not proved sufficient to assess whether there are similar trends there.

The emphasis on regulating toxics from pipes discharging to the bay is natural, since these are the sources best covered by law (the federal Clean Water Act). Yet it is well to note that significant toxic impacts to the bay system may come from at least three other sources not touched by such regulatory actions. First, the worst toxic threats have not always been from wastes or by-products but from products that were deliberately introduced widely into the environment because they were considered beneficial. Examples are lead in gasoline (an effective antiknock ingredient); the "miracle pesticide" DDT; chlordane (about the only sure thing to kill termites); TBT (the extremely effective boat antifouling paint, now banned for most uses); even PCBs, globally distributed for their superior insulating qualities in electrical transformers. Another such product, which probably has killed more ducks and geese than all other toxics combined, is the lead shot in shotgun shells, consumed by feeding ducks where it falls on the bottom in shallow marshy areas.

The second source is pollutants from the air, which are undoubtedly having toxic impacts on the bay. Acid rain is the most familiar example, but the next section discusses others. Air pollution now is regulated mostly for its impact on human health, not on water quality.

The third source is agricultural pesticides, which are turning up in groundwater that ultimately ends up in the bay. (See Figure 2.7.) Monitoring of such subsurface flows from one agricultural watershed in Virginia (Owl Run) found seventeen pesticides, some of which exceeded human health advisory levels established by EPA. A very incomplete national survey in 1988 by EPA detected forty-six pesticides in the groundwater of twenty-six states. (Many states, including Virginia, were not surveyed.) At least six of these chemicals were found in Maryland and Pennsylvania. Although the average concentrations were well below human health guidelines, there simply are no guidelines for the health of life in the bay. In Pennsylvania, a recent study of groundwater by the U.S. Geological Survey found that "a significant amount of herbicide remains in the soils and is leached to the groundwater system after the growing season."

Kepone, an ant and roach poison that contaminated dozens of miles of the James River after an Allied Chemical plant dumped it at Hopewell during the 1960s and 1970s, illustrates the special problems involved in controlling toxic chemical discharges from industry. Environmental regulators did not even know this chemical was being manufactured in the region, so there was no monitoring for it. Moreover, it came from a tiny and obscure manufacturing plant (being operated for the giant Allied Chemical). With polluting nutrients, the bigger the sewage plant, the bigger the flow of nutrients that can be controlled. With toxics, however, regulators cannot just concentrate on a few giant plants that produce the bulk of the waste stream.

Could another kepone spill happen, or be happening today? It does not seem as likely, but no one can guarantee that it won't. There are roughly 65,000 chemicals already in commercial use in this country, and 1,000 new compounds are developed each year. EPA concedes that fewer than 2 percent of these have been adequately tested for their effects on human health and the environment. Permits for dischargers thus do not include limits on all the chemicals being discharged. In fact, EPA only tries to address 126 "priority pollutants" in its control strategies.

Maryland and Virginia have made progress (and Pennsylvania is beginning to) in the use of *biomonitoring* techniques that expose fish or other aquatic life to the actual discharges from plants around the bay. Rather than scrutinizing a laundry list of chemicals, each in tiny amounts with little-known levels of toxicity, biomonitoring in effect "asks" the fish what it feels like to be in the plant's total waste stream and determines whether the discharge permit is strict enough. Virginia has also been notably innovative in its development of *fingerprinting* techniques, which examine the water in various rivers for a large range of potential toxics. Problems are then traced back to individual dischargers.

Beyond Toxics

It seems likely that the revolution in chemicals that has made our lives better while causing many unintended environmental impacts

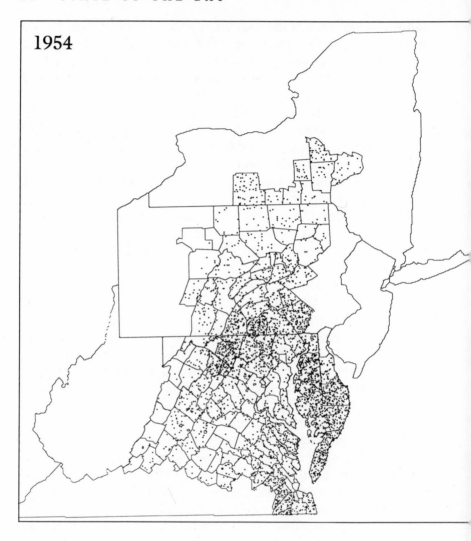

1954

will be repeated in coming decades with biotechnology, including the genetic engineering of many living organisms. Maryland clearly is pursuing this future. Already there are experiments and proposals for such undertakings as transferring cold-resistant genetic material from winter flounder to striped bass—with unknown potential to alter the habits of that species and others with which it interacts in the environment. Other researchers are interested in producing strains of bigger and faster-growing "trophy fish" of various species.

1987

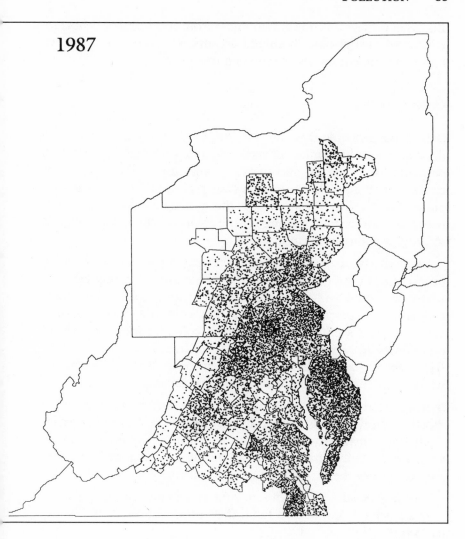

FIGURE 2.7. PESTICIDE USE TRENDS IN THE CHESAPEAKE WATER-
SHED: 1954–1987   *Pesticide use has more than tripled across the bay's water-
shed in recent decades, from 3,500 tons in 1954 to 13,000 tons in 1987.
However, 1987 applications actually represent a decline of about 20 percent from
1974 tonnages. Note: Each dot = 1 ton* [By S. Tennenbaum and R. Costanza,
Chesapeake Biological Laboratory, University of Maryland]

But what is the risk to the environment from accidental or deliberate releases of such genetically altered organisms? It is not clear that we have independent means of assessing this issue.

CONCLUSIONS

□ It seems probable that the year 2000 will still find us unable to discover the subtle links between acid rain and rockfish, between pesticide use going up and oysters going down. Therefore, with toxics more than perhaps any other bay problem, it seems crucial to place the burden of proof on the pollutant—to prove it is harmless—rather than waiting for the environment to turn belly up to prove a pollutant harmful.

□ Similarly, we are seeing strong warning signs—in fish tumors, precancerous growths, and localized restrictions on eating fish—of where we could end up if we are not strict in controlling toxic chemicals. At present, however, the bay, even in its more polluted areas, has not seen the levels of toxic contamination of seafood experienced in New England waters, the Great Lakes, the Hudson River estuary, and Puget Sound. To an overwhelming extent, its seafood still meets current federal health standards.

□ Regulation of toxics entering the system is extremely limited— mostly to heavy metals from industrial discharges and to industries discharging metals to sewage treatment plants. Organic chemicals are generally still not regulated and monitored adequately; neither are toxics from the air or from agricultural and lawn chemicals.

□ Techniques such as biomonitoring and fingerprinting of toxic discharges are beginning to fulfill their promise and should be expanded.

□ Major toxic threats to the bay in the future will not necessarily come in the form of wastes or industrial by-products. They may well be beneficial products—like leaded gasoline or, perhaps in the future, genetically engineered substances—that are deliberately distributed in the environment.

□ Acid rain (see the "Air" section) is almost certainly involved in some of the bay's fish declines, but the scope of its impact is not known.

OIL SPILLS

"It can't happen to me."

—JOSEPH HAZELWOOD, motto printed next to his yearbook picture
at New York Maritime College, where he graduated with honors

In 1976 an oil barge spilled 250,000 gallons of its cargo into the middle Chesapeake Bay, killing thousands of wintering waterfowl and contaminating areas of the bay's bottom with hydrocarbons. In 1988 a similar spill, of similar size, occurred again—almost in the same location. There had been very little progress in the intervening thirteen years to make oil transport on the bay safer. Meanwhile, more than 1.4 million tons of petroleum products are being shipped up and down the estuary and its rivers annually.

The bay is immensely vulnerable to pollution from a large spill on several counts. In the first place, it is quite shallow—average depth less than 22 feet. In other words, anything spilled into the bay doesn't have to move very far to contaminate the bottom. And most of the life in and around the bay either lives on the bottom or depends on it for food and habitat.

Furthermore, the bay's shoreline tends to be either marsh or beach, with huge acreages of shallow grass beds and tidal mudflats adjoining them. Spilled oil, once it hits these shores, is almost impossible to clean up and can persist with damaging environmental effects for years. On a 1 to 10 scale of shoreline vulnerability to oil spills developed by the federal government (with 10 being the most vulnerable), most of the bay rates 9 or higher. By contrast, none of the shoreline hit by the *Exxon Valdez* disaster in Alaska ranked more than 7 (much of it 2 or 3); yet thousands of workers after many months had not been able to clean it satisfactorily. In fact, there is evidence that the cleanup efforts there did more damage than if the shores had been left to nature's weathering and washing.

And, finally, the bay's only wintering and spawning area for blue crabs, its most valuable single fishery resource, lies in a high-traffic area for shipping, including oil transport, near Norfolk, Hampton Roads, and Virginia Beach. According to the Virginia Port Authority, the threat of vessel collision is very high there.

Barges, Tugs, and Drilling

While a great deal of attention is now being directed toward better regulation and design of oil tankers in the wake of the Valdez disaster, most of the oil traffic on inland and coastal waters moves in barges (75 to 90 percent on the Chesapeake), which are less regulated than tankers. For example, barges (which are not manned but towed or pushed by tugs) generally carry no alarm or indicator system to alert someone on the tug if they are losing oil or overflowing during loading. A major spill occurred several years ago in Baltimore Harbor for lack of a simple alarm system. A barge being fueled simply filled up and ran over because of inattention to the loading process. In many years, much more oil goes into the water through small-to-moderate spills from barges than from the more spectacular spills from supertankers. In 1983 and 1984, for example, the Coast Guard reported that tank barges spilled 4.3 million gallons nationally compared to 2.1 million from tanker ships.

The Coast Guard, charged with ensuring the safe transport of oil nationwide, has been cut back on personnel and budget and assigned higher-priority missions such as drug interdiction—with predictable results. An internal investigation sharply critical of that service's marine inspection methods nationwide says the Coast Guard coddles oil shippers. An example locally was the spill of about 200,000 gallons of gasoline and heating oil from a barge off Smith Point, Virginia, in August 1988. The thirty-year-old barge, which nearly broke in half while under tow, had been found to be in marginal condition in 1986 as to the thickness of its steel plates in decks and the hull; but the Coast Guard allowed it to continue operating as long as "recommended" additional testing was undertaken. It was not.

Neither do the operators of tugs towing and pushing oil barges up and down the bay carry pilots with local expertise, as larger ships are required to do. The threat of collision is unacceptably high, especially in the heavily trafficked region around the bay's mouth at Norfolk and Hampton Roads. "Vessel collision is much more probable than catastrophic groundings," said the Virginia Port Authority in assessing the likelihood of an *Exxon Valdez* event on the Chesapeake. But oil spills are not always the big ones that get the most publicity. Between 1979 and 1983, for example, in a period when no large spills occurred on the bay, the Coast Guard reported 360,000 gallons of oil spilled into the bay, mostly from numerous errors while loading or in handling oil at land-based terminals.

Another oil-related threat to the bay is from drilling for oil. Although drilling is currently banned in the actual waters of the bay, neither Maryland nor Virginia is equipped to deal with the many direct and indirect impacts of oil discovery in the region. Drilling can cause pollution from toxic drilling muds and other wastes, from unexpected blowouts of wells, and from air quality degradation. Additionally, the indirect impacts of oil discovery—industrialization and boom development in rural coastline areas—make it one of the less desirable forms of economic growth the states might attract.

The Issue of Response

Nor is there any reason to feel comforted about our ability to clean up or contain a large oil spill on the bay or one of its rivers. The Valdez spill made it painfully obvious that even the best of the nation's "contingency response plans" for reacting to a spill was little more than a paper exercise. Faced with poor weather or a huge spill (and ships containing as much as 21 million gallons of oil ply the bay), any existing cleanup ability would simply be overwhelmed.

Ironically a recent Coast Guard review found the response capability inadequate for large spills and mentioned that a likely scenario for such an occurrence was the mouth of Chesapeake Bay—and several months later, there was a collision between two ships there. Fortunately the spillage of oil was limited, and it did not occur in the area that was populated with spawning blue crabs.

CONCLUSIONS

□ Chesapeake Bay is extremely vulnerable to a large oil spill—both because of its shallowness and marshy coastlines and because large quantities of petroleum products are shipped on its waters daily.

□ Regulation of oil shipping (and safety standards for vessels) is too lax—particularly so for barges, which carry the bulk of petroleum throughout the bay system.

□ Oil drilling, a real possibility for rural areas of the bay's shoreline, carries both direct and indirect threats of environmental degradation.

□ The small, everyday spillage of oil around the bay, though it does not get the attention of a big spill, contributes significant quantities of oil to the water.

□ The Coast Guard is not carrying out its job of ensuring marine safety with regard to oil transport. Nor is it being given the resources and the directives to do it right.

□ There is no program that adequately addresses prevention of collisions, a severe threat to pollute the bay with oil.

□ There is no capability to contain and clean up a large oil spill under difficult conditions.

AIR

This most excellent canopy, the air.

—SHAKESPEARE

Across every square inch of their 2.6-million-acre surface, the bay and its tributaries are in constant contact with the atmosphere. And the atmosphere these days is no longer so excellent (as Shakespeare would have it). Air pollution is heating it up like a greenhouse, ripping holes in the ozone layer, and turning the heavens sour with acid rain.

Just as the health of its waters is dictated by the health of its watershed, so is Chesapeake Bay also a creature of what we may call its "airshed." The airshed has no precise borders; it changes with the direction of the wind. But for most of the year, the net flow of air to the bay is from west to east. The bay thus receives the fallout of pollutants emitted to the air from the urban centers of Baltimore, Washington, Richmond, and Norfolk—from as far afield as the great industrial complexes of the Ohio River valley and other midwestern points. These pollutants come when rainstorms wash them from the air—and also as "dryfall," the steady, slow sifting down from above during the rest of the year, much like dust accumulates on the window ledge. Additionally, at least a part of whatever air pollutants fall on the lands of the watershed also wash into the water during rainstorms.

The bay states and the nation have, of course, been working for decades, with mixed success, to control air pollution. But virtually all our efforts have been governed by concern for what affects human health. For the most part, it is a different set of pollutants that harms the bay—or possibly lower levels of them than would concern human health.

The air pollutes the bay in several ways. A major way is delivery of nutrients—nitrogen and phosphorus—which are implicated in the decline of bay grasses and its low-oxygen problems. As early as 1982 scientists with the EPA Chesapeake Bay Program speculated that as much as 15 percent of the nitrogen reaching the main bay resulted from direct deposits on the water's surface from the air. More recently, studies by the Environmental Defense Fund and EPA have suggested the problem may be even larger—up to 25 percent.

Some rough calculations done by the Washington Council of Governments (COG) estimated that nearly 6 million tons of nitrogen and a quarter million tons of phosphorus fall on the waters of the Potomac River basin each year from the air. That is equivalent to about 9 percent of the nitrogen and 5 percent of the phosphorus from all sources—sewage, agriculture, and forestland—running into the river and, ultimately, the bay. In addition, COG has estimated that more than three-quarters of all the nitrogen and up to a third of all the phosphorus running off urban areas in stormwater to the Potomac come from what the air has deposited on paved-over areas.

The true amounts of nutrients and other pollutants dumped from the air to the bay are not well understood, but the indications suggest they are substantial. We need a better answer quickly, because currently the baywide pollution cleanup goal of a 40 percent reduction in nutrients does not recognize airborne sources as controllable. If they are as substantial as they seem to be, our current strategy—attacking mainly sewage and agricultural sources of nutrients—may be less successful than projected.

The outlook for reducing many airborne nutrients has improved in recent months with passage of the new federal Clean Air Act. Projections up until 1990 showed nothing but a steady increase in emissions of nitrogen oxides, a source of acid rain and nutrients to the bay. The new revisions will alter that scenario for the better, but the new act still does not put an ultimate limit on nitrogen oxides, the bulk of which come from automobiles. Unless we change our driving habits and patterns of sprawling land development, we are certain to repeat our previous history—offsetting any positive impacts of cleaner cars with increases in driving and auto ownership. (See the Washington Bypass case study in Chapter 6.) For example, the total "vehicle miles traveled" in Maryland and Virginia have risen by 31 and 40 percent, respectively, in just the last decade. Pennsylvania has seen a more modest 10 percent increase. Continued increases like this—and all projections show the current trends continuing—will outstrip our new air quality regulations in less than a few decades. (See Figure 2.8.)

Moreover, the new Clean Air Act phases in slowly over several years. Its full benefits in some areas—such as controlling toxic emissions from places like Bethlehem Steel's huge works in Baltimore—will not kick in before the year 2020. Most cities, which do not yet comply with the air quality standards of the 1970 Clean Air Act, now get another fifteen years to meet the even tougher standards of the new act.

Acid Rain

Acid rain is another airborne threat to the bay that may have a serious toxic impact on its fish. During the last twenty years, rain falling across much of the Northeast has become substantially more acidic. One long-term monitoring station below Annapolis shows a tenfold increase in acidity between 1974 and 1985. Similarly, rainfall across Virginia has an acidity (pH of 4.7 on average) that is frequently ten times that of unpolluted precipitation. Sulfates, pollutants that come from fossil fuel burning by industries, power plants, and home heating, run eight to twelve times higher than in unpolluted rain in precipitation across Virginia's Blue Ridge Mountains. Pennsylvania has recorded acid rain with a pH as low as 3.69. (Every one-point rise or fall on the pH scale of acidity is equivalent to a *tenfold* change in acidity.)

Thus severe storms can cause pulses of highly acidic water to enter streams and rivers, stressing or killing little fish and fish eggs as well as aquatic species important as food for young fish. Since acid rain that falls in forested watersheds may percolate more slowly through the forest floor into streams, the resulting acid levels may be less drastic—but they may also create a longer-term stress on life in the water. Acid rain also can release aluminum, one of the most abundant elements in the earth's crust, from streamside soils. And aluminum in the water can be lethal for aquatic life in quantities as low as a few parts of aluminum per every billion parts of water.

Several species like shad, herring, yellow perch, and to a lesser extent white perch and rockfish, spawn in upstream reaches of tributaries that may be vulnerable to acid problems. Research linking acid rain and fish declines has been mixed. Although acid rain has not been established as a major, baywide factor in the decline of any species, it does seem clearly linked in studies by the Smithsonian Institution to the virtual wipeout of yellow perch in certain streams on Maryland's western shore. Virginia and Pennsylvania both have documented extreme vulnerability of their freshwater trout streams to acid rain. A Virginia survey in 1987 of 349 trout streams, for example, found that 93 percent were at risk of acidification and 10 percent already were acidic. (Trout are extremely sensitive to a drop in pH.) "Acid rain will, over the next few decades, reduce Virginia's wild trout habitat and threaten the survival of Virginia's remnant trout populations," the study concluded.

Vulnerability of streams and rivers used by bay species that run upstream for spawning varies widely, depending on the capacity of each stream's soils to buffer the impact of acid rainfall. Generally, coastal plain streams of the bay's western shore and the lower Eastern Shore seem most vulnerable. Perhaps acidification explains the rather mysterious depression of shad and rockfish and herring populations in the Eastern Shore's Nanticoke River, which to all appearances is one of the bay's most pristine waterways. Since the effects of an acidic pulse can be short-lived, it is unlikely that we are picking up all of acid rain's impacts with the random, sporadic monitoring that has been done to date. (See also Chapter 3 for acid rain and its impact on fish.)

Airborne Toxics

Water quality goals tend to focus on controlling toxic pollution by regulating industrial and sewage discharges to the water, but there is some evidence that we may need to focus on more than just the pipes

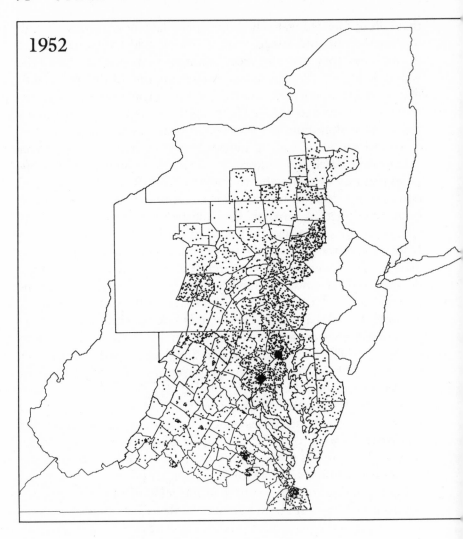

1952

from plants. The air also pollutes the bay through a wide range of toxic materials, mostly by-products of fuel burning and industrial processes.

Although the airborne sources of toxics are huge, they have been only roughly documented to date. Preliminary data, for example, show that industries in the watershed emit tens of millions of pounds annually of more than 400 different chemicals such as

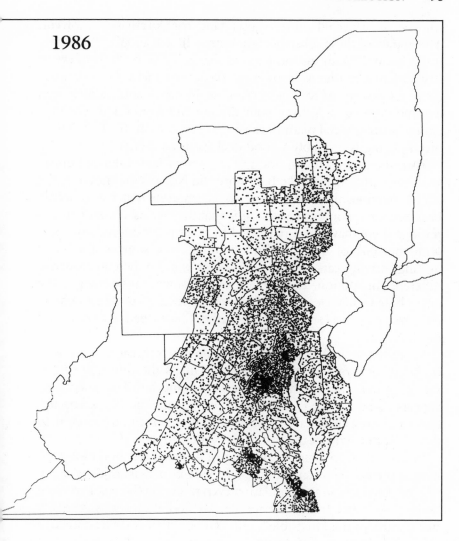

1986

FIGURE 2.8. TRENDS IN AIR POLLUTION (NO$_x$) IN THE CHESAPEAKE WATERSHED: 1952–1986 *Nitrogen oxides, a contributor to acid rain and to nutrients entering the bay, have risen sharply, from 234,000 tons to 618,000 tons, despite increasingly tighter pollution controls on sources such as automobile exhausts. More cars, driven more miles, have overwhelmed the regulations. Note: Each dot = 50 tons* [By S. Tennenbaum and R. Costanza, Chesapeake Biological Laboratory, University of Maryland]

toluene, a suspected cancer-causer, and trichlorethane, a solvent. The impact of these substances on human health and the bay simply is not known. Many airborne toxics also come as much from everyday human activities as from industrial smokestacks. On a national basis, 52 percent of toxic air pollutants in urban areas comes from automobiles—that is, from your driving and from mine. The next closest source, metal plating, causes 10 percent. (In the bay region, metal plating is probably a good deal less than that.)

Thus the heavier distribution of many toxic air pollutants in bay sediments around areas like Baltimore and Norfolk may not have the simple relationship to industrial concentrations that has generally been assumed. Some scientists think that the increased toxic concentrations there may be more related to sheer population densities— with the bulk of the pollutants coming from sources like home heating, driving cars, and so forth. This is more than an academic difference of opinion. The implication is that we may be entering the next phase of bay cleanup with strategies focused too narrowly on industrial pipes and smokestacks—rather than targeting all of us and our lifestyles.

There is one final facet of the airborne toxics threat that needs to be better understood: the *microlayer*. This is the thin film of bay surface water, the interface between bay and air. The microlayer appears to be a place that gathers both aquatic life (including fish eggs) and toxic chemicals in concentrations many times greater than they exist throughout the rest of the water's depth.

In sum, then, our understanding of atmospheric pollution is as hazy as the air that often hangs over the region. Scientific investigation has been sparse and regulation even rarer. Yet there is a growing body of evidence from Chesapeake Bay and elsewhere suggesting that control of this "invisible" source of pollutants may be critical to success in cleaning up the bay.

CONCLUSIONS

□ Airborne pollution of the bay from nutrients and from toxics, including acid rain, is a potentially substantial source of degradation to the bay and tributaries that needs to be quantified and understood immediately.

□ The new version of the Clean Air Act will help substantially to reduce airborne impacts on the bay from autos, toxics, and acid rain. But it will not be completely implemented to produce its full benefits for more than a decade at best.

□ Although the Clean Air Act does not directly address the impact of nutrients on water quality, there may be modest reductions in them anyhow.

□ Current bay goals for nutrient reduction do not include the air as a "controllable" source.

□ The root causes of air pollution, particularly increasing automobile use, still are not being confronted by air quality laws. As a result, gains made in cleaning up individual cars are likely to continue to be offset or even outstripped by growth in vehicle miles traveled. This is particularly true in the bay's watershed, given the projected large increases in population.

□ Regulations aimed at reducing airborne toxics from industrial sources may be too narrowly aimed. Sources such as home heating and automobile use need a closer look.

RECREATIONAL POLLUTION—BOATS

There is nothing—absolutely nothing—half so much worth doing as simply messing about in boats.

—RAT, introducing Mole to the river in Kenneth Grahame's *The Wind in the Willows*

Every weekend from May to October, tens of thousands of recreational boaters cruise Chesapeake Bay and its many tributaries. In the evening many of these vessels can be found at anchor in secluded coves or tied up at marinas in communities such as Oxford, Maryland, or Irvington, Virginia. The problem of controlling the discharge of human waste from these vessels—the equivalent of a small city's sewage flows on peak boating weekends—has been one of the more glaring failures to obey the mandates of the nineteen-year-old federal Clean Water Act and the more recent goals of Maryland and Virginia.

An "Embarrassing Failure"

The Clean Water Act contemplated essentially two forms of managing boaters' wastes: either an onboard system to treat and disinfect waste before pumping it overboard or installation of a holding tank to let wastes be pumped out at onshore locations. Enforcement was turned over to the U.S. Coast Guard with few provisions for state enforcement. Faced with decreasing budgets and rising duties regarding the traffic in drugs, the Coast Guard has virtually ignored these responsibilities.

Onboard treatment has proved to be a complicated, smelly, and, to some extent, environmentally questionable practice. The use of chemical disinfectants has come under widespread attack because of their potential to kill living organisms in the water to which they are discharged. Moreover, disinfection is often not complete—with consequences for bacterial pollution of shellfish beds and swimming waters. The holding tank and pump-out approach, which appears the best alternative, has seriously lagged in Chesapeake Bay. Marinas and nearby communities have vigorously resisted the installation of pump-out facilities.

Boaters' wastes are often said to be a minor pollutant compared to sewage treatment plants and agricultural runoff. This is true. But the observation begs several important issues. In local circumstances, such as marinas and anchorages poorly flushed by currents, human waste can seriously degrade both water quality and the boating experience of others. Moreover, to ignore pollution sources that are relatively small is to encourage the already powerful tendency to point the finger at someone else—industry at agriculture, farmers at sewage plants, and on and on. Boaters have no more right than midnight dumpers of toxic chemicals to put their wastes in public waters. The essential question is not the quantity of pollution but ethical behavior toward the environment.

In the last two years Maryland has begun to take the initiative by requiring pump-out facilities at all new or expanded marinas of over ten boat slips and the creation of a governor's commission on boat waste. Efforts in Virginia have focused on voluntary pump-out at marinas. Progress in the District of Columbia has been slow. Overall, an EPA official calls it "perhaps the single most embarrassing failure of all our [bay cleanup] commitments." Recently a panel on boat pollution convened under the Chesapeake Bay cleanup agreement has put forth the first comprehensive recommendations for restricting discharges of wastes from boats baywide.

Related Threats to the Bay

Recreational boats and their use also pose a broader range of direct and indirect threats to the bay. They are one of the fastest-growing sectors of bay use—tripling in Virginia since 1967 (62,138 to 196,119) and rising almost as fast in Maryland (62,206 to 167,451).

The paint used to prevent their hulls from fouling is a source of toxic metals to the bay's sediments. The demand for ever more marinas for docking space puts more pressure on development of shoreline marshes and open space. Marinas, because of boat sewage disposal, are responsible for about 4,100 acres of shellfish beds being condemned in Virginia, for example. Outboard motors, which mix oil with gasoline, are sources of up to several quarts of oil per day, per boat, discharged directly through their exhausts to the bay's waters. Boat repair yards and marinas seldom have adequate controls to prevent runoff from carrying solvents and old paints into waterways.

Finally, pleasure boats are increasingly competing for space with the boats and waterfront needs of the bay's watermen. Usually the pleasure boaters win. These problems are not baywide, but they tend to be worrisome in areas like Annapolis, Middle River, Rock Hall, Solomons, and Urbanna, where extraordinary concentrations of pleasure boating have developed.

CONCLUSIONS

☐ Discharges of human wastes from pleasure boats represent a failure of federal, state, and individual commitments to clean up the bay.

☐ Pleasure boat usage competes directly with watermen for space in many ports around the bay—with the yachts usually overwhelming the workboats.

☐ Boating is a source of oil and toxic metal pollution to the bay. It is not a major polluter, but it is a sector of bay usage that is growing rapidly.

DISSOLVED OXYGEN

We don't pot the deep water anymore in summertime . . . the crabs just aren't there.

—TANGIER SOUND WATERMAN, 1988

Dissolved oxygen, which is just as essential to the bay's life as air is to ours, is the literal bottom line of pollution problems in Chesapeake Bay. It is one of the major reasons we are trying to reduce the flows of nutrients down the Susquehanna and other bay rivers.

During the summers of the 1980s, as much as 40 percent of the bay's volume on occasion did not meet the standard for healthy oxygen levels—greater than five parts oxygen per million parts of water. (See Figure 2.9.) In one of those summers, up to 20 percent of the bay's volume was *hypoxic*—that is, oxygen was less than 2 ppm, a condition bad enough to kill or severely stress most aquatic life. And volumes of *anoxic* water, water virtually devoid of any oxygen, reached as high as 8 percent of the total bay.

During such times, the bay looks no different to the observer crossing it by bridge or boat. But to fish and crabs, parts of the bay have become as hostile as a desert. Even the volumes of water that are less than anoxic can cause subtler stresses, such as changes in

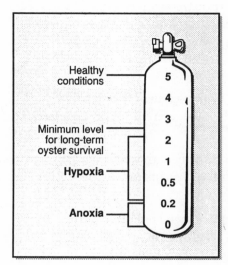

FIGURE 2.9. DISSOLVED OXYGEN CONCENTRATIONS *Clean water laws generally set 5 parts oxygen, dissolved in every million parts of water, as the minimum healthy level for aquatic life. At 2–3 parts per million, stress becomes severe—and in anoxic conditions, few life forms can survive.*

feeding behavior documented with bottom-dwelling worms that make them more susceptible to being eliminated by predators.

Nor is this "bad" water, as bay watermen call it, confined always to the deep channels (though that is where the bulk of it occurs). Winds pressing on the surface can cause the bay, in effect, to tilt from east to west, sloshing bad water from the deeps across vast acreages of the highly productive shallower areas, where it stresses oyster beds and other species. Oxygen-poor water from the bay's main channels may also intrude for miles up the mouths of rivers. Local versions of the low oxygen in the main bay have been documented in the Patuxent and Choptank rivers.

Thirty Years of Flux

In 1983, perhaps the single most graphic piece of evidence for the bay's decline put forth by EPA and the states was a chart showing the volume of the estuary with oxygen deficiencies in the summer of 1950 versus the volume with problems in 1980. It showed a fifteen-fold expansion of bad water. Not surprisingly, a primary goal of our current bay restoration is to return oxygen levels to something approximating that 1950 picture.

Thus far there is no evidence that we are seeing such a return. At the same time, it is beginning to look as if dissolved oxygen levels aren't as tidy an indicator of the bay's health as presented in 1983. Since then, scientists have learned more about the complex mechanisms that create low oxygen conditions in the bay. The data behind the 1950–1980 comparisons have been reanalyzed. The simple picture of a fifteenfold decline has gotten more complicated.

We know that nutrients (and possibly silica in soils) entering the bay are causing excessive growth of plankton. And we know that the plankton, falling to the bottom of the bay and decomposing, are consuming oxygen from the water. But the timing and quantity of water flowing down the Susquehanna and other rivers each spring seem to be just as important, regardless of nutrients and sediment. A wet spring causes high river flows. This causes the bay to become stratified—strongly defined layers of fresh water near the surface, saltier water near the bottom. Combined with a lack of strong winds, this layering can put a "lid" on the system that prevents new oxygen from reaching the deep waters to replace that being lost by plankton decomposition. Thus in both 1958 and 1965 (see Figure

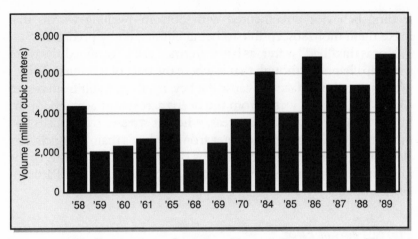

FIGURE 2.10. DISSOLVED OXYGEN: THREE DECADES OF TRENDS
Data for volumes of low oxygen in the bay's waters have been sketchy and subject to interpretation until better monitoring programs began in 1984. Years not listed here either had no data or the data were deemed unreliable. [Adapted from William Boicourt, Horn Point Environmental Laboratory, University of Maryland]

2.10), well before it was considered widely polluted, the bay experienced levels of low oxygen not unlike some of the worst of more recent years. These were years of high river flow.

It is not uncommon, as discussed in Chapter 1, for the extreme natural variability that characterizes an estuary like the Chesapeake to make it hard to separate natural from human effects. As noted earlier, it's like trying to pick out a weak but important radio message amid tremendous static. But what does this say about our attempts to reduce nutrients and resolve the dissolved oxygen problem anytime soon? Most scientists suspect that man-made pollutants have worsened the oxygen problem in the bay, though they can't say by how much. Studies of the bay's *benthos*, or bottom-dwelling creatures, indicate they are more stressed by low oxygen now than they were in the 1970s. It also appears that the duration of low oxygen in bay waters has increased since the 1950s. Further, there is widespread anecdotal evidence from crabbers who have increasingly had to change the location of their traps during recent decades—from deeper water, which is more likely to be devoid of oxygen and crabs, to the shallows.

Some of the most recent scientific thinking goes like this: We have so saturated the bay with nutrients that until we reduce them substantially, we won't see a response in the water. Meanwhile, the ups and downs that we do see in dissolved oxygen probably are driven by wet and dry springtimes. Think of it as adding salt to a glass of water until the water cannot absorb any more—and then adding more and more even though the excess salt just settles out on the bottom. Now begin removing salt from the glass. You can remove a good deal before the water begins to reflect your progress by actually getting less salty. So it may be with nutrients and dissolved oxygen.

CONCLUSIONS

□ "It is likely that reductions in nutrient loading will not be reflected in improved water quality until nutrient inputs are reduced to some unknown level [which] could be 10 percent or 90 percent and will vary depending on other factors," says the draft of a recent University of Maryland analysis of the oxygen problem. The real bottom line is this: Eventually we are likely to see a clear trend of improving oxygen levels, and eventually we can probably say the improvement was aided by pollution controls; but from one year to the next, probably for several more years, the annual variations in oxygen levels in the bay may not be a good indicator of our progress (or lack of it). This is not as satisfying as a neat chart showing that if we turn the nutrient screw this much, the dissolved oxygen level moves that much. But natural systems simply are not tidy affairs.

□ Nutrients and sediment have such clearly adverse impacts on other parts of the bay's health—on submerged grasses, for example—that we would need to reduce them just as urgently even if their effects on dissolved oxygen were no problem at all.

CHAPTER 3

Harvests

There is a story told of Ed Ricketts, the eccentric marine biologist immortalized in John Steinbeck's Cannery Row. *After listening for days at a conference to theories of what caused the crash of the West Coast's sardine fishery, Ricketts stood up, a shiny object half concealed in one hand.*

"You want to know where all the sardines went?" he said. "I'll show you. We put them all in these little tins."

Acid rain, toxic chemicals, loss of habitat, disease, natural cycles—all have likely played roles in the declines of the Chesapeake's fabled abundance of fish and shellfish. But we often tend to underestimate the extent to which both sport and commercial fishermen just took fish out of the bay faster than it could grow new ones.

The Chesapeake fisheries, based on commercial catches of the last twenty-five years, suggest a dismal picture of decline from traditional harvest levels: American shad, down 60 percent in Virginia and 90 percent in Maryland (fishing banned in Maryland since 1980); rockfish, or striped bass, down 80 percent in Virginia and 64 percent in Maryland (fishing banned or heavily restricted in Maryland since 1984 and restricted in Virginia); river herring, down about 93 percent baywide; white perch, down 47 percent in Virginia and 63 percent in Maryland; yellow perch, down 90 percent in Virginia and 71 percent in Maryland (fishing banned in some tributaries); American eel, down 40 percent in Virginia and 9 percent in Maryland. Hickory shad have almost ceased to be a viable species in many of the bay's waters where they abounded only a couple of decades ago; sturgeon, which grew to more than 12 feet and whose numbers supported caviar factories at the turn of the century, are rarely caught in the bay nowadays. (See Figure 3.1.)

DECLINES

Poor shad, where is thy redress?

—HENRY THOREAU

All of these species are either year-round bay residents or depend on the bay's rivers and creeks to reproduce and to nurture their young. (Species like the bluefish and menhaden that are less dependent on the bay and its rivers in their vulnerable early life stages have not generally experienced such drastic declines.) To some extent the problems of the bay-dependent species may reflect a deterioration of habitat and water quality in the upstream sections of the system, where impacts of human populations and pollution caused by acid rain and possibly other chemicals are more prevalent. But at least as great a factor has been the extreme vulnerability of most of these species to overfishing. All of them are characterized by spawning migrations—moving in great concentrations, at predictable times of the year, up into the narrower, upstream portions of the estuary's rivers and creeks (except the eel, the only one that runs downstream to the oceans to spawn).

It did not take a fisheries scientist to see how the spawning corridors for shad and herring, rockfish and perch, and in earlier decades sturgeon, were routinely curtained off with the nets and traps of fishermen until very recent years—or how the little spawning streams for yellow perch were lined with sportfishermen and the herring streams with dipnetters. "Gauntlet fishing" it was called by one biologist, and it remained the norm until, one after another, the fish populations began to crash. In addition to being caught as they spawned, many of these species were also being caught at sea, caught as they migrated through other coastal states, caught by recreational and commercial fishermen alike. No single state or management agency was totaling the score.

The rockfish, or striped bass, one of the bay's (and the whole East Coast's) premier sport and commercial species from colonial times until the last decade, illustrates the problems that have affected

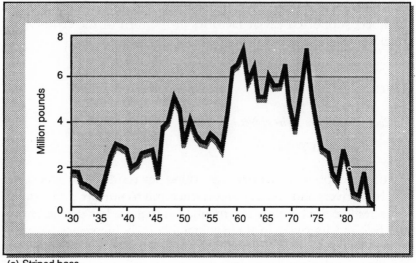

(a) Striped bass

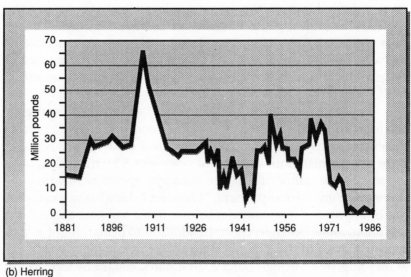

(b) Herring

FIGURE 3.1. DECLINES IN THREE MAJOR BAY FISHERIES. [From Maryland Department of Natural Resources and Virginia Marine Resources Commission; adapted by Joseph Hutchinson]

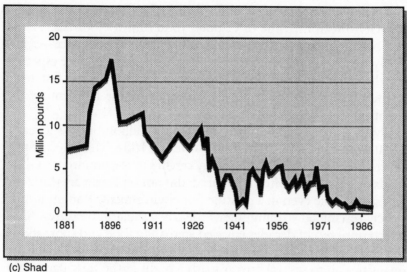

(c) Shad

several species. It is now thought that during the heyday of the fishery in the 1970s, more than half of the rockfish born each year were being harvested as soon as they reached legal size (at two to three years of age). This halving, and halving again, and so forth, carried out for several years before the females matured at age six or seven, meant that only a tiny fraction ever survived to reproduce themselves.

Sportfishermen on the bay caught just as many as watermen, at least through the 1960s. A picture of the "good ole days," circa 1960, that recently ran in an Eastern Shore newspaper exemplifies this: two anglers squat proudly in their boat, while the third grins up from a pile of rockfish that have been arranged to cover him, head to toe, with plenty more spilling off the sides of the pile. It took them just three hours to make the catch. No sportfisherman ever thought he was as much a threat as the few thousand watermen who used up to 5 or 6 miles of nets and sometimes returned with a daily harvest measured in tons. And he wasn't—but there were more than a million of him. The decimation of the rockfish populations that occurred during the 1970s alone cost the East Coast an estimated 7,500 lost jobs and $220 million in lost economic activity, according to a Department of Commerce Study.

There was ample precedent for fishing the Chesapeake beyond its capacity. From the time of Captain John Smith's journals, the bay had been framed as a place of incredible natural abundance—with a heavy-handed implication that it was a table set by Nature especially for the colonists to exploit. The early settlers were too few to do serious damage to the bay's fisheries, but by the last century that situation had changed dramatically.

Oyster harvests soared from less than a million bushels a year in 1840 to an incredible 20 million bushels in 1884. That all-time peak of harvest, with which modern-day catches in the hundreds of thousands of bushels are often compared, did not represent anything that was sustainable even in a pristine bay environment. Rather, it more closely resembled stripmining of the bay's shellfish treasures. Shad, which until recent decades enjoyed status as a food and sport species the equal of any, were being netted and shipped out of Crisfield in quantities up to several boxcar loads a night in the early part of this century. From the time of George Washington, who ran a fish netting operation out of Mount Vernon on the Potomac, large sections of the bay were virtually closed off by nets during spring. One shad fishing operation in the early 1900s regularly strung a huge net across nearly half the upper Chesapeake in the rich spawning grounds just below the Susquehanna River's mouth.

There was nothing unique to the Chesapeake region about fishing as if there were no tomorrow. Nationally and internationally, to this day, the oceans and coastal waters have been seen as the last frontiers of limitless abundance and overexploited for everything from sperm whales to surf clams. Examples of timely conservation measures are still the exception rather than the rule. "Every species of food finfish in the United States' marine waters is now fished at or above its capacity to replace itself," said a recent report by the Sport Fishing Institute. It noted that the number of Americans who fish has increased two and one-half times in the last thirty years.

Equally as troubling as the declines in catches have been declines in the ability of some species to reproduce by spawning successfully. Rockfish are one of the few species for which there is a good historical record of spawning success (back to 1954). They tend to spawn with uneven success from year to year, depending on periodic extraordinary spawning success, or "dominant" years, to maintain their populations. The rockfish, whose spawning areas until recently supplied an astounding 90 percent of the East Coast population, averaged a dominant year (in the Maryland part of the bay, the main spawning grounds) about every two and a half years in the sixteen years between 1954 and 1970. But they did not have another one for nineteen years—in the spring of 1989. (See Figure 3.2.)

One of the theories that held sway for the first several years of this reproductive drought—and is still voiced about other, still-healthy species in the bay—is that fish produce so many eggs, often millions per female, that as long as even a few are left to spawn, they can reproduce huge numbers of young, "bring the species back," as long as environmental conditions are right. The problem is that many of the bay's species are, in effect, gamblers who spread their bets. Environmental conditions are almost never uniformly right for success across what may be hundreds of miles of spawning waters scattered throughout widely separated river systems. But if all the areas are flooded each year with spawning fish, some are bound to hit the jackpot. Conversely, if too many spawners are removed from the action, their ability as a species to cover all their bets, or possi-

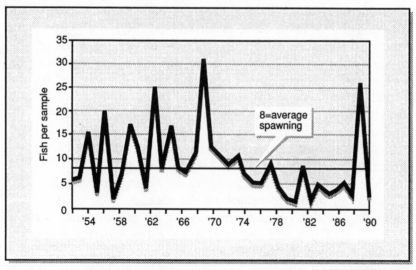

FIGURE 3.2. STRIPED BASS SPAWNING IN MARYLAND: 1954–1990
Striped bass, or rockfish, tend to experience "dominant years" in reproduction—in these years the number of young, as measured by a standard sampling net, is far above the average year's success. From 1970 to 1989 no dominant year occurred, and continued harvesting pressure decimated rockfish populations. [Adapted by Joseph Hutchinson from Maryland Department of Natural Resources]

bilities for success, goes down. And at some point so too does spawning success.

The extreme example of this pattern is the American shad, fished so hard in Maryland that by 1980, when fishing was closed, the shad landings were at less than 1 percent of historic levels. It seems likely that there were literally too few fish left to "restart" their population, although the effects of acid rain may also have been a contributing factor. After a decade of no fishing for the species, accompanied by heavy stocking of hatchery-raised young shad, their estimated numbers in the part of the bay near the Susquehanna River's mouth have finally begun an encouraging upward trend. But a fishing season is still probably years away, and some great shad rivers like the Nanticoke on Maryland's Eastern Shore have shown no real upsurge.

We may have acted to conserve the rockfish before it was too late. Numbers were quite depressed, but not nearly so much as the shad, when fishing for the rockfish was banned in 1984 in Maryland and restricted in Virginia and along the rest of the East Coast. The aim was to preserve the young females from what was barely an average reproductive year in 1982 until most had matured sexually and spawned at least once. (This occurred by 1990.) With virtually no fishing to eliminate them, the relatively modest amounts of little rockfish born in 1982 have become the largest population of the species in the modern history of the bay. By 1989 they had become virtually a nuisance to fishermen, who often cannot keep the now illegal rockfish out of their nets and off their hooks. And when the females born in 1982 first began to spawn in large numbers in 1989, the result was the first "dominant" spawn in nineteen years—and the second best in thirty-five years of recordkeeping.

While factors other than stopping the fishing pressure shouldn't be ruled out in the comeback of the rockfish, biologists say it is compelling evidence that overharvesting has played a major role in the decline of this and probably many other fisheries. But is the rockfish now securely back? The answer is an emphatic no. Eighteen years of generally poor spawning followed by one huge success does not equal a clear comeback trend. In fact, spawning in 1990 was well below average. This is not surprising, though, since the species has never produced two dominant spawns back to back.

How long, then, must we severely restrict fishing before we know rockfish are firmly reestablished? A key point in the rock's comeback will occur when spawning females of many different ages once again exist. This is important because rockfish live for decades, and the older females, those twelve to fifteen years and more, produced a huge proportion of the eggs before the great declines of the 1970s and 1980s. While we have made progress toward restoring the spawning stocks of rockfish, the age spread of spawning females is not as diverse as biologists would like to see it. Having different-age spawners is also another way for the fish to spread their "bets," since different age groups appear to take advantage of different environmental conditions at spawning. If conditions one year are not good for younger females, they may be fine for older ones (or vice versa).

The rockfish, among all species in decline in the bay, is the one for which we have the most information and have made the most progress in managing to position it for a comeback. In one sense the case of the rockfish is not typical, since much of the impetus for better management came from federal legislation. (The fish migrates through several states and hence became an issue in Congress.) Nevertheless, the lessons we've learned do apply to the other species.

Thus it is notable that when very restricted fishing seasons were opened in Maryland and Virginia in the autumn of 1990 on the strength of the 1989 spawning success, there were firm limits placed on catches—both the number per angler each day and the total take of fish. Maryland in fact closed its season early when it looked like the total catch was being reached faster than expected. All this might not seem extraordinary to the inland fisherman, who has long been limited on the daily number of trout, bass, and other species taken from rivers and streams, but it is one of the first times we have acted as if the bay had limits on its capacity to supply fish.

Traditionally, Maryland and Virginia always have come at the controversial issue of limits through the back door—limiting catches by limiting catching gear, that is, by specifying the type and size of nets, traps, and other devices used to take fish. Seldom was there a limit set on catches. But this strategy was overwhelmed in large part by a combination of technology and numbers: bigger, faster, all-weather boats; extremely sophisticated electronic fish-locating and navigational devices; burgeoning numbers of recreational hook and line fishermen.

Even the historic old wooden sailing vessels called skipjacks—the only "gear" Maryland allows to dredge for oysters—now often have electronic navigation devices in the cabins that enable a captain to relocate a choice oystering spot in fog or darkness with precision down to a few yards. Such technology has made both sport and commercial fishermen much more efficient. An expert skipper with the right electronics can locate a school of fish and catch virtually all its members. The bay is suddenly smaller and less of a hiding place than it used to be. The impact is just as devastating as an increase in pollution or destruction of habitat.

RESTORATION

There may well be more rockfish in the bay in 1990 than at any time in modern history.

—MEMO FROM A FEDERAL FISHERIES BIOLOGIST

The limits imposed on the number of pounds of rockfish that could be caught, as well as the abrupt closing of the 1990 season when quotas were reached, may well represent the future of bay fishing—a first taste of what Maryland and Virginia have proclaimed as a new era of jointly managing the bay's species on a sustainable basis. Never again can we afford to return to the days of wide-open exploitation, this new philosophy of management says.

The primary tools for achieving this goal are an array of management plans that are being written for most of the important recreational and commercial species of fish, shellfish, and crabs. These plans, unlike the lip service that has always been paid to conservation of the bay's resources, are meant to develop excellent biological information, set catch quotas, and open and close fishing seasons as needed to ensure the long-term health of each species. They will be complemented by other programs aimed at improving water quality and restoring habitat. But with the exception of rockfish, most of these plans don't yet exist in any substantial form. Nor is our scientific knowledge adequate for managing many species (see Figure 3.3).

The other (even less predictable) half of fishery management is the task of mustering the political will and leadership to specify plans and enforce them. Our track record here is not good. There has never been a case of successful fishery management in the bay before. Additionally, certain wide-ranging species such as shad must be managed better in the ocean waters of the bay states if management of the fish in the bay is to reach its potential. Virginia and Maryland

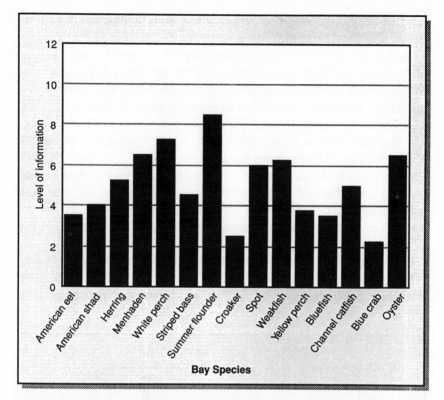

FIGURE 3.3. STATE OF KNOWLEDGE FOR MANAGING SELECTED FISH-
ERIES *Information needed to manage most of the bay's fisheries is incomplete.
This chart rates each species according to our knowledge of twelve critical areas
including reproduction, growth rates, natural mortality, and commercial and
recreational catch rates.* [Adapted by Donna Malloy from EPA, Chesapeake
Bay Stock Assessment Report]

have been slow to control the expansion in commercial fishing for
shad that migrate close to their ocean coastlines on their way to
spawn in the bay. This failure has probably delayed comebacks in
the bay.

Crabs

An upcoming test case of whether or not we have truly entered
the "new era" of fishery management will be to see what happens
with the blue crab, whose situation is discussed in more depth in

Chapter 6. Since crab catches are still relatively healthy, all experts agree that this is the ideal time to establish a conservation strategy.

Although catches have remained high for several years (Figure 3.4), there has been an ominous rise in the effort it has taken to sustain these catches. Biologists call this *catch per unit effort*. It is a truer measure of the abundance of a species than catches. While crab catches have remained level, for example, the number of crab pots on the bay has risen by nearly 50 percent in the last six years to more than a million. Thus catches per unit effort are down, even though catches aren't. Moreover, Maryland and Virginia estimate that growing numbers of recreational crabbers—all of us and our kids with their chicken necks on strings—are taking as much as 21 million pounds of crabs a year, nearly a quarter of the commercial catches.

The states have promised to effectively limit the crab harvest at what they think is a sustainable level within the next year or two. This effort will be controversial. It will also be a precedent if it

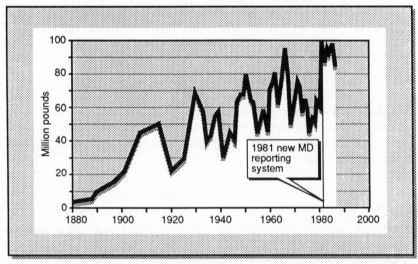

FIGURE 3.4. TRENDS IN BLUE CRAB CATCHES: MARYLAND AND VIR-GINIA   *Blue crab harvests, always highly variable from year to year, have shown no downward trend in recent decades like so many bay fisheries. The leap in catches in 1981 is thought to be at least partly the result of a more accurate reporting system in Maryland.* [Adapted by Joseph Hutchinson from EPA, Chesapeake Bay Stock Assessment Report, and Maryland Department of Natural Resources]

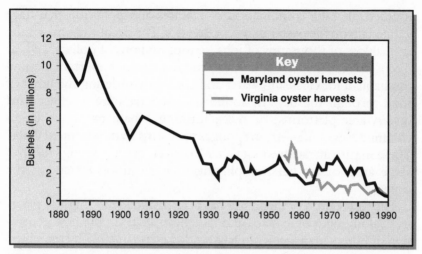

FIGURE 3.5. THE BAY'S DWINDLING OYSTER HARVESTS.   [EPA, Chesapeake Bay Stock Assessment Report]

succeeds—the first time measures have been taken to conserve a species *before* it was in decline.

Oysters

Chesapeake, or Chesepioc, is an Indian word for Great Shellfish Bay. Oysters are what the bay, as much as anything, was all about. "Oysters there be in whole banks and beds . . . some thirteen inches long," wrote William Strachey, an early visitor to the bay in 1612. "The abundance of oysters is incredible . . . there are whole banks of them so that the ships must avoid them. . . . I often cut them in two, before I could put them into my mouth," wrote a Swiss traveler, Francis Michel, a hundred years after Strachey.

And so it would continue to be for nearly another two centuries. It was not until the 1880s that gross overharvesting (see Figure 3.5) propelled the landings of oysters to a peak that crested, like a huge tidal wave, just before the twentieth century—then broke on a downward trend that in the last decade has left a harvest as thin as the lap of receding surf. Maryland and Virginia had the authority for virtually all this time to regulate harvests more strictly but failed to do so.

What overfishing and mismanagement began has been all but

finished off by a combination of diseases and pollution that have ganged up on the oyster in recent decades. The decline has meant the annual loss of thousands of jobs, tens of millions of dollars, and, as discussed in Chapter 4, the destruction of an important natural mechanism for cleansing water and efficiently ordering the flows of food through the bay. In addition, oyster bars are in effect hard underwater platforms, or reefs, forming a base for much larger communities of life—from sponges to worms to the young of crabs. These in turn attract feeding fish. Moreover, other filtering creatures settle atop oyster bars, amplifying their cleansing effects on the water.

The restoration of the oyster has been assigned the "highest priority" (along with blue crabs and American shad) in the new generation of fishery management plans embarked on in 1987 by the states. Yet, at this point, the specter of disease nearly obscures everything else. Both MSX, which appeared out of nowhere in the 1950s, and "dermo" disease, both caused by microscopic parasites, have reduced oyster harvests during the 1980s to their lowest levels since commercial harvesting began around 1839. Actual numbers of oysters are estimated to be about 1 percent of their historic populations.

Three decades of research have not yielded a solution to the oyster diseases, rendering restoration in the near term a moot question. Considering the importance of the oyster to the Chesapeake, research budgets aimed at the disease problem are relatively modest, in the hundreds of thousands of dollars annually. The disease problem does not appear directly related to pollution, but stresses from low oxygen and low levels of toxic chemicals common throughout the bay may have made the oysters more vulnerable to disease.

The dilemma has focused debate on ways to "manage around" the disease problem. Virginia has pushed the introduction of a non-native oyster from the West Coast that might be disease resistant. It might also outcompete the native bay oysters, however. Some say the risk is worth it—that we have very little left to lose. Others, including the state of Maryland, are not willing to risk the future of a species that has been well adapted to the Chesapeake environment for thousands of years.

For more than a century the argument has raged over aquaculture of oysters as opposed to the "wild" harvest practiced by free-ranging watermen. Virginia long ago adopted a dual system that resulted in substantial numbers of "private" oystermen who leased bottom from the state and planted and harvested oysters. Maryland's watermen, fearing the "little man would be forced out of the industry," have effectively resisted widespread adoption of private leases.

Aquaculture today means much more than just leasing bottom. It means procedures like growing hatchery-raised young oysters in floating rafts and pushing them to market size in a short enough time that the disease will not kill them before they are harvested. Hybrid oysters that grow faster but do not reproduce—and so do not pose a threat to native species—might also be used in such aquaculture. Genetic engineering might be able to produce an oyster of uniform size and shape, enabling machine shucking. Even with the disease problem, "we now have enough tools to make dramatic differences in the production of oysters" concluded a recent plan on the future of the American oyster industry.

Whether to endorse aquaculture of oysters wholeheartedly—and whether to give up on the traditional harvesting methods—are major policy decisions that may be soon forced on the states by the current desperate status of wild oysters. These are decisions with much larger implications than just private versus public enterprise. Curtailing the present practice of spreading shells on the bottom to support traditional oystering and adopting a raft-based system, for example, might boost harvests significantly. But it might also result in the decline of the reef system of oysters on the bottom that makes such excellent habitat for many other species. Moreover, in areas like the West Coast, vaunted for its productivity from private oyster farms, pesticides are used to keep other growth from fouling the oysters. The difference between this system and the current wild harvest is the difference between a one-crop farm and a forest that supports an abundance of diverse life.

In the meantime, the proposed baywide management plan that is to conserve what oyster stocks are left does not yet have anything in it but good intentions. It proposes to set harvest quotas and to open and close oystering areas based on conservation; but there is nothing specific in it to date. As of 1990, Virginia was still permitting its oystermen to harvest dwindling stocks of oysters in the James River despite a report from the Virginia Institute of Marine Science warning that collapse of the populations there was imminent. (See Figure 3.6.)

Maryland too has continued its normal oyster harvest—even though catches and reproduction both are clearly heading toward

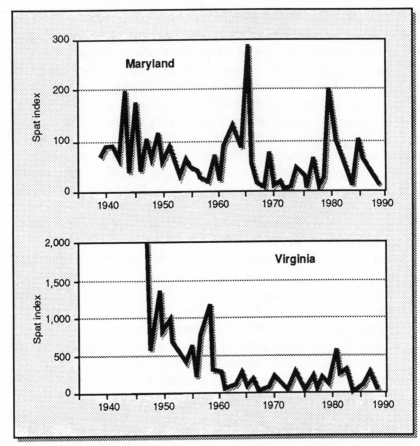

FIGURE 3.6. REPRODUCTIVE SUCCESS OF OYSTERS: MARYLAND AND VIRGINIA.   [Adapted by Joseph Hutchinson from Maryland Department of Natural Resources and Virginia Marine Fisheries Resources Commission]

levels that soon may scarcely support any commercial fishery at all. An internal memo written by an oyster scientist at Maryland's Department of Natural Resources in 1989 advocated banning or restricting harvests immediately on large areas where there still were enough survivors of the diseases to possibly bring back the population. The survivors might have some genetic resistance to the diseases, the memo said, adding: "The most cost effective mechanism . . . is to leave them alone and let Mother Nature provide the recovery." But in the winter of 1990, with watermen coming off one of their worst summers in a long time (plenty of crabs, poor prices),

CAMPAIGN UPON THE QUINEPIAC

The following account, taken from old oyster journals, tells of oyster exploitation in Connecticut during the early 1800s. It was after exhaustion of the New England oyster beds that businessmen there sent the large fleets of ships that began overexploiting the Chesapeake's shellfish:

> It was a time of great excitement, and nowhere greater than along the Quinepiac. . . . As midnight approached, men dressed in oilskin and carrying oars, paddles, rakes and tongs collected all along the shore, where a crowd of women and children assembled to see the fun.
>
> No eye could see the face of the great church clock on the hill, but lanterns glimmered upon a hundred watch-dials and then were set down, as only a coveted minute remained. . . . It was like an electric shock as the great bell struck a deep-toned peal. Backs bent to oars and paddles churned the water. From opposite banks, waves of boats leaped out and advanced towards one another in the darkness, as though bent on mutual annihilation.
>
> Before the twelve blows upon the loud bell had ceased their reverberations, the oyster beds had been reached, tongs were scraping the long-rested bottom and the season's campaign upon the Quinepiac had begun.
>
> . . . A week of this sort of attack, however, usually sufficed to clean the bottom so thoroughly that subsequent raking was of small account. . . . At the present time the bed does not yield marketable oysters.

neither state showed any inclination to bite the bullet and protect the remnants of what was once the richest oyster bay in the world.

Watermen

Perhaps the ultimate reflection of the state of the bay's fisheries is the Chesapeake Bay waterman. There are now about 9,000 full-time watermen in Maryland, according to the Maryland Watermens Association, and perhaps 5,000 in Virginia, based on estimates by individual watermen. The very term *waterman* recognizes the fact that the bay's seafood harvesters tend to specialize in no single fishery, instead relying for a living on shifting frequently among catching everything from crabs and clams to rockfish, terrapin, eels, even bloodworms.

Watermen are a paradox. On the one hand, they are as powerful a symbol as exists of the bay we want to preserve and their own preservation is a powerful thrust behind the current bay restoration programs. Marylanders and Virginians (and vacationing Pennsylvanians) all love the images of the men and the boats and the independent lifestyle of watermen, still attuned to natural forces as the rest of us punch clocks and live lives increasingly disconnected from nature. Bay residents have a luxury that few developed regions enjoy—not just eating oysters on the half shell, but oysters caught by salty captains under full sail in century-old wooden skipjacks; not just rockfish stuffed with crab meat, but rock and crab that come from little communities along the bay's edge where quaint language persists and the harbors are the stuff of picture postcards.

On the other hand, having watermen around can be a little like having a shark in your aquarium. It is their nature to be very, very good at exploiting any and all fishery resources. Working as they do at harvesting a commons—that is, public waters which are open to all comers—it is not in the interest of any individual waterman to catch less than he can, for whatever he leaves would just be fair game for someone else. Thus although many watermen today recognize the need for conservation, such a mentality is not fostered by the arena in which they have to work. In the absence of strong fishery management, watermen are capable of quickly overwhelming the natural resource.

Some sportfishing interests respond to this danger by advocating getting rid of commercial watermen so there will be more fish for sportsmen. They have some compelling, if sometimes self-serving, arguments. In Maryland and Virginia there are about 14,000 watermen—probably fewer than that who are full time—and well over a million sportfishermen. With species like shad and rockfish, maximizing sportfishing and tourism opportunities clearly outstrips any conceivable economic value of commercial harvests.

Watermen meanwhile face other problems. Throughout the bay, their communities and lifestyles are crumbling or under severe stress. There are many forces behind this pressure besides the state of the bay's water quality, including modern expectations and college op-portunities for their youth and competition with condo builders for waterfront space. On remote Smith Island, Maryland, 12 miles out in the bay, more than a quarter of the watermen's homes now are owned by New Yorkers, Washingtonians, and other "foreigners" from Norfolk, Richmond, Baltimore, and Pittsburgh. A high-speed ferry already is running tourists from Baltimore's Inner Harbor to the watermen's village of Rock Hall, Maryland, which is two hours by car from the city but only forty-five minutes by boat—and the ferry's promoters want to turn it into a year-round commuter boat.

Increasingly, as oysters and fish decline, the watermen are also losing the diversity of species that has so typified their traditional fishing. Nowadays they must depend on one species, crabs, for the bulk of their income. That is a dangerous proposition, since even the hardy crab, like everything in nature, has its limits. There have been severe depressions in crab catches in the past that were unrelated to pollution. If such a crash were to come now, or if a disastrous oil spill at the bay's mouth wiped out the crab spawning grounds there, the waterman would have little alternative but to leave the water.

Waterfowl

The twenty-nine species of waterfowl—geese, ducks, and swans—inhabiting Chesapeake Bay are among the most visible indicators of environmental conditions in and around the estuary. In their feeding and breeding they depend on a range of bay habitats, from upland fields and streambanks to the marshy edges, shallow grass beds, and shellfish colonies of the channel edges.

Except for a handful of commercial hunting guides, no one's livelihood depends on waterfowl, nor do they play an important part in our diets anymore. Nonetheless, for hunter and birdwatcher and anyone who thrills each autumn to the music of geese aloft, water-fowl are as much the essence of what makes living in the bay region worthwhile as any creatures below or above the bay's surface. Eco-nomically, tourism and hunting related to geese and ducks have become a major industry for the region. Some farmers fortunate enough to have waterfront cornfields can make more renting them for shooting in the winter than they can from the crops they grow on them.

Given the dramatic and widespread environmental declines of the bay in recent decades, it might seem surprising that waterfowl populations fell by less than 10 percent between the 1950s and the 1980s. Then, as now, the bay was home to about a million waterfowl each winter—about a third of the entire population along the East Coast. The overall numbers, however, have masked a tremendous decline in the diversity of waterfowl (see Figure 3.7). Canada geese and snow

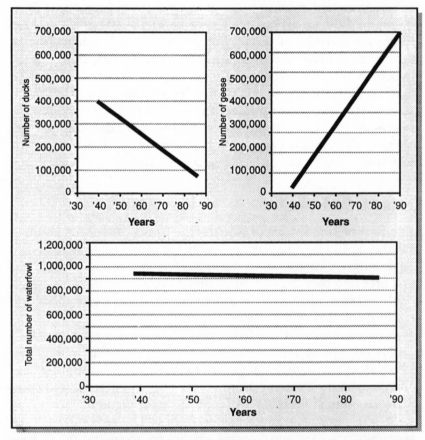

FIGURE 3.7. CHESAPEAKE BAY WATERFOWL TRENDS: 1930–1989
Although waterfowl numbers in the bay region have remained fairly constant, a great loss of diversity has occurred. One species, the Canada goose, has increased dramatically, but most of the bay's twenty-seven or so varieties of ducks have trended downward. [Adapted by Joseph Hutchinson from EPA, Chesapeake Bay Liaison Office, State of the Bay Report, 1990]

geese, which accounted for less than 20 percent of all bay waterfowl during the 1950s, made up 65 percent of the total during the 1980s. Meanwhile, seventeen of the twenty varieties of ducks surveyed annually declined, many of them to a mere remnant of former numbers. The declines were triggered by the water pollution that killed the majority of the bay's submerged aquatic grasses, food for the great majority of waterfowl on the bay. The losses of both nontidal and tidal wetlands habitat, where the fowl fed in shallow ponds and potholes, also hurt.

Equally critical, however, was the ability of waterfowl to adapt to the declines. This ability varied tremendously. Canada geese, for example, had already begun in the 1950s to change feeding habits to take advantage of the growing acreage of corn harvested by machine instead of hand. The mechanical harvesters not only enabled farmers to put more acres in grain like corn but also left a good deal more corn on the ground. (Ironically it was the increasing pollution from these farms, along with increases in human sewage and runoff from developed lands, that killed the underwater grasses.)

Tundra swans, the largest and most majestic of the bay's waterfowl, changed to feeding in grain fields and also extended their migration south to the Carolinas, where more grasses remained. Their populations have remained stable on the bay since the 1950s. Canvasback ducks, which have little ability to feed on land but can dive several yards deep, changed their diet from about 90 percent grasses to about 90 percent hard-shelled clams and snails on the bay bottom. They have declined sharply since the 1950s but appear to have stabilized in recent years at lower population levels.

Species like redhead ducks and American wigeon simply could not adapt and have almost vanished from the bay. (This raises a wider and most intriguing thought: To an extent the dominant bay species of today, the rockfish and the crab, the wild goose and the great blue heron, are *what is left*—the toughest and most adaptable of a much larger assortment of creatures that did not make the adaptations. That even these survivor species are beginning to show strains may be an indication of how far humankind has pushed the Chesapeake ecosystem.)

Black ducks, a prime game species and one of the few waterfowl that breeds in the bay watershed (although most migrate north), have suffered from the widespread destruction of habitat by development and by changes in agriculture from hayfields, where they once nested, to grain. The sea ducks, which feed mainly on bottom-dwelling snails and mollusks and on fishes, have on the whole fared better than the other classes of duck. Possibly this is because they have not been desired by hunters owing to their fishy-tasting flesh. Recent increases in sea duck hunting may indicate how far other, more preferred, species have declined.

Hunting of waterfowl on the bay in modern times has been a sport—not a livelihood like fishing—and regulation of recreational waterfowlers has proved a good deal easier and more effective than fishing, where commercial, recreational, and charter boat fishermen compete for the same natural resources. This is not to say that waterfowl management has been unflawed. As population has grown and along with it leisure time, sport hunting pressure has intensified and become somewhat of an industry complete with tourism and commercial hunting guides. The latter now invest hundreds of thousands of dollars in renting waterfront farms in some cases and must run a large number of customers through to recoup their investment. They have lobbied hard for extended hunting seasons and larger bag limits. (The federal and state governments set shooting limits each year based on each species' population and success in breeding. Although states cannot raise the federal limits, they can be more restrictive.)

It is easier to manage waterfowl than fish for the simple reason that you can see them and, from an airplane, count them. We know with some precision how many geese and ducks there are in our part of the world, and how they are doing each summer on the breeding grounds. That level of knowledge, vital for management, is not approached for most fish that swim in U.S. waters. In sum, our ability to regulate harvests of waterfowl is substantially better than our ability to manage fishing in the bay.

The tougher issue is restoring habitat. The goal set in the 1987 Chesapeake Bay restoration agreement among the states and EPA is to bring waterfowl populations back to where they were in the 1970s. This would mean, for the most part, only modest increases. But any increase is ambitious, given that many species are also losing habitat to agriculture and development where they breed in Canada and the northern prairies of the United States. Both Maryland and Virginia are targeting tens of thousands of acres of waterfowl habitat for protection and enhancement—this in addition to about 120,000 acres of habitat in the two states currently in refuges and wildlife management areas. But unless water quality improves enough to bring back the submerged grasses, prospects for a major recovery of many bay waterfowl seem unlikely. Moreover, some of the most critical habitat degradation is beyond the control of the bay states and even the federal government. This is the conversion of prairie potholes where many of "our" ducks nest across Canadian provinces like Saskatchewan and Alberta and Manitoba.

Even the success story of the Canada goose's adaptation to cornfields, which has sustained waterfowl hunting in the bay watershed more than any other factor, is shakier than it seems. Just as watermen have grown dangerously dependent on a single species in the water, the blue crab, so are hunters now quite dependent on the goose. For both fishing and hunting, the major impact of pollution seems to have been the loss of diversity. In just the last few years the Canada goose has experienced poor breeding success, apparently the product of purely natural climatic events on its Labrador nesting grounds. The result has been a dramatic dip in populations, forcing the states to curtail hunting seasons and reduce the number of birds that can be shot. Yet pressure from commercial guides and many hunters has caused state legislatures to urge their game agencies to allow more harvesting than is biologically proper, given the current dip in goose populations. As with fishing, we cannot rule out environmental problems when waterfowl decline, problems like habitat loss and ingestion of toxic lead shot. But often we are simply killing them faster than they can reproduce.

Moreover, the goose's high populations are quite dependent now on a human agricultural system that could change quickly to growing other products in response to shifting markets. Compare this unreliable source to their natural food supply—the grasses that persisted for thousands of years until polluted. Even if farmers do not shift their production from corn, the goose's favorite food, the future for farms in the region is downward. All projections for the bay's watershed show development in the next thirty years taking hundreds of thousands of acres of agricultural land out of production.

Finally, the shift from hunting over water to hunting over land has implications for other wildlife. While this is scarcely a major impact, it is a fascinating illustration of the complex way in which human activities become intertwined with the natural world. With the decline of waterfowl that fed in the grass beds offshore, there has been a huge decline in the number of offshore duck blinds—essentially wooden boxes mounted on poles and covered with pine boughs for camouflage. Wildlife managers say these blinds provided not only wintertime hunting but in spring and summer were fine nesting places for ospreys, owls, black ducks, and green herons, and sometimes for all four species at the same time.

CONCLUSIONS

☐ The fishery resources of Chesapeake Bay, virtually across the board, are either in sharp decline or under severe pressure. We are currently exploiting the bay's fish and shellfish resources close to the breaking point or beyond. Fishing in the Chesapeake, both sport and commercial, has always been characterized by no limits on total harvests of any species.

☐ Although pollution and habitat destruction certainly have contributed to the declines in many important bay fish, an equal or greater culprit has been simple overfishing. In taking fish faster than the bay can replace them, both commercial and sport fishermen have played substantial roles. The impact of sportfishing, not well quantified, has probably been underestimated.

☐ The striped bass, or rockfish, has shown encouraging signs of a comeback, but it will be several more years before we can judge whether they are firmly reestablished.

☐ The American shad, fished into commercial extinction in the Maryland part of the bay, is finally showing signs of coming back after a ten-year fishing moratorium and restocking efforts. But it will be years before a season can be safely opened on the species.

☐ Traditional means of attempting to limit catches of bay species by limiting the types of fishing gear have consistently been overwhelmed by technology: better boats, electronic fishfinding, and high-tech navigational gear.

☐ Although catches of blue crabs appear healthy, the amount of time and gear needed to catch the same number of crabs has skyrocketed in recent years.

☐ Both Maryland and Virginia continue to endorse overfishing of oysters, which have declined in a century to about 1 percent of their estimated historical abundance. Apart from their economic importance and good eating, oysters have been a key part of the bay's resilience with their ability to clarify large volumes of water and order the flows of food energy through the bay. The physical structure of oyster bars used to provide enormous and rich habitat for crabs, fish, and other shellfish.

□ Disease and low abundance mean there is little prospect in the near future for a major oyster comeback.

□ Maryland and Virginia are on the threshold of implementing a new era of scientifically managed fishery harvests, but only in the case of the striped bass is there anything yet resembling the kind of plans and policies that will be needed for each species. And because the striped bass migrates coastwide, the intelligent management here was in large part a product of national legislation, not local efforts. Blue crabs, which both states have pledged to begin managing conservatively while the population still is relatively healthy, will be a test case for our resolve to manage other species.

□ Some fundamental choices will have to be made in this decade regarding how much the bay should continue to be harvested by traditional watermen and how much it should be farmed by aquaculturists.

□ Watermen, whose preservation has been a major thrust of our bay cleanup efforts, are beset by a variety of attacks on their traditional lifestyles and livelihoods. The decline in water quality is only one among many problems.

□ Just as watermen have become dangerously dependent on a single species (the blue crab) as diversity of the bay's resources has declined, so have waterfowl hunters become too dependent on the Canada goose. The goose has adapted famously to pollution of its traditional food by switching from eating underwater grasses to feeding in cornfields. Many species of ducks have not been so adaptable, however, and their numbers are in sharp decline.

□ Waterfowl hunting has gotten to be bigger business in some areas, principally Maryland's Eastern Shore, increasing pressure to keep bag limits high and maintain longer seasons on wild geese than are biologically prudent.

CHAPTER 4

Resilience

If we were to present a citation to nature for a near-victory in her struggle of resistance against the works of man, I hope this Conference would vote unanimously the Chesapeake as the recipient. The valiant way in which the vast ecology in the waters, in the marshes, on the land, and even in the sky, has fought against the poison of pollution and man's rank disregard for the living values makes one stand in awe of the power of nature.

—Rogers C. B. Morton,
congressman from Maryland

We have always put a lot of faith in the bay's resilience—in its ability to bounce back from environmental insults. The history of the estuary is full of examples of this species or that being knocked back by natural events or pollution, only to resurge to record levels. It was partly our expectations of this resilience that delayed recognition during the 1970s that the bay had dropped to a lower plateau of environmental quality.

In June 1972, Mother Nature delivered the bay a fierce blow—the worst rain and flooding in perhaps two centuries. Across the vast watershed the floods blasted the bay for days on end with unheard-of volumes of choking silt, farm chemicals, sewage from ruptured lines, and fresh water—too much of the latter just as deadly as any other pollutant to many bay creatures.

Tropical Storm Agnes would have shocked the bay's system in any era, but coming at a time when many of the bay's original systems of resilience were depleted or stressed, it sent the estuary into a tailspin from which it still has not recovered. It was as if an aging prizefighter had suddenly found that he could no longer take a punch and come back.

In retrospect, it was not so surprising. For example, the forest that once covered most of the watershed was about 40 percent gone. This represented the loss of a superb filter and regulator of the bay's environment. Rainstorms trickling through a forest canopy soak into the deep organic matter of the forest floor. Less rain runs immediately off the land, and in dry times there is plenty stored in the forest water table to feed rivers by seeping in from underground. And far less pollution, from sediment to nutrients, escapes from each acre of forest than from any other land use. As a result, flows of water to the bay from forestland are cleaner, steadier, stabler, and less subject to wild fluctuations in storms than from any other land cover, from pastures to pavement.

Gone, too, was far more than half of the watershed's original inland and coastal wetlands. These not only harbored rich wildlife, they also played a role at least as great as forests (per acre) in filtering pollutants running from the land and buffering the bay against the extremes of flood and drought.

Along the shallow edges of the bay and its rivers, more than a hundred thousand acres of submerged grasses still grew, as they had for thousands of years. But by the time of Agnes they were weakened and under severe stress. And the rush of pollutants that clouded the bay's water, cutting off light needed for grass growth, had been picking up sharply since the 1950s. The grasses, like the wetlands and the forest, were most obviously vital habitat for a variety of bay species. But they played an even more important, if less understood, role in trapping sediments and absorbing nutrients to clarify and cleanse the bay's waters.

In slightly deeper water lay what little was left—perhaps less than 10 percent in 1972—of the bay's fabled oyster beds, which once grew in reefs thick enough to pose navigational hazards to shipping. We value them as hors d'oeuvres and a source of employment for watermen. But by filtering water through their gills to feed, the bay's original oyster populations could remove pollutants like sediment every few days from a volume of water equal to the whole bay, thereby helping to clarify the water.

Altogether the forests, the wetlands, the grasses, and the oysters once constituted a marvelous system of buffers and filters, stabilizers and regulators. They lent the bay a tremendous capacity to absorb environmental insult and snap back. Even today people will sometimes remark of this or that aspect of the bay's decline that "things haven't been the same since Agnes." But the problem wasn't just Agnes. It was the extent to which we had reduced the modern bay's ability to take the punch.

The following sections set out the ways in which we must measure progress in addition to water quality and fisheries abundance if we are to maintain a healthy Chesapeake. Perhaps we can continue reducing the bay's resilience even further, without immediate consequence, if the next decade is without huge storms and no other unforeseen environmental stresses occur to the estuary. It will never be possible to argue to a scientific certainty that developing this patch of forest will kill so many rockfish or building a highway over that little marsh will stress submerged grasses a hundred miles distant. But if the bay continues to lose resilience, when the next heavy blow lands we may find that the fight has all but ended.

FORESTS

Rain forests . . . coral reefs, ocean depths . . . are not separate and independent entities; they are interrelated parts of the total system of the world of life, of the biosphere.
—MARSTON BATES, *The Forest and the Sea*

To the modern timberman, an oak tree is in its prime at around sixty to eighty years. Beyond that time, it is no longer adding wood as rapidly, and delaying its harvest will only risk disease or injury from lightning or wind.

To the squirrel, the same oak is just coming into its own after about 150 years, when its acorn production begins to peak—a peak it may sustain for another century.

To woodland birds, vireos, warblers, and the like, a forest studded with oaks two, three, and even four centuries old is living at its finest. The remarkable habitat afforded by the canopy and structure of the climax, old-growth forest provides the maximum number of niches for nesting and feeding.

The forest itself might say that the most productive oak is the dead one—the old giant that has spanned half a millennium, nourished generations of squirrels, cradled millions of songbirds, died, rotted, and, at long last, crashed to the ground. The sizable pit created by the oak's uprooting, and the bulk of the fallen tree, create unevenness on the forest floor, trapping and filtering water, damming up leaves that will rot into rich piles of compost, regenerating forest soils. The "dead" carcass of the oak bristles with new communities—mosses, fungi, lichens, beetles, ants, microbes. A whole new ecosystem has been created, further enriching the diversity of life.

Finally the bay, which ultimately depends on the quality and quantity of the rainwater that runs from the lands of its watershed, would say that no other land use—pasture, cornfield, suburban lawn, or urban street—consistently delivers the clear, pure water that has filtered first through the forest.

The Great Green Filter

We can only speculate on the quality of freshwater flows to the pristine bay that existed when the virgin forest covered almost all of the bay's watershed from New York state to Norfolk. Forests that have not been logged and otherwise altered by humans are so rare and scattered nowadays that even professional foresters often have never studied their workings. Our whole concept of a healthy and mature forest now applies to something that once would have been considered inferior and scraggly. Nonetheless, study after study confirms that even today forested lands of the watershed result in cleaner, clearer water flowing down the bay's tributaries than any other use to which we put land.

We can get a tantalizing hint of what the original, pristine bay was like from Young Woman's Creek, a 99.7 percent forested sub-watershed of the bay in north-central Pennsylvania. (See Figure 4.1.) It is part of the larger, Susquehanna River portion of the bay's watershed. Notice how, as rainfall increases runoff to the stream, the low levels of pollutants leaving the Young Woman's watershed rise only slightly.

Now look at the behavior of another Susquehanna subtributary, Conestoga Creek in southern Pennsylvania, whose watershed is nearly 65 percent agricultural, 14 percent forest, and about 22 percent developed. Extensive animal agriculture in its watershed produces enough manure to put 8 tons annually on every acre of farmland—more nutrients than crops can possibly use. The water running off these lands is hugely sensitive to increased rainfall. There

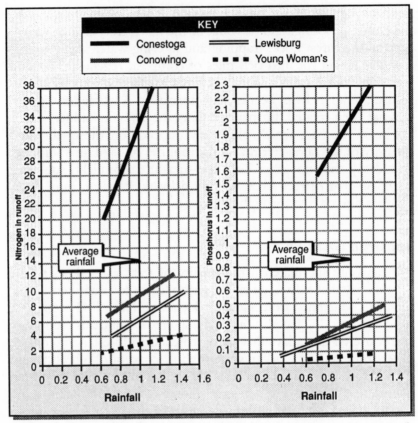

FIGURE 4.1. POLLUTION AND LAND USE *As rainfall increases, more nitrogen and phosphorus run into waterways from all four sections of the Susquehanna River charted here. But pollution loads are highest—and increase most rapidly with rainfall—in agricultural drainage basins like the Conestoga as compared to those with more forest cover like Young Woman's Creek.* [Adapted by Joseph Hutchinson from Susquehanna River Basin Commission reports]

is not the leaf litter of the forest floor to slow it and absorb it; and it carries more than twenty times the concentrations of nitrogen and phosphorus, both major pollutants of the bay, as Young Woman's Creek.

Notice the levels of nutrients in water from the Susquehanna's west branch, which enters the main river at Lewisburg. Nitrogen in runoff, for example, is about 40 percent less there than in flows from the fourth watershed in Figure 4.1, which represents the flow of the whole Susquehanna (measured at Conowingo near its mouth). It just happens that a major goal of our bay restoration program is to reduce nutrients flowing to the bay by 40 percent. If the whole river basin could be made like its west branch, victory would be ours. What is the west branch's secret? Some of it lies in the fact that its watershed has remained more in forest—about 20 percent more— than the watershed of the whole river.

Forests in Decline

To a large extent the efforts discussed in Chapter 3 to control the contaminated runoff from farms and developed lands are imperfect attempts to mimic what the forests once did quite naturally. It is clear that, to date, we have no adequate substitute for the forests we have destroyed. Meanwhile the amount of forestland in the watershed is on the decline, falling to both development and agriculture, and there are no prospects in the foreseeable future for reversing it. Among the principal bay states (Maryland, Virginia, and Pennsylvania) and the EPA, there are now formal programs to restore the bay's fish, oysters, and underwater plants, as well as programs to protect its wetlands and programs to reduce pollution from farms, urban pavements, sewage, and industrial plants. But there is no coherent policy to protect and enhance what is "least polluting" in the first place: the forest.

Statistics on forest decline across the bay's watershed are not as

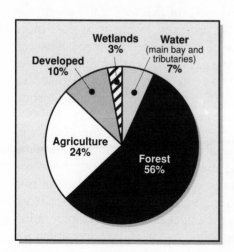

FIGURE 4.2. LAND USE AND WATER IN THE CHESAPEAKE BAY WATERSHED. [Adapted by Joseph Hutchinson from EPA, Chesapeake Bay Liaison Office, Land Use Statistics for the Chesapeake Bay Watershed]

precise as we would like, but gross forest acreage, we will see, may not be as important as how that forest is distributed in the watershed. (See Figure 4.2.) The watershed now is forested over about 24.5 million acres, or roughly 60 percent of its 64,000 square miles of land. (If that sounds like a lot, keep in mind that New York City is nearly 20 percent in trees and parkland.) Agriculture accounts for 29 percent and developed lands account for most of the remaining 11 percent of the watershed. So we have lost, since Indian times, nearly 40 percent of the bay's forest cover. The loss has not been a straight line. Intensive agricultural clearing and timbering by 1830 are estimated to have reduced forests in Maryland and Virginia to 4 or 5 million acres below current coverage. Pennsylvania had far less forest in 1920 than it does now.

Why wasn't the bay's health worse then than now? One reason is that the increased pollution this triggered was largely limited to sediment. In recent decades, runoff from cleared or developed land has included a much more potent range of chemicals—pesticides and concentrated fertilizers from farms and lawns; pollutants from septic tanks; toxic metals and compounds from our polluted air that wash from the impervious surfaces of cities instead of being trapped in soils and vegetation. In other words, there are two aspects to the forest filter's role in bay resilience: the size of the filter and the nastiness of what needs filtering. Additionally, the bay of a century and a half ago had much more of its other natural filtering mechanisms intact—wetlands, submerged grasses, and oyster beds—to deal with the huge influxes of sediments.

Having regained some forest during the first half of this century as agriculture reverted to trees, we are now losing it again—more permanently this time in the case of losses to development. Between 1978 and 1985, EPA estimates the bay lost more than 800,000 acres of trees from its watershed. Of this, the agency estimates that Virginia accounted for about 410,000 acres and Maryland around 68,000. (Maryland had lost much larger amounts, around 380,000 acres, during its boom development period during the 1960s and early 1970s.) Pennsylvania officials say EPA's estimates showing 370,000 acres of forest loss in the Susquehanna River basin are faulty. State foresters say that forest trends in the last decade or two probably have been "stable" there, with losses in the lower basin balanced by significant gains in the upper basin. (Development has accounted for losses; farms abandoned to forest have accounted for gains.) In New York and West Virginia's parts of the watershed, forest has increased since 1978, largely the result of marginal farms reverting to natural vegetation.

A decade or even two is not always long enough to see clear trends in forest change. Some suburban counties in Maryland, for example, showed surprising gains in forest during the 1960s and early 1970s. But this gain represented farms bought by speculators who let them revert briefly to forest before clearing and paving them. Given the bay's growing population and our present patterns of sprawl development, it is difficult to see anything but more forest loss in the next century.

A Matter of Location

Although more forest is always better for the bay than less forest, the *location and distribution* of that forest are perhaps more critical than overall acreage. Conversely, although we don't want to lose forest anywhere, there are some places where it is worse to lose it than others.

Scientific study increasingly is establishing what one would intuitively guess—that forests growing between bay tributaries and polluting land uses like farms or developments will trap and filter and detoxify polluted runoff before it reaches the water. In addition, they appear to increase the pH of the runoff (that is, reduce its acidity)—important in an era when acid rain is lowering the pH of some waters with harmful effects on fish. It is precisely in such streamside locations—where forest would have the greatest beneficial impact on water quality—that forestland is the most scarce in many portions of the watershed. Pennsylvania foresters point out that these "critical" acreages, whose value to water quality far outweighs their gross size, are what is being lost the fastest in the Susquehanna basin.

We do not have data to quantify how many of the bay's stream and river miles have inadequate forest buffers. We are just beginning to get a feel for how large these buffers should be. But it is clear from aerial observation that where the forests are needed most is where they exist least. Scientists in Pennsylvania and Maryland have had extreme difficulty in even finding stream watersheds well buffered with forests in developed and agricultural areas to serve as controls in their runoff experiments.

The most concerted efforts to control the loss of waterfront forest in Maryland and Virginia have occurred around the edges of the bay proper and its lower, tidal rivers (Maryland's Critical Area Act and Virginia's Chesapeake Bay Preservation Act). These objectives are worthwhile for a number of reasons. But for controlling major bay pollutants like agricultural fertilizers they will not be nearly enough. About 90 percent of such pollutants enter the bay from lands *above* these coastal zones, running off the watershed via the vast network of small streams and creeks and rivers far from the main bay.

Mapping of forest density by county within the watershed shows how unevenly distributed they are. By state, the parts of Virginia and Pennsylvania that lie in the bay's watershed are more than 60 percent forested while Maryland's portion is about 45 percent. But these figures can mislead. Pennsylvania, for example, has its relatively high percentage of forest lumped into counties like Potter and Wyoming that are heavily (84 and 75 percent) forested. Meanwhile counties like Lancaster, a huge source of polluting agricultural run-off to the bay, have only 13 percent of their forest remaining. (Even the District of Columbia has 8 percent forest remaining.) Here are some other examples of these disparities in forest distribution (taken from EPA's 1985 land use figures):

County	% Forested
Pennsylvania	
Adams	29%
Bedford	65%
Centre	77%
Cumberland	36%
Dauphin	48%
Lancaster	13%
Lebanon	35%
Potter	84%
Wyoming	75%
Maryland	
Baltimore	28%
Carroll	29%
Frederick	31%
Garrett	72%
Montgomery	30%
Queen Annes	25%

County	% Forested
St. Mary's	55%
Wicomico	50%
Virginia	
Accomack	67%
Essex	65%
Fairfax	34%
Gloucester	69%
King and Queen	80%
Loudoun	32%
Middlesex	70%
Rockingham	60%

Fragmenting the Forest

Across most of the bay watershed, forests can be cleared at will by farmers, homeowners, developers, and loggers. Except in the special coastal zones of Maryland and Virginia, there are seldom restrictions against cutting nearly to the edge of the water. (A protective buffer, by contrast, may need to be 100 feet wide or more.) Even regulations considered at the forefront of environmentally sound land use in the watershed merely slow losses of forest—as opposed to holding the line or even increasing acreage. For example, Prince Georges County, Maryland, recently passed a law that requires builders to save from 10 to 50 percent of the trees on a development site, depending on the type of development; Virginia's Chesapeake Bay Preservation Act, which mandates a natural buffer of 100 feet between the water's edge and other land uses, has numerous loopholes (see the "Edges of the Bay" section).

Commercial timber firms generally do replant an acreage equal to what they harvest, but they control less than 10 percent of forestland in Virginia, about 20 percent in Pennsylvania, and less than 10 percent in Maryland. And one of the largest single timber owners, Chesapeake Corporation, has formed a development company to begin subdividing its choicer, waterfront forest holdings as shorefront real estate has soared in value.

Losses of open space, which will be split between farms and forests (percentage of each unknown), are projected to run nearly

1.2 million more acres during the next thirty years unless development patterns change, according to the "2020 Report" prepared for the governors of Maryland, Virginia, and Pennsylvania. The loss of these forests represents more than a loss of pollution filters. Forests are home to wildlife in the watershed from black bears to warblers. They are at the base of a huge hunting and outdoor recreation industry. And they are the key to maintaining cool temperatures in the thousands of miles of prime trout streams in Maryland, Pennsylvania, and Virginia.

Here, too, gross forest acreage statistics sometimes miss the real story of impacts on wildlife. More rapidly than they are being cleared, forests are being fragmented—crisscrossed and isolated by roads, powerline corridors, interstate highway fencing, housing development, even by wildlife management in some cases. Many species of songbirds need the forest interior for successful breeding. If they are too close to a forest edge, their nests are easier prey to raccoons, bluejays, opossums, and cowbirds. One study by the Wilderness Society that compared such "edge" losses on deep-woods nesters found impacts on 70 percent of all nests in suburban Maryland, but only 2 percent of nests in the Great Smoky Mountains. Forest fragmentation, along with the loss of wintering habitat in the tropics, is thought to be a factor in general declines among many eastern songbirds since the 1940s.

The fragmenting of forests also diminishes them as habitat for many mammals. The state of Maryland is developing a program to protect and enhance "greenways," maintaining forests along stream corridors, to provide paths for animals from one block of forest to another. This measure also provides pollution control. To date, the state has protected about 300 miles of such corridors.

Since nature is nothing if not diverse, there are also species of wildlife that thrive on cutover forest and on the creation of edges created by clearing fields next to forest. When these species happen to be popular with hunters—deer and wild turkey are two—the many other values of the intact forest often can't compete. An example of tunnel vision management is a recent Maryland Wildlife Administration proposal, announced in its internal newsletter, for clear-cutting (in phases over a period of years) more than 3 square miles of public forest in the Potomac River basin primarily for enhancing wild turkey habitat. (Deer, squirrel, and grouse are named as minor beneficiaries.) Wildlife managers note that the cutting will occur on steep slopes with highly erosion-prone soils. The forest removal will be permanent; the land is to be kept in grassy vegetation and mowed. A much wider problem is that years of management of deer herds to accommodate hunters' desires for an antlered buck have helped to create a tremendous overpopulation of the animals across the bay watershed—to the point that they are now a significant source of destruction to timber and parkland in all three principal bay watershed states.

Despite their status as the watershed's least-polluting land use, trees can cause serious pollution when they are harvested—especially given the clear-cutting methods much in favor today. New roads may have to be constructed to reach remote cuts. Cutting may occur without leaving adequate forested buffers next to waterways, and heavy equipment can cause erosion and compaction of forest soils, degrading their capacity to remove pollution for a time even if they are replanted. To their credit, forestry agencies in much of the watershed are putting a new emphasis on harvesting with an eye to maintaining water quality. Publicly managed commercial forests account for less than a quarter of Virginia's forest acreage, however, and considerably less than that in Maryland and Pennsylvania.

Of the rest, thousands of individuals make up most of the ownership. And whether they follow excellent harvest practices is mostly voluntary (or not subject to adequate enforcement). In Virginia, for example, a state credited with making a serious effort to push environmentally sound harvesting practices, Chesapeake Bay Foundation field observations in 1990 indicated great variability in voluntary pollution controls during logging. Even the best operations were judged somewhat lacking in pollution control. A key problem was that enforcement generally was left up to the landowner.

The lack of contact between forestry experts and landowners is a particular problem in Virginia and Pennsylvania. (Maryland, by way of contrast, has hired more than twenty "bay foresters.") In Pennsylvania, erosion and sediment control regulations for forestry still are not implemented. The Keystone State arguably is the part of the watershed where improvement in harvesting practices is going to be most critical in the next decade. The state now has vast acreages of hardwood trees (oak, cherry, maple)—the largest hardwood resource in the United States—coming of age for cutting. The forestry activity may rival anything seen there since the early years of this century.

Trees that are not cut down have a multitude of other values besides maintaining the bay's resilience. They remove air pollution; they shade homes and commercial buildings, helping to cut air conditioning demand; they remove carbon dioxide from the air, thereby helping to reduce one of the principal causes of the greenhouse effect, thought to be causing global warming. One tree can remove 20 pounds of carbon. One acre of trees can remove 4 tons annually. (Total U.S. emissions of carbon are about 1.5 billion tons per year.)

Finally, trees make our great urban areas more livable. They do our hearts and minds good just to look at them. A 1984 study published in *Science* magazine found that over a nine-year period, gall bladder patients in a British hospital who could see a cluster of trees instead of a brick wall outside their window had shorter postoperative stays and took fewer painkillers. "The hunger for trees is outspoken and seemingly universal," wrote Kevin Lynch in a UNESCO study, *Growing Up in Cities*, that interviewed children from Argentina, Australia, Mexico, and Poland. Unfortunately, studies indicate that most urban areas in the United States are planted to only about half their potential acreage of trees. In addition, many cities are no longer planting at a rate to keep up with trees removed because of death or damage.

CONCLUSIONS

☐ The bay watershed's forests are its least polluting land use. They are a basis for much of our wildlife, a renewable economic resource, a major source of recreation and tourism, an air pollution filter, a carbon bank working to reduce global warming. They are vital to maintaining clear, clean water and in maintaining stability and resilience in the bay ecosystem.

☐ They are also about 40 percent gone since colonial settlement and still declining. And we have no policy for their protection or any goal for their maintenance and restoration outside a few parts of the watershed.

☐ The situation is worse than gross forest acreages indicate, because high-pollution areas that need the forest buffer most tend to have the least. Distribution and location of forest are at least as critical as the total amount.

☐ Forests still are managed too often for narrow or short-term purposes—such as wildlife production for certain huntable species—and not enough for their multiple values.

☐ With forest ownership spread among tens of thousands of private landowners, our ability to ensure environmentally sound harvesting techniques and provide guidance on stewardship to forest owners is still far too limited.

NONTIDAL WETLANDS

What would the world be, once bereft,
of wet and of wildness? Let them be left.

    —GERARD MANLEY HOPKINS,
      Poems, no. 56

Nontidal wetlands have all the forest's values for bay resilience, and then some. They are, like the forest, a "least polluting" land use. They filter and cleanse and improve the quality of water flowing through them. Whenever we turn a nontidal wetland into pasture or cornfield or homesite we are virtually certain to increase the pollution running off the land to the bay.

The word *wetlands* conjures for most people images of the broad expanses of tidal marshes that extend, often spectacularly, along the edges of the bay and lower parts of its rivers. Recognized by science and in state and federal law for their extraordinary environmental values (see the "Edges of the Bay" section), tidal wetlands in the bay region have enjoyed substantial protection for more than a decade.

Nontidal wetlands, though no less valuable, are their poor cousins. Scattered from coastal plain to mountaintop, they officially comprise about a million acres, or about 3 percent of the watershed. Such wetlands range from peat bogs to cypress swamps to cattails fringing a pond in the highway median strip. They even include slight depressions in the middle of farm fields that are not even distinguishable to the layman until they become saturated periodically with rainwater, instantly attracting life ranging from spring peepers to breeding ducks and great blue herons and muskrats.

Nontidal wetlands, despite their relatively small coverage of the bay's watershed, are home to an extraordinary number of the bay region's rare plants and animals, species unable to exist outside these isolated pockets of wet and wildness. They also afford flood protection and recharge areas to replenish underground water supplies. (Think of them as sponges.) And, finally, they add diversity, interest, and character to the landscape.

Not all nontidal wetlands are visually spectacular, however. "Is This a Wetland?" asks a recent flyer published by environmentalists to aid in identifying these important areas. "Are the bases of the trees swollen? Do the leaves on the ground look matted, washed with silt, grayer than those on adjacent sites? Are bottles and cans lying on the site filled with mud? Are there leaves or trashy debris that look like they've been washed up against roots?" Still, even these inconspicuous sites can miraculously spring forth with a variety of life, from peeping frogs to ducks and geese and muskrats, not to mention plant species, when they become saturated or water-filled. And if current agricultural alterations of their normal hydrology were to cease, many such places would become spectacular pockets of wildlife on a full-time basis.

EPA estimates that we lost about 60,000 acres of nontidal wetlands between the 1950s and the late 1970s, and there is little reason to think that rate slowed significantly during the 1980s. (See Figure 4.3.) Indeed, losses probably have been greater than these numbers indicate, given the difficulty of identifying seasonally saturated areas that qualify as nontidal wetlands. (Standing water is not necessarily required for lands to perform as nontidal wetlands.) Virginia alone, for example, estimates losses (57,000 acres) nearly equal to the official estimates for the entire watershed.

Development, agriculture, and the building of ponds and reservoirs have been major destroyers of nontidal wetlands (Figure 4.4). State and federal highway construction programs have also been remarkably indifferent to preserving nontidal wetlands that get in their way. Destruction can be direct, through filling or paving or draining, or indirect through overloading with sediment running from a nearby construction site. Alterations of surface and belowground drainage patterns—sometimes by a ditching or quarrying or pumping project some distance removed—can also destroy or degrade wetland values. These indirect threats are not, for the most part, covered by the federal Clean Water Act's regulations aimed at protecting nontidal wetlands.

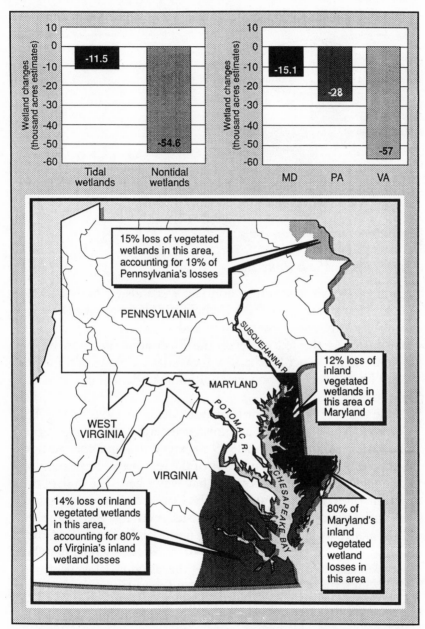

FIGURE 4.3. EXTENT OF WETLANDS LOSSES IN THE CHESAPEAKE BAY
WATERSHED—MID-1950S THROUGH LATE 1970S. *Note: State totals may
be larger than watershed.* [From Kiner, USFWS; *Mid-Atlantic Wetlands:
A Disappearing National Treasure*]

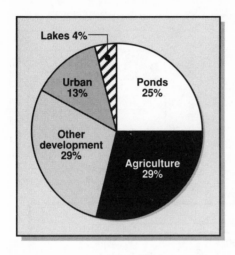

FIGURE 4.4. CAUSES OF NON-TIDAL WETLANDS LOSS SINCE THE 1950s. [From Kiner, USFWS]

Lofty Goals, Weak Protection

The goals set for protecting nontidal wetlands by Maryland, Virginia, Pennsylvania, and EPA in their 1987 Chesapeake Bay agreements are lofty ones: "no net loss" and a "net resource gain" in the long term. At the federal level, the Bush administration has also announced a "no net loss" policy for wetlands. None of these goals seems likely to be met, however, without substantial improvements in wetlands protection.

One reason is the abrupt turnabout made in 1990 by the Army Corps of Engineers, which administers federal wetlands regulations. The Corps had proposed in 1989 to extend its regulatory authority to several hundred thousand acres of the less-visible or recognizable nontidal wetlands throughout the bay watershed. The bulk of these areas involved agricultural lands. The Corps' decision did not interfere with farming where it already existed, even if it was in soils that, if left alone, would revert to being nontidal wetlands. But once a farm went up for sale for development, these areas would have been extended standard regulatory protections as nontidal wetlands.

Although the impacts fell only on land speculation—not on agricultural operations—they created such a firestorm of protest that the Corps reversed its proposal in 1990. It was followed in this decision by the state of Maryland, the only one of the three principal watershed states to have a comprehensive nontidal wetlands law. In the short run, the Corps and Maryland's actions will mean little, since farmers could still have continued to plow and plant and drain as usual. But as hundreds of thousands of acres of farmlands are developed, as projected by EPA between now and the year 2020, a huge potential for allowing natural wetlands to revert to performing their fullest ecological functions will be lost.

It became obvious during the recent debate over new nontidal wetland protections that the Corps is too understaffed to perform its role in administering even the present law, which requires permits for any dredging or filling that might harm nontidal wetlands. In addition, the federal law does not adequately protect wetlands from the impacts of drainage, excavation, flooding, or devegetation. Federal programs that give farmers money to build ponds, for example, have actually resulted in the destruction of thousands of acres of nontidal wetlands in recent years. A major problem, enforcers say, is people who build on nontidal wetlands, either intentionally or unintentionally, without applying for a permit. To a large extent, no conceivable level of regulation will redress this problem without concerted public education about the importance of nontidal wetlands.

There has, however, been progress in protecting nontidal wetlands. A federal "swampbuster" provision aimed at farmers threatens the loss of subsidies if unfarmed wetlands are converted to crop production. Maryland recently became the first of the watershed states to enact a state nontidal wetlands law designed to shore up some of the weak points in the federal provisions. Virginia, while lacking a comprehensive law, has increased staff and extended limited new protection to nontidal wetlands, particularly in the coastal plain. Pennsylvania is in the process of strengthening its wetlands regulations to provide some added protection as it debates a comprehensive wetlands law.

These measures all seem likely to slow the destruction of nontidal wetlands. Yet it appears unlikely that we will reach the no-net-loss goal in the foreseeable future—and actual gains in nontidal wetland acreage seem far off indeed. Maryland's law, for example, the toughest protections in the watershed, still exempts agriculture and forestry, activities that occur across nearly a third of the state's land surface, from applying for permits. They are expected to minimize damage to wetlands voluntarily. Moreover, activities such as home building that destroy less than 5,000 square feet of nontidal wetlands are not required to compensate for the loss by creating new wetlands nearby.

Such compensation is already being used by agencies such as Maryland's highways department to comply with the goal of no net loss of wetlands. But such creation of nontidal wetlands is a relatively new and unproved technique, as much art as science, and not subject to long-term monitoring to determine whether it really is successful. According to an EPA report, "Wetland Creation and Restoration: The Status of the Science," we are currently unable to create a fully functioning wetland in many cases. And a recent U.S. Fish and Wildlife Service survey shows that approximately 70 percent of the compensation projects in Virginia, Maryland, and Delaware were not completed or failed to fulfill their permit requirements.

Currently the Army Corps of Engineers and the state of Maryland have allowed Maryland's highway administration to build up "IOUs" for 269 acres of destroyed wetlands (both nontidal and tidal) in an effort not to hold up projects. About 60 acres have been replaced so far, and plans are under way for another 140 acres; but there is no assurance that they will all work in the long run as well as what was destroyed. Pennsylvania and Virginia both are substantially further from "no net loss" than Maryland, although Pennsylvania is making a laudable attempt to regulate the hydrological changes (alterations in drainage above or below ground) that can degrade nontidal wetlands.

In the meantime, local jurisdictions, spurred by concerned citizens, have sometimes moved ahead of the state and federal laws. Several Virginia counties, for example, have protected the Dragon Run, in the Piankatank River watershed, which is one of the finest and most scenic bottomland hardwood wetlands in the bay region.

Conclusions

☐ Nontidal wetlands are a vital part of the bay's resilience with their ability to filter and improve the quality of water flowing through them, as well as cushion the extremes of drought and flood. They help the bay rebound from both natural and human disturbance. They are a haven for wildlife; although covering only a small fraction of the watershed's lands, they harbor an extraordinary proportion of its rare plants and animals.

☐ We have lost hundreds of thousands of acres of nontidal wetlands since colonial times, and at least 60,000 acres in recent decades.

Continued losses seem assured—especially given the recent decision by the Army Corps of Engineers not to regulate nontidal wetlands scattered across millions of acres of the watershed's agricultural croplands. This area involves large acreages of potential wetlands that currently are altered by farming. The rules now abandoned by the Corps would not have changed that, but they would have brought these lands into the wetlands regulatory process whenever they were sold for development.

☐ Only Maryland has a comprehensive nontidal wetlands law. It does not appear strong enough to meet the goal of no net loss, however, let alone the long-term baywide goal of a net gain in nontidal wetlands. The state has indicated it will follow the Corps' lead in backing down on agricultural wetlands regulation.

☐ The Corps of Engineers is too understaffed to carry out its role of protecting wetlands.

☐ Additional (if inadequate) protections being extended by all three watershed states should slow the rate of decline of nontidal wetlands.

☐ Creation of new wetlands to replace those destroyed by highways and other development is an unproved process without any long-term assurance of adequately replacing or enhancing wetlands values.

EDGES OF THE BAY

We feel the greatest personal freedom is to be able to walk all the way down the waterline. Freedom for you is buying land all the way down the waterline.

—BENGT-OWE JANSSON, Swedish scientist visiting the bay

Edges have always been among the most interesting and vital phenomena in nature. Many scientists think humankind evolved along the edge of the African jungle and savanna, a friendly intersection that allowed tree-dwelling apes the safety of the forest and access to the abundant game of the plains. Hunters, human and animal, frequently find that the edges where one type of vegetation gives way to another, such as forest and field, are especially rife with game. The edge seems to create an abundance and diversity of life that adds up to more than the sum of the habitats on either side of it. (See

Figure 4.5.) Nowhere do these qualities of edges come together more gloriously than where the lands of the bay's watershed slope down to the beaches and bluffs and tidal marshes of the coastlines. And nowhere do human pressures and pollution clash more directly with prime habitat for the bay's plant and animal life.

One of the bay's most striking features is the way in which land and water intertwine, forming a shoreline that wanders more than 8,000 miles down and back the 195-mile length of the estuary (including its islands). No other bay on earth has so much shoreline for its size. Try this experiment during the summer months from any marsh or beach along the bay or river shoreline. Pull a small seine net—say 25 feet long—through the shallows. If you do it properly, you will likely come up with a wriggling mass of minnows, crabs, jellyfish, hogchokers, baby spot, menhaden, perch, and perhaps dozens of other fish—all this harvested in minutes from a patch of water little bigger than your bedroom at home. Multiply it by the times your bedroom would fit along more than 8,000 miles of shoreline and you will begin to get an appreciation for life at the bay's edge.

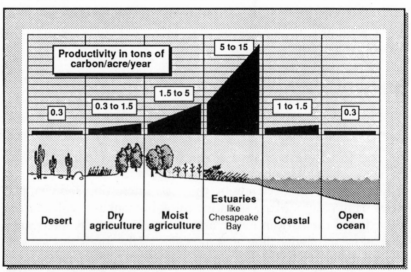

FIGURE 4.5. PRODUCTIVITY OF THE LAND/WATER EDGE *The biological productivity, measured in tons of carbon, of estuaries is among the highest measured anywhere on the planet.* [Adapted by Joseph Hutchinson from Odum, *Fundamentals of Ecology*]

It is not in the middle of the bay or at its mouth or in its depths where the most life lies. It lies in these warm, food-rich, protective seams of marsh and tide flat where land and water knit together, where crabs shed their shells and the young of fish reside and the eagles and ospreys and great blue herons feed. (See Figure 4.6.) The natural habitat of the forest and river edges, marsh and forest, also helps to lend the bay a measure of resilience in absorbing and rebounding from both natural and human environmental insult.

But from the modern human perspective, this edge is better known as waterfront real estate. And it is every bit as attractive to growing numbers of people as it is to crabs and ducks and rockfish. Nearly two-thirds of all Americans live in the 50-mile-wide ribbon of land that borders the Atlantic, Pacific, Gulf of Mexico, and Great Lakes coasts. In the Chesapeake Bay region, power plants seek the edge of the bay and its tributary rivers for cooling water; sewage plants locate there for a ready source of dilution for treated wastes (Figure 4.7); marinas want expansion to accommodate a growing demand for boat access. In Maryland, a survey in the early 1980s showed that nearly 20 percent of all development activity in the state was occurring within approximately a thousand feet of the edge of the bay and its tidal rivers. The competition for use of the edge—all along the nation's and the world's coasts—is immense. And in this conflict Chesapeake Bay's long, productive, and embattled shore-lines are second to none.

In recent years Maryland and Virginia have increasingly recognized the special importance and special pressures surrounding their Chesapeake edges. The rest of this section applies our measures of progress to see how we are doing in preserving this unique aspect of the bay ecosystem.

Tidal Wetlands

Currently about 250,000 acres of tidal wetlands remain in the Chesapeake watershed, according to EPA and the U.S. Fish and Wildlife Service. It is estimated that during the last century Virginia lost 42 percent of its wetlands, tidal and nontidal, and Maryland lost 73 percent. Tidal wetlands were still being destroyed by development at the rate of more than a thousand acres a year until the last two decades. (See Figure 4.8.)

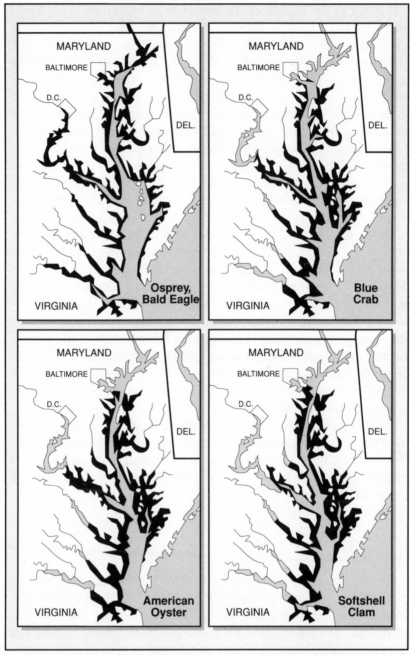

FIGURE 4.6. LIFE ON THE EDGE   *For species after species in Chesapeake Bay, the prime habitat for spawning, feeding, and living is most often in the shallows, on the very edge of land and water.* [U.S. Army Corps of Engineers; USFWS]

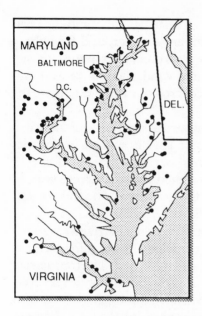

FIGURE 4.7. LOCATION OF MAJOR
SEWAGE TREATMENT PLANTS *More
than wildlife uses the bay's edge. It is also
the most convenient place to locate sewage
treatment plants, because of the dilution
it affords wastes.* [U.S. Army Corps of
Engineers]

That trend represented the decline of some of the richest habitat
on earth for a variety of plants and animals. It was also another
decline in the bay's ability to cleanse and stabilize itself—another
loss of resilience. Tidal marshes, for example, which are mostly
found along the shorelines, also provide excellent protection against
erosion by absorbing wave energy and stabilizing sediments. They
are also capable of absorbing and filtering pollutants that wash from
farms and urban areas. And they provide flood control by absorbing

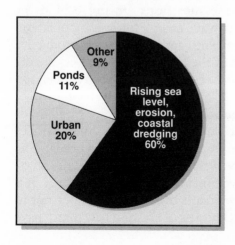

FIGURE 4.8. CAUSES OF TIDAL
WETLANDS LOSS SINCE THE
1950s. [From Kiner, USFWS]

excess runoff in storms. Not least of all, marshes are beautiful. Their broad expanses along the bay's edges are a playground for light, a canvas that changes color and texture with every shift in the intensity and angle of the sun and moon. In the wind, they ripple as sensuously as the great prairies that once covered our Midwest before the advent of the steel plow.

During the 1970s state and federal laws designed to curtail marsh losses took effect. The impact of these laws is evident in statistics kept by Maryland. Losses before the laws were estimated at 948 acres a year. Since 1978, they have averaged about 13 acres a year. In addition, the state has permitted the filling of about 40 acres per year of open waters (submerged wetlands) since 1978.

The actual destruction of tidal marsh by human activities is somewhat greater than 13 acres per year. The state often requires creation of 1 or 2 acres of new marsh for each acre destroyed. Thirteen acres is the *net* loss after "compensation." The state has authorized an average of 24 acres per year of new marsh establishment, some of it reflecting compensation, some of it simply a landowner's desire to create a marsh where none had existed. Such compensation, however, is a relatively new procedure. There is some question about how long it takes newly created marshes to fully replace all the values of the marsh that has been destroyed—or if they ever do replace them fully. The state performs no long-term follow-up of "created" marshes to find out.

One of the major sources of this much-reduced but continuing wetland loss is the desire of waterfront property owners to "harden" their shoreline against erosion with vertical steel or wooden bulkheads or other devices. This measure stops erosion behind the bulkhead, but it can also deflect wave energy hitting the bulkhead downward, causing rapid scouring and erosion of productive shallow-water habitats in front of the bulkhead. Moreover, the deflected energy can speed erosion of adjoining, unprotected shoreline.

Since 1978 Maryland has authorized construction of bulkheads and revetments (stone piles also known as "riprap") along 20 miles of bayshore each year (some of it replacing existing bulkheads). The mileage is split about equally between the bulkheads and the revetments, the latter having a less harmful impact on natural habitat. It is state policy to "encourage" revetments over bulkheads, but not to require them. Since 1982, as techniques of creating new marsh have become more accepted, an average of 2 miles of shoreline in Maryland has been protected against erosion by marsh planting—by far the most preferable strategy from an environmental perspective. As with revetments, the state encourages marsh creation wherever possible but does not require it.

Virginia has presumed a good measure of success in stopping tidal wetlands losses since the 1970s, but only in 1990 did the Virginia Institute of Marine Science (VIMS) actually begin compiling results of its permit programs. They show that permits were issued allowing the destruction of about 5 acres of marsh in 1988 and about 9 acres in 1989. In 1988, about 17 acres of shallow-water wetlands habitat had bulkheads and riprap placed on it; in 1989, about 24 acres was lost. (Virginia scientists note that riprap does provide some habitat, so these losses are not as total as those from bulkheading or from filling or dredging a marsh.)

As in Maryland, the bulk of Virginia's wetlands losses comes from installing shoreline protections: riprap and bulkheads. VIMS calculates that 413 miles of its tidal shoreline, or about 10 percent, has been hardened with bulkheads or riprap. In 1988 and 1989, about 20 miles of new and replacement riprap and an equal mileage of bulkheading were approved. Like Maryland, the state encourages riprap but does not require it. (In some areas, such as narrow canals, the more destructive bulkheads are the only means feasible.)

The wetlands policy established in 1987 by the states and EPA to restore the bay sets a short-term goal of "no net loss" from human impacts and a long-term goal of "resource gain." For the foreseeable future, however, trends in both Maryland and Virginia (Pennsylvania has no tidal wetlands in the watershed) seem likely to continue to be net losses. These losses may seem small enough to be tolerable, but wetlands are also being lost to natural forces such as erosion— and these losses seem to be accelerating. For example, in the last half century more than 5,000 acres of marsh has simply disappeared— turned into open water—within the Blackwater National Wildlife Refuge in Maryland. Investigators who studied the Blackwater Marsh think that the losses there may be only the first signal of a much more widespread problem.

Similar declines, averaging more than 120 acres per year for the last fifty years, are now being documented in the vast tidal marsh along the Nanticoke River at the head of Tangier Sound. (See Figure 4.9.) We have, of course, been losing tidal marsh to erosion

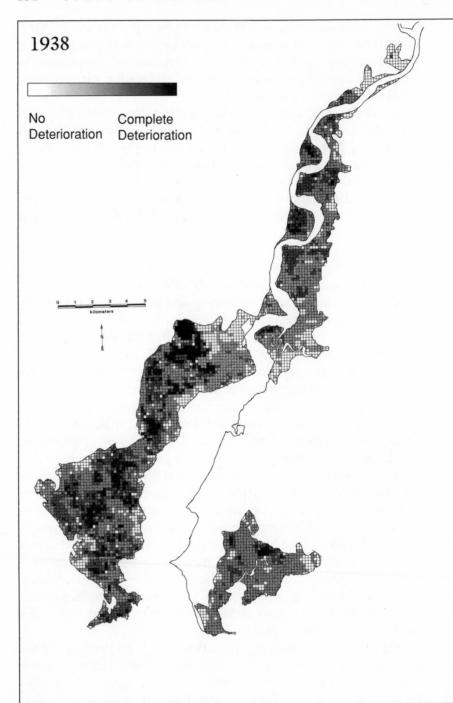

1938

No
Deterioration

Complete
Deterioration

0 1 2 3 4 5
kilometers

1985

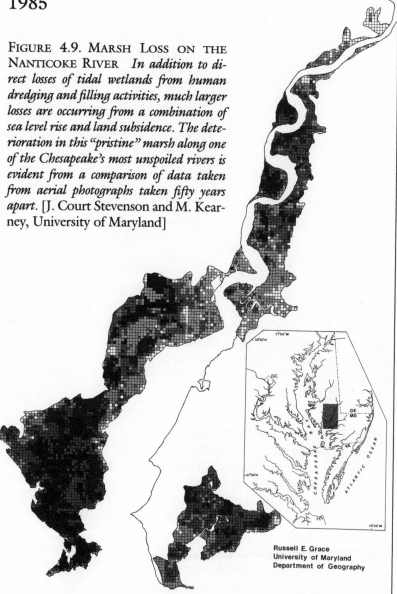

FIGURE 4.9. MARSH LOSS ON THE NANTICOKE RIVER   *In addition to direct losses of tidal wetlands from human dredging and filling activities, much larger losses are occurring from a combination of sea level rise and land subsidence. The deterioration in this "pristine" marsh along one of the Chesapeake's most unspoiled rivers is evident from a comparison of data taken from aerial photographs taken fifty years apart.* [J. Court Stevenson and M. Kearney, University of Maryland]

Russell E. Grace
University of Maryland
Department of Geography

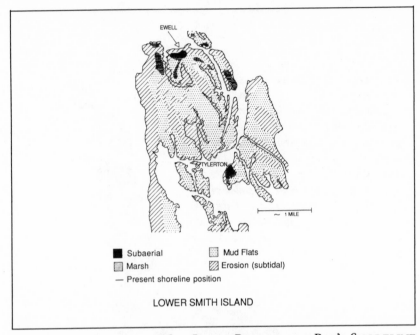

FIGURE 4.10. IMPACTS OF SEA LEVEL RISE ON THE BAY'S SHORELINE
BY 2100   *At the most conservative estimate, the level of the bay relative to the land will be 3 feet higher within the next century—with dramatic impacts on many areas of the bay's shoreline.* Some bay islands will be left with almost no land above water (subaerial). [J. Court Stevenson and M. Kearney, University of Maryland]

by wind and waves since the bay was formed; but something new and ominous appears to be operating in more recent times. There is preliminary scientific evidence that the submergence of the shoreline around the mid-Chesapeake Bay began accelerating about a century and a half ago and picked up even more rapidly in the 1930s. The explanations for this phenomenon are rising sea levels plus subsidence of the land.

Sea level is rising faster in recent decades than it has for thousands of years, probably because of a global warming trend. (See Figure 4.10.) The causes of land subsidence around the bay can only be guessed at, however. Two possible causes, scientists speculate, may be increases in groundwater pumping and the sheer weight of all the sediment that has flowed into the bay since humans began clearing the surrounding forests. The weight of billions and billions of tons

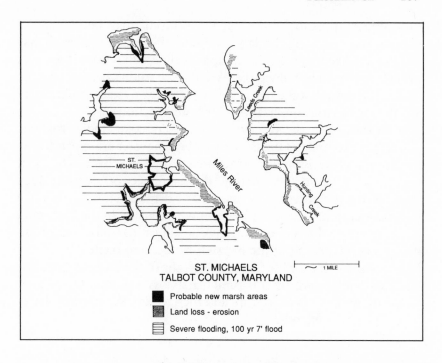

ST. MICHAELS
TALBOT COUNTY, MARYLAND

■ Probable new marsh areas

▨ Land loss - erosion

▤ Severe flooding, 100 yr 7' flood

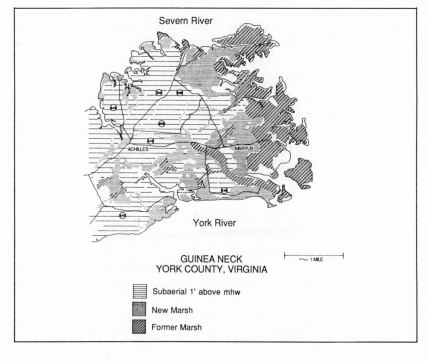

Severn River

ACHILLES   MARYUS

York River

GUINEA NECK
YORK COUNTY, VIRGINIA

▤ Subaerial 1' above mhw

▨ New Marsh

▧ Former Marsh

of sediment, pressing down on the bottom, may be enough to depress the edges of the lands around the estuary. Not all bay marshes are likely to suffer such rapid decline, but tens of thousands of acres appear to be vulnerable. While more studies need to be done to quantify how fast the bay is losing wetlands to such causes, there are already obvious implications for human actions.

It appears from the Blackwater and Nanticoke studies that the marsh loss proceeds as small patches of open water are expanded by wind and wave erosion into larger areas. Anything that creates open water, or expands the existing drainage network within such marshes, has the potential to hasten their demise. Mosquito control programs currently being carried out within many of the bay's tidal wetlands create the very conditions that appear to lead to long-term marsh loss. (Ditching of the marsh for mosquito control has never been evaluated for adverse impacts in light of the recent marsh loss studies.) The certainty that natural marsh loss is picking up makes it all the more imperative to stop, and then to reverse, all controllable destruction of wetlands.

Virginia's Chesapeake Bay Preservation Act

In 1988, Virginia enacted a law which, in concept, says that the uses of land around the bay and its tributaries—from forestry and farming to development—should never increase water pollution and in many cases should actually reduce it. The Chesapeake Bay Preservation Act applies to the twenty-nine counties and more than fifty cities and towns in the state's coastal areas, though nothing prohibits other local jurisdictions from adopting it. The law and its accompanying regulations have been seen as a sweeping breakthrough for environmental protection on several counts:

- The Preservation Act gives local jurisdictions for the first time the broad authority to regulate land use to protect water quality.
- This authority, while focused on protecting the shoreline, could be applied to the whole county.
- It requires that a 100-foot buffer of natural vegetation be kept along the edges of waterways to filter pollutants from other land uses.
- Its goals—holding the line or even reducing water pollution around the tidal Chesapeake—address the biggest issue in the

bay's future: how to keep it healthy as an additional 2.6 million
people move into the watershed by the year 2020.

Will it work? Counties and towns did not begin implementing the
act until the end of 1990. Nevertheless there is a consensus in
Virginia that it is a major—almost radical—step forward in linking
land use to water quality. Certainly land use and development will be
managed on a more environmentally sound basis throughout coastal
Virginia. A number of counties are including broad geographic
areas and have begun to identify sensitive land areas from wetlands
to erodible slopes. Specific improvements contained in the Preservation Act include the limitation of new shoreline development to
"water-dependent" uses (such as boat repair facilities or seafood
companies) and the setting of much stronger standards for septic
tank installations.

At the same time, Virginia's Preservation Act is littered with
"shoulds" rather than "shalls" regarding what the local jurisdictions
are supposed to do. It seems likely to fall well short of its ambitious
goal of no new pollution. In other words, it may prove to be yet
another law that falls into the category of so many environmental
protection strategies of recent decades—making progress at four
knots upstream while the current runs downstream at five knots.
Some examples:

- The 100-foot buffer along all land/water edges is not required
  to be forested, only kept in "indigenous vegetation." Yet forest
  has much higher values for overall pollution control than other
  vegetation.
- Existing forest buffers can be cut to improve landowners' "sight
  lines and vistas" of the water. Moreover, trees may be cut for
  several feet back from the banks of waterways if an owner wants
  to bulkhead the shoreline for erosion control.
- Commercial logging can take place in the buffer nearly to the
  water's edge, as long as foresters voluntarily abide by the state
  forestry agency's erosion and sediment pollution controls. Inspection and enforcement are not now adequate to ensure this is
  done. Nor are controls nearly good enough to replace a 100-
  foot forested buffer.
- Farmers may reduce the vegetated buffer protecting waterways
  to 25 feet (from 100) if they have a government-approved

conservation plan covering the runoff of pollutants and the use of pesticides and animal manure. But the current range of such approved pollution controls does not appear to be nearly so effective as claimed. (See the discussion of agriculture in Chapter 2.)

- In some areas, many more lots than expected were subdivided in anticipation of the Preservation Act and will be "grandfathered" out of its provisions. An example: Lancaster County, in the rural Northern Neck between the Potomac and Rappahannock rivers, still has a sleepy look about most of it, to judge from what is built. But the rate of land subdivision (that is, the authorization of building lots) has recently exceeded the rate of actual building by a factor of four or five. A true look at land use in Lancaster County would have to take the existing residential development and multiply it several times, even if no more building was ever approved.
- The act was not intended to be a growth management law. Thus it provides no incentive or guidance for rezoning land to promote less of the low-density sprawl development that is gobbling up open space around the bay's watershed. (See Chapter 5.) But the two are so linked—growth patterns and environmentally sound land use—that it is hard to see the Preservation Act fulfilling its ambitions in the long run without complementary growth management: another case of attacking the pollution without confronting its root source.
- The act also allows numerous variances and exceptions from its land use protections—for road construction, for the placement of utilities, and for replacing parts of the buffer with "alternative" pollution controls.
- The act contains few mechanisms short of legal action that can be used to prod a county to perform well in implementing its share of the Preservation Act.

Virginia's Chesapeake Bay Preservation Act, in a nutshell, allows a county or town to be virtually as good as it wants to be in protecting the bay's water quality by regulating land use. But it also provides ample opportunity for jurisdictions to underachieve the lofty goal of no new pollution.

A CHANCE TO DO IT RIGHT

A prime example of the Chesapeake Bay Preservation Act's promise and its limits is Richmond County in the Northern Neck, a peaceful and lovely place with virtually all of its long shoreline in forest and marsh—a place with fewer people than it had in 1730, where you can see four or five eagles at a time, and where there are scarcely enough realtors and developers yet to mount opposition to the exemplary way the county is trying to use the new legislation.

Richmond County is trying to take the new act and run with it. It is proposing to preserve all prime farm soils, about half the county's farmland, with a 20-acre minimum lot size. Its proposed subdivision ordinances and development guidelines, discouraging strip zoning and eliminating steep slopes from development, would be models for most Virginia counties, let alone one that is still totally rural and has never before even had zoning.

The county is proof that a jurisdiction need not wait until waves of poorly planned development wash over it to begin shaping its future. But there are still severe limits on what even the most dedicated county government can accomplish, Richmond County officials acknowledge. Surrounding counties are not moving nearly so vigorously—and if they develop poorly, it will be difficult for Richmond County to avoid the consequences (such as traffic congestion) and pressure to follow suit. Moreover, the county still is going to have tens of thousands of acres of forest and farmland that are essentially easy targets for unplanned sprawl. "I've looked far and wide [for alternative models] and I'm still looking," says a county official.

Most land use experts in Virginia say that without strong regional or statewide growth management, the best efforts of a single county to make the most of the Preservation Act may be severely eroded in the long run, as population pressure inevitably rises.

Maryland's Critical Area Act

Maryland's attempt to protect the bay's edge, the Critical Area Act of 1984, amounted to a sweeping rezoning by the state to restrict and improve development in a zone 1,000 feet back from the water around the entire bay and its tidal rivers—about 10 percent of the state's land surface. The act substantially usurped land use powers that traditionally had belonged to the counties. Not only did it expressly limit forest clearing for development, but it also recognized protection of wildlife habitat as a legitimate reason to limit development. Perhaps its most far-reaching premise, which foreshadowed current baywide attempts at growth controls, was that "the number, movement, and activities of people" can cause serious environmental degradation even if traditional pollution sources are all controlled. (See Chapter 5.)

Maryland's Critical Area Act, like Virginia's, mandates a 100-foot vegetated buffer (up to 300 feet in some cases) between tidal shorelines and other land uses. Although it is plagued with far fewer loopholes than Virginia's law as far as development goes, like Virginia's it contains sizable exemptions for agricultural and forestry activities.

Opponents claimed the law would end all growth along the state's highly valuable waterfront. Supporters hailed the law as the keystone without whose passage a wide-ranging package of other legislation to clean up the bay would fail. In fact, after its first two years of operation, it appears that the restrictions on development in the critical area will be considerably less than its opponents feared—and the potential for growth will be considerably more than the law's backers thought.

The Maryland Critical Area Commission, the state agency that administers the law, estimates a long-term potential to add about 53,000 new dwelling units around the bay's tidal shoreline. This is about 10 percent of the new housing anticipated in Maryland between now and the year 2020—and on about 10 percent of the state's land (the acreage within the 1,000-foot zone). This is still far less than the development that would have occurred in the highly desirable shoreline areas of the bay without the Critical Area Act. (Development there before the law was running at about 17 percent of the state total.)

But the value of the Critical Area Act is only partly in how much development it allows. Potentially just as important is its aim to make that development occur more compactly, saving open space and least-polluting land uses such as forests. A review of the last few years of experience in enforcing the Critical Area Act's provisions, done with the assistance of the state's Critical Area Commission, indicates definite and encouraging improvement in protection of natural resources near the bay shoreline. In Prince Georges County, a D.C. suburban area, there has actually been a net increase in forest in the 1,000-foot critical area: 110 acres of trees removed by development and 153 acres replanted. In Dorchester County, a rural part of Maryland's Eastern Shore, a landowner planning to clear-cut a prime forest area was influenced to protect 30 of its 73 acres and use selective cutting on the rest to protect its integrity as a forest ecosystem. In Kent County, near the head of the bay, more than 122 acres of forest has been protected from development.

The aim of compact placement of housing appears to have lagged, however, especially in the more rural counties. Out of 245 single homes built in the critical area in Dorchester County, most have been on 2-acre lots; in Kent County, virtually all the building permits have gone for single-family homes. Even so, performance standards of the new law such as limits on the amount of impervious surface from development (which has adverse impacts on stream flows and water quality) appear to be working fairly well.

Another key in assessing how the counties are doing is to see what use they are making of the 5 percent portion of each one's undeveloped shoreline that the act allows them to use for new intensive development. This "growth allocation"—a political compromise made during debate in the legislature—diluted the original hope of restricting all development in the remaining natural shoreline areas to an average of one house per 20 acres. Counties are supposed to treat this 5 percent growth allocation as a precious and nonrenewable resource—the "last" unspoiled shoreline where high-intensity development could occur—and parcel it out judiciously and only to development that would be of greatest benefit, economically and environmentally.

What was the status of the growth allocation as of July 1990? Seven of the sixteen counties with tidal shoreline had not handed out any of their 5 percent. Reasons included sparse demand for it in some rural areas like Caroline County and delays in areas like Cecil County so that waterfront developers could prepare competing plans, with the allocation going to the best plan. Six more counties were using their growth allocations at a relatively rapid rate. Their rationales vary widely. Prince Georges County, which had relatively little such area to begin with, decided to allocate most of its 5 percent to one large and environmentally controversial commercial/residential complex on the Potomac. Anne Arundel County, with the highest rate of shoreline development in the state, had exceeded its 5 percent between passage of the state law and development of local regulations for administering it. (Under the law, development during that interim still counted toward using up the allotment.) At the other extreme, Dorchester County on Maryland's Eastern Shore had been rapidly frittering away its allocation with low-density sprawling growth as usual.

Officials of the Critical Area Commission say they fully expect a major test of the law by 1992 as some counties begin asking the legislature to expand the growth allotment in the conservation parts of the critical area. In overall efforts to comply with the spirit and law of the program, nine of the sixteen counties and Baltimore City have put forth what the Critical Area Commission terms "top-notch efforts." Efforts by the other seven have ranged from merely lackluster to outright opposition.

As of 1990, the state had intervened on ten projects in the critical area where it thought counties were not meeting the law's standards; seven cases had been settled satisfactorily out of court with what the state commission deemed suitable protection of shoreline habitat. But from interviews with both state and county officials it seems clear that even though the law gives the state a good deal of authority to see that local jurisdictions protect their critical areas, the political reality is that only full support of the law by both county officials and their planning and zoning commissions will result in good long-term performance.

In sum, then, there is little doubt that the Critical Area Act has brought a new level of land use planning and environmentally sound development to coastal Maryland. Yet it will allow substantially more development than was intended because of "grandfathering" of existing subdivided but unbuilt lots and because the growth allocations in practice have been interpreted liberally. Political acceptance at the local level is still quite uneven and (especially in rural counties) constitutes a hindrance to achieving the law's full potential. It is an open question whether the state commission charged with administering the program has the staffing and the political backing to confront several counties who have made it obvious they will drag their feet on implementing the law. Another question is whether newer and tougher environmental laws, as they are adopted, will be applied to the 1,000-foot critical zone. For example, protection for nontidal wetlands in the zone is not as comprehensive as Maryland's recent new wetlands law allows in the rest of the state. The critical area is excluded from the law.

Shoreline Erosion

A major pollutant of the bay is sediment—soil washing from the land. It turns streams and rivers brown and cloudy, smothering and choking aquatic life and cutting off sunlight needed for growth of the bay's submerged grass beds. Traditionally, our pollution control programs have aimed to control this pollutant through techniques that filter or halt the runoff of soils during rainstorms from farm fields and construction sites. But studies have shown that in the main stem of the bay and the lower portions of its rivers, a majority of the sediment entering the water comes from another source: natural erosion of the banks and cliffs along the bay's extensive shoreline.

Arguments are sometimes raised that, in light of the shoreline's contribution, we should not concentrate so much on controlling sediment from farms and development. But the large input of sediment from shoreline erosion does not mean that shoreline erosion is the majority of the bay's sediment problem. Upland sources cause widespread and well-documented damage to thousands of miles of streams and rivers. Moreover, stopping these sources of sediment also stops other pollutants (such as farm chemicals) that may make their way into the bay independent of sediment movements. In addition, it is not clear that these upland sediments stay trapped forever in the bottoms of streams and rivers, isolated from the main bay. It appears that huge storms like Tropical Storm Agnes in 1972 may periodically flush much of this accumulated sediment from its "final" resting place throughout the bay.

Furthermore, in certain areas of the bay the contribution of sediment from upland sources is still quite large—about 50 percent of total sediment in Maryland's upper bay comes from uplands because of the huge drainage basin of the Susquehanna River and its extensive agricultural lands. As one moves farther down the bay, however, toward the tidal portions of many of its tributaries, shoreline erosion is the overwhelming source of sediment.

In other words, there are extensive areas where sediment is a problem—destroying submerged grass beds, for example—and in these areas our current, upland-based control strategies are not very effective. One way to deal with shoreline erosion, a method often endorsed by shorefront landowners and developers, is to create physical barriers—stone riprap, bulkheads, dikes—along as much bayfront as possible to stop erosion. Some politicians have taken this a step further, saying we need to encourage as much waterfront development as possible to generate the tax base to pay the high expense of such extensive "armoring" of the shoreline. Such a policy, however, in addition to being hugely expensive, would destroy large acreages of shallow-water habitat, some of the bay's most productive area. It would also run counter to attempts in both Maryland and Virginia to protect the bay's edge from explosive development.

There is a better way to look at the problem: Shoreline erosion has always been occurring in the bay, yet it is only since we lost other parts of the natural system in the estuary that it has become an increasing problem. The thick growths of submerged grasses that once lined much of the bay's shallow edge were a highly efficient means of clarifying sediment from the bay's waters. This may sound like the "chicken or the egg" situation—the grasses stopped the sediment, but the sediment killed the grasses. In fact, the grasses died because of the combined effects of sediment along with increasing amounts of other pollutants like nitrogen and phosphorus from sewage and land runoff. Reducing these two pollutants might well let the grasses get reestablished—and that in turn would control sediment, leading to more grasses. A resurgence of the grasses would reduce shoreline erosion dramatically in many areas. Growing so long and thick that they literally lay matted on the surface, the underwater grass beds were highly effective buffers against waves battering the shoreline and eroding it.

The issue of controlling sediment pollution is not an either/or situation. Traditional upland sources like agriculture and development must continue to be reduced, but strategies like planting marsh and restoring submerged grasses to buffer shoreline erosion naturally must also be a priority.

CONCLUSIONS

Tidal Wetlands

□ The edges of Chesapeake Bay and its tidal rivers are a concentrated version of the larger battle to reconcile the region's natural resources with a growing human impact on them. In the marshes and the shallows of the edges lies the bay's greatest productivity, while along the waterfront is where most of us are drawn to live and to site our power plants, marinas, and sewage treatment facilities.

□ The tidal marshes—the key to the environmental quality of the edges—are still being nibbled away by human development, although there has been a dramatic slowing of losses in Maryland and probably also Virginia since the largely unregulated days of the 1960s and before. (Virginia has just begun tracking how its tidal wetlands protection laws are working, so it is difficult to make comparisons before 1988.) Baywide goals of no net loss and a long-term gain in tidal wetlands are not likely to be met with current programs in either state.

□ Natural losses of wetlands, meanwhile, appear to be accelerating—probably on a wider scale than most of us are aware of. Possible reasons include sea level rise and subsidence of the land. Unless there is open space available on the landward side of submerging marshes to form new marsh, such natural losses will far outstrip losses from human impacts.

□ Projects like mosquito control ditching that create open water amid marshes appear to make the marsh even more prone to disappear from the impacts of sea level rise and wind erosion.

□ Bulkheading to protect private property along the waterfront is a major cause of human destruction of tidal wetlands in both Maryland and Virginia. Neither state requires more environmentally sound alternatives wherever possible.

□ As they are doing with nontidal wetlands, the states are depending on creation of new marshes to compensate for those destroyed as part of their no-net-loss strategy. But there is no long-term monitoring or scientific documentation to assure that this approach works well.

Virginia's Preservation Act

□ Virginia's first attempt at extending statewide protection to its environmentally critical bay shoreline and adjacent lands has been a bold step that should reduce the impacts of pollution caused by development. Yet it represents only the first step needed to restore the bay to health in the long run as population continues to grow.

Maryland's Critical Area Act

☐ Maryland's attempt to protect its bay shoreline from development and pollution is tougher and more mature than Virginia's, although the area it covers (1,000 feet back from the shoreline) is narrower in many instances than in Virginia.

☐ The act currently represents state-of-the-art land use in the region and clearly is having numerous beneficial impacts in practice. It is turning out to allow more development than its supporters had thought, however, and several counties are not acting in the spirit of the law. What seemed a radical step in controlling growth five years ago now seems increasingly like a solid but only modest step if the bay is to absorb millions more people and have any chance of regaining its health in coming years.

Shoreline Erosion

☐ Although the majority of the sediment washing into Chesapeake Bay comes from shoreline erosion—not from the land-based runoff where we aim most of our sediment control programs—there are abundant good reasons to continue these programs. There are also good reasons not to rush to armor the shoreline with bulkheads in the name of pollution control.

BOTTOM OF THE BAY

Men who never wrote a line
Are the greatest poets ever.
Verses of love inscribed upon
The bottom of the cove.

—GILBERT BYRON

The most important fact about the bay's bottom is that it is very close to the surface. Water that extends horizontally about 1 million feet (200 miles) and more than 100,000 feet (20 miles) across averages only about 21 feet deep. If we were to represent the whole estuary on the scale of a regulation football field and fill it to scale with water, the deepest spot in its main shipping channels would be a little over 1 inch and its average depth would be the thickness of three dimes—scarcely enough to dampen the field's turf.

What this means for the health of the Chesapeake is that its bottom—the sediments and also the grasses, oysters, and abundant other life there—is very much influenced by its water quality. And the state of these bottom communities in turn exerts a huge influence on water quality. These two-way "conversations" between the bay's watery domain and its bottom communities are constant and loud . . . and all because the bottom is so extraordinarily close to the top.

We have seen how the bay's resilience, its ability to handle environmental insult, has suffered from changes in its watershed— clearing and paving the forests, saturating the soils that drain to its rivers with excess agricultural fertilizers and manure, laying bare the soil to erosion through poor development and farming techniques. In the same fashion the estuary's degraded condition also reflects changes we have caused to its bottom.

This section assesses the state of the bay by measuring three parts of the bay's bottom that are especially significant to the estuary's health: the grasses that grow in its shallows; the *benthos*, the oysters and clams and worms and other creatures that inhabit the bottom muds and clays; and the sediments themselves.

Underwater Grasses

The dramatic disappearance, beginning two decades ago, of submerged grasses in Chesapeake Bay (Figure 4.11) was our strongest indication that a system-wide failure was occurring in the bay. Even so, it was ignored for years. Had a similar catastrophe occurred in the forests of the watershed, it would have drawn immediate attention from all over the world; but even the shallow water of the bay keeps problems out of sight and out of mind.

The grasses respond quickly to changes in water quality, and analyses of old pollen grains in the bay's deep sediments show they had existed successfully throughout the estuary for hundreds and probably thousands of years until the early 1970s. Nowadays, many scientists think a comeback of the grasses would be one of the best indicators that the bay as a whole is coming back.

The grass beds are critical to the bay's health in several ways. They lend resilience to the system by interacting with the bay's waters— absorbing nutrients like nitrogen and phosphorus when they are abundant at certain times of year and then releasing them at other

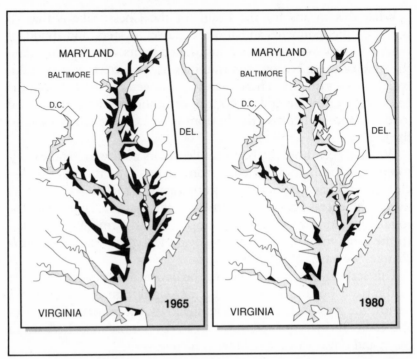

FIGURE 4.11. LOSSES OF UNDERWATER GRASSES: 1965–1980
Between the 1960s and the 1980s, the bay lost most of its underwater grasses, and there has not yet been any system-wide return of this vital part of the ecosystem. [EPA, *Chesapeake Bay: A Profile of Environmental Change*]

times when they are scarce. It has been estimated by EPA that the underwater vegetation in Chesapeake Bay thirty years ago could have absorbed about half of all the nitrogen and phosphorus in sewage being discharged to the bay in 1982. Moreover springtime storage, when high river flows are delivering great pulses of nutrients, reduced the growth of polluting levels of plankton, which also feed on nutrients. Summer and fall releases of nutrients, when the river flows are usually low, made nutrients available to the food web at a time when they were otherwise relatively scarce.

The grass beds also filtered large quantities of sediment suspended in the water flowing into the bay, settling it out and stabilizing it around their roots. The net impact of all this was to clarify the water, which in turn allowed sunlight to penetrate, creating better growth conditions for the grasses. In effect, the bottom of the bay was actively regulating the environment of the water above and around it, much as a large forest can create a microclimate of moist conditions that favor its continued survival.

The grasses are alive! If you ever saw a Maryland or Virginia soft-crabber pull up a huge roll of grass in his "scrape" (or dredge)— watched it vibrating and wriggling with shrimp, little fishes, soft crabs, seahorses, terrapins, baby hard crabs—you would never again think of the grasses as just so many green plants. Losing grasses in the bay is as devastating for the estuary's life as burning the jungle is for life in the Amazon rain forest. The grasses are also food for ducks and geese and swans, and an indirect source for many other creatures, like egrets and herons and striped bass and speckled trout, that feed on crabs and shrimp and many other smaller creatures that inhabit the grass beds. And, finally, growing frequently just offshore in the bay's shallows, thick beds of grasses, whose tops literally mat the surface on low tides, are a highly efficient absorber of wave energy, thus preventing erosion of shorelines.

The grasses died primarily from a lack of light. Too many nutrients—from human sewage and agricultural chemicals, from urban runoff and air pollution—were entering the bay and causing so much growth of floating plankton as to cloud the water. Sediment flowing from farms and construction sites added to the problem. Algal growths directly coating the grasses' leaves provided the coup de grace. As the grasses weakened, their very decline led to a loss of the bay's capacity to absorb and filter the pollution, which in turn weakened the grasses further . . . and so the vicious cycle went.

Rock bottom for the grasses occurred in 1984, when EPA estimated their acreage in the bay and its tributaries at about 37,000 acres (Figure 4.12). Since then, comebacks in a few areas where nutrient controls have worked have raised the acreage to about 50,000 or 60,000. Their extent under healthy conditions is thought to have been about 600,000 acres—and this may be an underestimate, for it assumes that enough light for growth never penetrated depths of the bay below 6 or 7 feet. Yet there is abundant anecdotal evidence from watermen still living, who made catches of seafood from bay grass beds, that the water half a century ago was clear enough to grow grasses as deep as 10 to 15 feet. Additionally, significant portions of modern acreages of grass are characterized as "sparse growth." It is likely that more of the acreage a few decades ago was in dense growth.

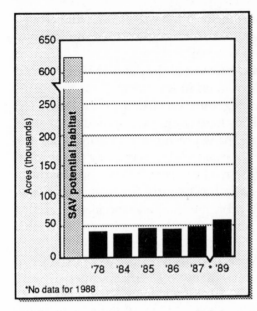

FIGURE 4.12. TRENDS IN UNDERWATER GRASSES: 1978–1989 *The bay's underwater grasses remain at less than a tenth of their estimated potential habitat of more than 600,000 acres. For 1988, no data were available.* [EPA, Chesapeake Bay Liaison Office, State of the Bay Report, 1990]

If the bay's grasses today remain far from healthy, there is solid if scattered evidence from the last five years that the prospects of a major rebound are far from hopeless. Since 1984 the bay has seen substantial returns of grasses in at least a few rivers, the Potomac, Choptank, and York. In the Potomac (see the case study in Chapter 6)—the river where reductions of nutrients from sewage have been most dramatic in the last decade—underwater vegetation went from almost nothing to covering about 4,000 acres between 1983 and 1987. As the grass beds proliferated, water clarity improved, as did the fishing and the populations of waterfowl observed on the river. (See Figure 4.13.)

One lesson from this is that reducing nutrients in the water, a major goal of the Chesapeake Bay cleanup program, is on the right track. Another lesson is that grasses can rebound quickly once conditions become favorable—and once established, they can further clear the water, creating even more favorable conditions for more grasses, and so forth. Just as environmental declines, once a threshold is crossed, sometimes accelerate out of control, so too may some environmental comebacks. The upper Potomac had been so bare of grasses for more than a decade that many wondered whether there was anything left to come back.

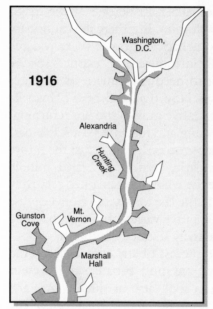

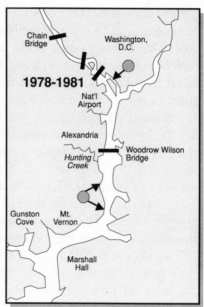

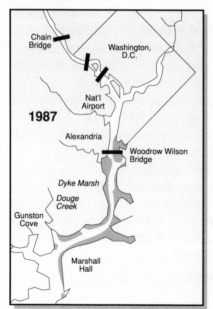

FIGURE 4.13. TRENDS IN UNDER-
WATER GRASSES IN THE PO-
TOMAC: 1916–1987 *The cleanup
of sewage discharges into the Potomac
below Washington brought the grasses
back in the late 1980s, following an
almost complete disappearance (1978–
1981). Earlier estimates, however,
show that they were once even more
extensive. Black bars show bridges
across the river.* [EPA, Chesapeake
Bay Liaison Office, State of the Bay
Report, 1990]

EPA considers the Potomac comeback to be one of the major "success stories" to date of the bay cleanup. But there is a cautionary note. The turning point in the comeback in grasses there was the explosive growth of an accidentally introduced, or "exotic," species called hydrilla, which seemed not to need the same level of water quality to thrive as the native grasses. Now that thick beds of hydrilla have further cleaned up the water, native grasses too are returning. But the hydrilla seems to be decreasing and may not be a stable part of the system there. It is thus perhaps too early to forecast the future of upper Potomac grass beds. Similarly, even in the broad, middle reaches of Chesapeake Bay, where the water has remained relatively clean, there has been a major shift in the last forty years from eelgrass to wigeongrass. The latter is also a native variety, but one that may be indicative of a more environmentally stressed condition.

The point is that in judging the success of any comebacks in the bay's grasses during coming years, we must broaden our present emphasis on quantity and learn to look also at quality. Are the grasses that evolved during centuries to do best in these regions the ones that are coming back? Are we regaining the same diversity, the mix of species that was there previously, or just one variety? And while the state of the grasses is one of our very best indicators of the state of the bay, we need to realize that like everything else about the estuary, a single year's observation will not tell us much.

In the Choptank River on Maryland's Eastern Shore, for example, the grasses made comebacks twice in the 1980s, only to die back dramatically in a succeeding year. How do we interpret such confusing messages of success followed by failure? Scientists say the resurgence and subsequent flop were mostly responses to climate rather than to effects of our pollution control programs. The increase in nutrients and sediment entering the bay from land runoff in a wet year, versus a normal or dry year, is enormous—more than enough to cause grass diebacks or, in dry years, to cause comebacks. The real test will be how the grasses hold up after several wet years— a test they cannot yet pass.

Benthos—the Bottom-Dwellers

Like the underwater grasses, the teeming assortment of clams, worms, sponges, corals, and other benthos lodged in the muds and sands and clays of the bay's bottom interact constantly with the water above them. Many species filter huge quantities of plankton and sediment from the waters of the bay as they feed. Estimates are that they filter from 28 percent to nearly 100 percent of all the water above them, depending on the region of the bay. It has been separately calculated by a University of Maryland scientist that the most famous member of the Chesapeake's benthic community, the American oyster, once had the capacity, as they fed by straining water through their gills, to filter and clarify the bulk of the bay's total volume of water every few days.

The decline of bay oysters is usually regarded as the loss of an economic and food resource and as contributing to the demise of the traditional lifestyle of the watermen who harvest them. But from the standpoint of the bay's health, the loss to the bay's resilience, its ability to absorb and rebound from pollution, is an equal or even more serious impact of the great oyster decline. As discussed in Chapter 3, the oyster has been reduced by pollution, overfishing, mismanagement, and disease to about 1 percent of its original population, and chances for a comeback seem bleak under current biological and political conditions.

To an extent, some of the oyster's capacity to cleanse the bay has been replaced by other species of benthos, such as *Corbicula* and *Rangia* clams, that have expanded their range dramatically in the more polluted conditions of the last few decades. But it still appears that the bottom of the bay is not nearly the vital filter that it was in more pristine times. In addition the oyster, like the underwater grasses, seems to have been a major "banker" and recycler of the huge pulses of nutrients that surged off the watershed in the wet springtime. It filters the lush, nutrient-fertilized spring plankton bloom through its gills, using some of it for growth, but also depositing nutrient-rich feces on the bay's bottom—a bottom which, you will recall, is never far from the top. Thus these nutrients packaged by the oyster's excretory system can be recycled into production again.

But just as the bay's oysters no longer filter much sediment from the water, neither do they still bank and package food for recycling as much. Estimates are that the pre-1870 oyster population could have removed 23 to 41 percent of the plankton blooms. Today that figure has fallen to about 0.4 percent. We might ask: where does the unfiltered plankton go nowadays? It appears that it goes to the bottom, where its decomposition can intensify the low-oxygen problems that plague large portions of the bay's deeper waters each summer. Ecologists will tell you that the bay is probably no less productive of life now than in less polluted times—but the productivity now is wrapped up more in plankton than in grasses and oysters, they add, and the result is a less diverse and less useful estuary.

Apart from these stabilizing or regulatory functions, a healthy oyster bed was also the bay's equivalent of the tropical coral reef, its hard surfaces and millions of crevices providing habitat for a whole host of other creatures (Figure 4.14). These in turn attracted feeding fish in warmer months and sea ducks and possibly loons in the winters. Young crabs also seem to prefer oystery bottoms as wintertime habitat over almost any other part of the bay. Similarly, all the benthos form a reservoir of food and habitat for fish and blue crabs and diving ducks, providing the majority of their diet. They are especially central to the diet of many fish during their vulnerable juvenile stages. A decline in the benthos may thus have every bit as much impact on fish populations as filling wetlands or damming a spawning river.

The benthos are also among the more valuable indicators of pollution in a region, because they spend their whole adult lives in the same place. Changes in levels of oxygen, toxic chemicals, sediment, and plankton all can be "read" by careful study of the bottom-dwellers over long periods of time. Comparisons of benthos in the Maryland portions of the bay between the early 1970s and the late 1980s indicate a few trends in the state of the bay:

- The abundance and diversity of benthos increased significantly in the middle and outer portions of Baltimore Harbor, apparently a response to reduced levels of toxic chemicals discharged there. But the benthos there were still not nearly as healthy as in comparable parts of the bay with cleaner water. (Problems with low oxygen in the harbor are worse today than they were in the 1970s.) In the Inner Harbor, there was only slight improvement in the benthos in two decades of monitoring.
- There were shifts among the kinds of benthos growing in deep, traditionally oxygen-poor waters to species that can tolerate less oxygen—indicating a worsening of oxygen deficiencies in the bay since the 1970s.
- There were increases in abundance of benthos, but no increase in diversity in the upper portions of the main bay, which are

FIGURE 4.14. THE OYSTER AS HABITAT   *Oysters originally were found in the bay in reefs. Today they are scattered widely over the bottom because of intensive dredging which broke apart the original "oyster rocks." This illustration from an early survey of virgin oyster reefs shows the diverse community of organisms that lived there along with oysters.* [From *Report of the Oyster Commission of the State of Maryland,* January 1884]

dominated by the flow of the Susquehanna River. This trend could reflect improvements in sewage treatment by Pennsylvania since the 1970s.

• The status of the benthos in the Maryland bay overall was characterized as "moderately healthy (excepting oysters)."

A similar study completed in July 1989 for the Virginia bottom of the bay was handicapped by having very little in the way of monitoring in years past from which to draw comparisons and trends. The report, based on samples taken between 1985 and 1989, did confirm that low-oxygen problems had reduced the quantity and diversity of benthos in two areas: the deep channel north of the Rappahannock River and the lower reaches of the Rappahannock itself.

"Memory" of the Bottom

The bottom of the bay is often thought of as the place where the buck stops—where the soils and toxic chemicals and nutrients from sewage and farms and city streets all over the watershed finally come to rest. But they do not simply rest there.

Consider, for example, one of the bay's largest problems: the excessive amounts of nutrients—nitrogen and phosphorus—that it receives each year from sewage and from runoff from farms and developed areas. These nutrients grow too much plankton, which in turn leads to oxygen depletion. In 1972, during Tropical Storm Agnes, the Chesapeake received some of the most intense rainfall in more than a century. The rivers delivered extraordinary volumes of water and nutrients during that time—more in days than the bay ordinarily gets in years. As expected, the bay experienced high growth of plankton that year. But the next year, when much less nutrient was flowing down the rivers, production of plankton surged even higher than in 1972. Apparently, nutrients in its bottom from the year before were released to fuel the plankton. The bay was, in effect, remembering Agnes. It may seem odd to associate "memory" with something so inert as the mud at the bottom of the bay. But the question of how long pollutants in the bottom will keep coming out to haunt us is of major importance, because we have been insulting the estuary for a long time now.

Scientific thinking in the early 1980s held that the bay was a literal "sink" for virtually everything that entered it, including nitrogen and phosphorus. What came into the system never left it. Even if we were to succeed in drastically reducing our flows of sewage and farm fertilizers into the bay, the thinking went, there was enough nutrient buried in the bottom to keep causing problems with plankton and oxygen for many, many years. (Lower summertime oxygen levels trigger the release of nutrient from bottom sediments.)

But now a scientific consensus seems to be building that the sediments are not the ultimate storage place for nutrients. Preliminary research is indicating that, far from being a total sink for nitrogen and phosphorus, the bay retains less than 20 percent of its nitrogen and related compounds and less than 70 percent of its phosphorus—and these numbers may drop as more is learned about the variety of physical, chemical, and biological processes that appear to transport them from the sediments into the atmosphere or out to sea. The implication for the bay cleanup is positive: The sediment's memory for nutrients now appears to be short term—on the order of months or perhaps a year or two at most. If we ever succeed in reducing the runoff to the bay of these two pollutants to levels compatible with good water quality, then we should see a comeback sooner rather than later.

For many toxic chemicals and industrial metals, which bind permanently to sediments, the bay's bottom does appear to be more of a final sink. This long memory for toxics is all the more reason to be zealous in reducing our inputs to the bay. Even with toxics, however, there is hope for recovery if we can reduce inputs. The normal processes of new sediment settling atop the old will bury the contaminated layers. In fact, this is what appears to be happening to the poisonous kepone lodged at the bottom of the James. Nearly a decade after the dumping of this pesticide was halted, the river finally has been declared open to fishing again. But a cautionary note is called for: If we are not careful, dredging can stir up these poisonous substances.

CONCLUSIONS

☐ The bottom of the bay, from its grass beds to its oysters and worms and muddy sediments, is intimately and continuously influencing—and being influenced by—the water. The water, of course, is in large part a product of what rain carries off and percolates through the lands of the watershed.

It is all connected. We may never be able to relate with legal precision the destruction of an upland forest acre with the decline of an underwater grass bed downstream or equate the dumping of excess manure on dairy farms with the lack of habitat for bottom-feeding fish. But the general connection is all too clear. As we have eliminated and overloaded the buffering and filtering capacities of forest and soil on the land, so we have also eliminated and over-loaded similar systems such as the grasses and the benthos on the bay bottom. And the rather thin film of water in the middle—what we (too narrowly) define as the Chesapeake Bay—has suffered, and will continue to suffer, until both watershed and water's bottom are restored to a greater degree of their natural functioning.

☐ The bay's underwater vegetation has been reduced by pollution to about 10 percent of the area it covered only a few decades ago. To date it has shown no strong trend toward baywide recovery, though there are signs in a few rivers that it can rebound rapidly when water conditions are right.

☐ The grasses' sensitivity and quick response to local improvement in water quality, along with their vital role in the bay ecosystem, suit them better than almost any other part of the bay's plant and animal communities as an indicator of environmental success or failure.

☐ The current strategies to bring back the grasses—reducing sediments and nutrients—appear to be the proper courses to follow. Attempts to reestablish them by replanting don't yet have much promise on a large scale because efforts are so labor-intensive and water quality is not good enough.

☐ The benthos, the assortment of shellfish, worms, and other bottom-dwellers, is another excellent indicator of improving or declining water quality and should be monitored. Virginia especially needs to improve its database.

☐ Monitoring of the benthos indicates a worsening in oxygen levels in some parts of the bay between the 1970s and 1980s. But it also indicates a modest environmental improvement in Baltimore Harbor in recent years and a possible improvement in water quality coming down the Susquehanna River.

☐ The loss of 99 percent of the bay's oysters has meant much more than the loss of an economic and food resource. It has meant the loss of a vital part of the bay's resilience, its ability to rebound from environmental insult. Healthy populations of oysters, with their immense filtering capacity, can play as much a role in maintaining bay water quality as human technologies like sewage treatment.

☐ The bay's bottom is much less of a final resting place or "sink" for key pollutants such as nitrogen and phosphorus than was thought even a few years ago. (For other pollutants, such as sediment and the toxic chemicals that cling to it, the bay still appears pretty much a sink.) Generally, the fact that the bay is less of a sink for nutrients than thought is good news. It means that such pollutants from years and decades past should not come seeping back out of the sediments, degrading water quality for lengthy periods of time even after we reduce current inputs. In short, we can expect a faster positive response to cleanup efforts than was once thought.

UPSTREAM AND DOWN

. . . for the savory shad is seen no more
above Columbia's smoke-wrapt shore.
Through centuries we'll sing the psalm,
O dam Columbia! Columbia dam!

—FROM AN ANONYMOUS POEM
PUBLISHED AROUND 1899

Water quality is the aspect of the bay's rivers that gets the most environmental concern, but the physical flows of those rivers have in some cases been so manipulated by humankind as to pose greater perils than pollution. In this section we assess the damage.

Dams

The bay's resilience has been lost in varying degrees from the forests and wetlands of its watershed, from its marshy edges, and from its bottom. But nowhere has the loss been more complete—or more completely reversible—than on its blockaded rivers. (See Figure 4.15.) We think of the bay's vast drainage system as flowing always downstream to the estuary; but just as important are the springtime tides of migratory fish that surge in from the ocean or from the bay and its lower rivers, driven by a spawning urge to penetrate the

---

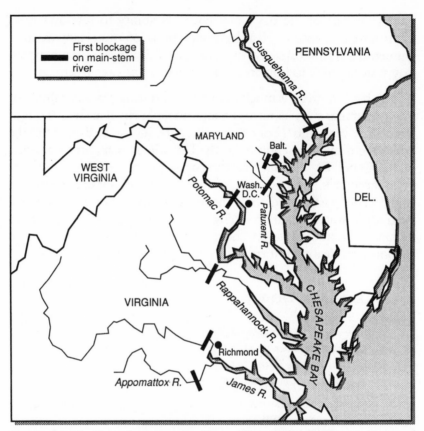

FIGURE 4.15. THE AMPUTATED BAY *Thousands of miles of rivers and streams that used to be spawning grounds for a variety of bay fish, including shad and striped bass and herring, have been cut off by dams in the last century and a half. Efforts to restore fish passage are now becoming a priority of the states.* [Alliance for the Chesapeake Bay]

watershed to its smallest creeks. These migrants include the herring and shad and rockfish and, to a lesser extent, the white and yellow perch.

For the fish, spawning is always a gamble, highly dependent for success on coinciding with just the right water temperature and just the right stream flows to wash food downstream at the perfect time to nourish the hatching larvae. In most places and in most years, the result is more bust than boom. The fish have evolved to cope with such difficulties in two ways. They lay a lot of eggs—millions in the case of female rockfish—and they spawn over hundreds and even thousands of miles of water, in effect placing their bets at many different windows, covering all the options. This strategy ensures that at least some of their species in some places each year will make a go of it.

In the vast network of different spawning reaches available throughout its watershed lay some of the resilience that sustained world-class fishing for shad, herring, and rockfish in the bay for more than a century. Herring and shad, the real long-distance runners, formerly flooded up the Susquehanna River as far as Binghamton, New York, 330 miles from the river's mouth, and up tributaries of Virginia's James River past Charlottesville. In the early years of this century, farmers in the Amish country of Lancaster County, Pennsylvania, landed as high as 400,000 pounds of shad.

The greatest river migrations are mostly gone now, as hydroelectric and water supply dams built from the 1820s through the 1930s have closed off hundreds of miles of major spawning river and thousands of miles of lesser streams. It was often remarked by the dam builders that they were finally making use of all the "wasted energy" in the water cascading downstream; they did not credit the upstream surges of migrating fish with any value. The era of highway building later in this century also took its toll, obstructing fish passage on streams throughout the watershed. Plenty of spawning areas lower down the rivers and in parts of the bay's main stem remained open—enough to sustain huge harvests until overfishing and pollution brought catches by the 1980s down to a shadow of their potential. Shad harvests baywide dropped from nearly 20 million pounds annually to less than a million. (Maryland catches dropped to 20,000 pounds by 1980.)

In the effort to restore the fisheries, begun in the 1980s, unblocking the dams has been given a high priority, along with improving water quality and managing overfishing. All three goals are vital, but in an important respect the restoration of historic upstream spawning runs carries benefits that go well beyond the enhanced quantities of fish that can be harvested. It is one of most vivid ways to reconnect inhabitants of the watershed who dwell far from the Chesapeake with the place to which their streams—and their wastes—all drain.

More than a thousand blocks to fish migration, ranging from road culverts to the 110-foot-high Conowingo hydroelectric dam on the Susquehanna, have been identified in Maryland and Virginia. A committee involving Pennsylvania, Maryland, and the federal government is now working to remove dam obstructions on the Susquehanna. Young shad have been raised and released for several years now to "imprint" them to the upper river. The hope is that when they mature at sea after a few years, they will return, salmonlike, to the river where they were born. Moreover, Virginia has established a revolving loan fund for removing obstructions to fish migrations and has breached two dams in the Richmond part of the James so far.

It is the goal of the bay restoration program to, "whenever necessary, restore natural passage for migratory fish"—a removal eventually of all blockages. But there are no specific schedules for accomplishing this, and the way can be strewn with blocks almost as solid as the great hydro dams. For example, Maryland and Pennsylvania have been negotiating more than a decade with the utility that owns Conowingo and the byzantine federal bureaucracy that regulates hydro dams. Only now do they seem assured of securing an adequate fish lift to get spawners upstream. And the costs can be substantial. Fish passage at a modest dam on the Patapsco River in Maryland is projected to cost $1.6 million, and breaching two dams at Richmond to allow fish through is budgeted at $1.5 million.

There are few other cases where lost habitat can be restored to the bay as quickly as by creating fish passage around dams. But at the current pace, significant restoration is going to take decades.

Low Flows

We know that water quality is important to restoring the bay, but water *quantity* can be critical also. The very essence of the bay is the dynamic balance it maintains between the salt ocean pushing up its channels and the freshwater rivers flowing down. The resulting mixture makes the Chesapeake neither river nor ocean but a good deal more productive of life than either one. If the flows of the rivers were to diminish permanently, the bay would not, of course, dry out; the ocean would just push up farther, maintaining the same volume as always. But the balance of fresh and salt would be altered—with dramatic impacts on aquatic life.

We are headed for just that situation, according to a study published by the Army Corps of Engineers in 1984. The study projected that by the year 2020, our growing use of fresh water would increase salinity in the bay by 2 to 4 parts per thousand on average. (The bay ranges from about 25 parts per thousand at its mouth to zero, or fresh, at its head.) A panel of experts called to evaluate the impacts of such a change on the bay's plant and animal life conceded that making such projections stretched the limits of science, but they nevertheless thought that many more bay species would be harmed than helped. Those species projected to suffer most included striped bass, oysters, shad, and redhead and canvasback ducks. Moderately favored by the change would be sea nettles, hard clams, barnacles, spot, and menhaden.

Since the study was published in 1984, it is apparent that the Corps misjudged the growth of freshwater losses by overestimating how fast we would need to build new power plants around the bay. Such plants are among the major causes of increasing freshwater losses. Even so, the issue of declining fresh water remains a real one. Only the timetable has been extended. It is not so much a matter of how much water is used—a large percentage of what we use for drinking, flushing toilets, showering, and cooling industrial machinery is returned fairly efficiently to the bay through sewage flows and industrial discharge pipes. Rather, the key is uses that cause what the Corps terms "consumptive loss." This is often evaporation, such as from watering lawns on hot days. By far the largest consumptive losses come from the cooling towers used by power plants and some industries.

The Corps study listed a number of "most promising alternatives" to stem the decrease of freshwater inflow to the bay: water conservation, growth restrictions, and increasing water storage capacity in upstream reservoirs. It did not list energy conservation—though the greatest "saving" of fresh water since 1984 probably has been through such conservation (the power plants we have *not* built).

Today a project looms on the horizon that potentially faces the bay with another loss of fresh water. This is the proposed widening and deepening of the Chesapeake and Delaware Canal, the shipping link between the upper Chesapeake and Delaware bays. This canal, first cut through the isthmus of the Eastern Shore more than a century ago, shuttles massive flows of water in and out of the upper Chesapeake through its 45-foot-deep channel. (At peak tidal flow, oceanographers must use 1,100-pound locomotive wheels to anchor their current-measuring meters in place.) Of course, the tides run equally in both directions, both from the Chesapeake and back to it.

But the *net* flow, because of the canal's slope, is out of the Chesapeake. Currently it is a small loss of fresh water, but any project to widen and deepen the canal will need to consider whether the net freshwater outflows from the Chesapeake would be altered.

Apart from causing system-wide impacts, the lowering of freshwater flows to the bay can cause serious local problems. Demands for Susquehanna River water, for example, already are so great that in a severe drought there would only be enough water reaching Conowingo Dam to meet current water quality standards 30 percent of the time. These standards involve release of a certain minimum flow through the dam to keep oxygen levels healthy in the several miles of key fishery habitat below the dam. This is especially important in light of the attempts in Pennsylvania and Maryland to restore the Susquehanna to its historic potential for spawning fish.

Currently Maryland officials are attempting to buy the rights to billions of gallons of water in upstream reservoirs in Pennsylvania. They would then be able to release it downstream in a drought crisis, at least partially staving off degradation of the waters below Conowingo. Despite such plans, there has been very little discussion among the bay states and EPA to form a coherent, long-term plan to avoid changes to the bay's essential balance of fresh water and salt. In addition, all three states have ongoing programs or laws intended to ensure enough freshwater flows down streams and rivers to protect aquatic life during droughts. But again they are looking at the problem piecemeal and not on a whole-bay basis.

CONCLUSIONS

□ The current baywide goal of reopening all historic spawning rivers and streams by removing dams that have cut off thousands of miles is an excellent one. Its value is both economic—increased commercial fisheries and huge recreational opportunities—and political. What better way to convince Pennsylvanians near the New York border and Virginians in Albemarle County they are part of the bay's watershed than to send them a gift of shad and herring every spring?

□ We are using the fresh water of the bay watershed in quantities that eventually will shift its salinity in ways that will harm more creatures than it will benefit. On the Susquehanna we are already at the point in freshwater consumption where a severe drought would compromise the amount of river flow needed to sustain good fish habitat below Conowingo Dam. A proposal to widen and deepen the canal linking Chesapeake and Delaware bays could cause an additional leakage of fresh water from the upper Chesapeake. We need a permanent cap on losses of fresh water from the bay. Water conservation and energy conservation must go hand in hand toward this goal, since power plants are a major source of the losses.

CHAPTER 5

The Ultimate Issue: People

*Colonists and Indians together began a dynamic
and unstable process of ecological change . . . ecological abundance and economic prodigality went
hand in hand: the people of plenty were a people of
waste. We live with their legacy today.*

> —*CHANGE IN THE LAND: INDIANS, COLONISTS
> AND THE ECOLOGY OF NEW ENGLAND*
> BY WILLIAM CRONON

In the spring of 1977, Maryland and Virginia were concluding the
first bistate conference on the health of Chesapeake Bay. The conference found the bay to be "fairly healthy" but noted several worrisome trends that in retrospect were warnings of a widespread and
worsening system-wide decline in the estuary. The speaker chosen to
summarize the conference, Dr. J. L. McHugh of the Marine Sciences
Research Center of the State University of New York, ended his talk
on a prophetic note:

> One theme has run like a thread through all the papers and discussions in
> this conference, as it does in all discussions of environmental manage-
> ment. It is an issue that is almost always evaded, and certainly never
> addressed seriously. Yet this is the root problem of the environment, the
> basic cause of all the other problems—the human population explo-
> sion. . . . If we cannot cope with it, maybe everything else will be in vain.

Assuming that we eventually handled that problem, Dr. McHugh
said, another set of problems might do us in:

188

That is our preoccupation with what we call "progress," which promises to add a growing load, per capita, of contamination to the environment.

He thus proposed two topics for consideration by all those who would save the bay: controlling the human population and reassessing our concept of progress. Future discussions may be sterile if we continue to treat these key problems as if they did not exist.

In the nearly fifteen years since that conference, these issues have become even more critical, but attempts to confront them have been disjointed, piecemeal, and often ineffective—examples all too often of our previous analogy of rowing four knots against a five-knot current. It is time—past time in many cases—to do better. The two sections in this chapter address population impacts and the way in which our current definitions of progress are forcing uneconomic and polluting use of the bay's watershed. They are both complex issues, but not so difficult to resolve as some would make them out.

To a large extent the rapid growth of population in the bay's watershed is the result of immigration, part of a nationwide influx of people toward the coastlines. Additionally, the adverse environmental impacts of population growth are greatly magnified by *how* we live, rather than by just how many of us are living in a place. The point is that we can go a long way toward confronting Dr. McHugh's "population explosion" without wading into the emotionally charged waters of birth control, abortion, and the like. Similarly, the alternatives to "progress" do not call for the abandonment of high-quality lifestyles. Rather, they entail giving serious thought and encouragement to achieving a quality, *sustainable* existence for us and our descendants. The antidote to gluttony, whether it involves food or natural resources, is not starvation but eating well.

INDIVIDUAL IMPACTS

We have met the enemy and he is us.

—POGO

If the enemy is us, the solution is near at hand. For those who wonder how many more people can ultimately live around Chesapeake Bay without degrading it, the short answer is this: Too many are here already. The bay is already degraded; its capacity to remain unpolluted and healthy is already exceeded. The real point, of course, is that population numbers can never be divorced from population impacts. What is our per capita consumption of natural resources? What is our per capita production of wastes and our disposal of those wastes?

Make no mistake, most of the problems with Chesapeake Bay are the cumulative impact of every one of the nearly 15 million people who live in its watershed. To indulge in the exercise of assigning the blame only to "industry" or "chemicals" or "developers" is to bury our heads in the sand. And environmental protection measures that do not consider the habits and lifestyles of individuals are generally assured of undershooting their target or failing outright. Some examples:

- We now plow far less land for agriculture than we did forty years ago; but we slather far more chemicals on each acre.
- We have dramatically reduced emissions from individual autos; but we each own more cars and drive them more than ever. Thus, as the bay region's population rose by 50 percent (1952–1986), air pollutants from cars increased by more than 250 percent.
- We have expanded landfills and built waste incinerators; but we have continued to generate more and more trash per capita. Residents in the watershed a few decades ago generated 2.2 pounds of garbage a day. In 1986 this figure had risen almost 50 percent to 3.3 pounds a day. (See Figure 5.1.)
- We currently plan and zone and lobby for "controlled growth" more than ever in history; but each of us has been using nearly twice the open space to live on as we did forty years ago—and each new resident averages nearly four times as much because of galloping sprawl development. More land in the watershed will be developed in the three decades between 1990 and 2020 than was developed in the three centuries between 1608 and the 1950s, based on projections from the recent "2020 Report" on population and land use.
- Energy consumption in the watershed has followed a course similar to waste—population up by 50 percent, but energy consumption up by 100 percent. (See Figure 5.2.)

And these numbers only hint at the ripple effects of an increasingly consumptive lifestyle—the added trees that were felled for the added roads needed for the added cars; the destruction of bay shoreline to site the added power plants needed to meet the added electrical demands.

Nationally the story is the same as locally: The U.S. population, 5 percent of the world's people, consumes a quarter of its vital resources, such as oil and industrial ores, and produces equally disproportionate shares of global pollution. Neither the world nor the bay could stand millions more people living as we do now. We bay dwellers and our fellow Americans are the hungriest resource-users ever to stalk the earth. The greatest of the dinosaurs by comparison were no more than nibbling mice.

The Way Out

Fortunately, the alternatives do not mean an impoverished existence; rather, they may lead to a higher quality of life. One example: Western Europeans, with a high standard of living, use about half the energy we do to generate one dollar of GNP. Similarly, reducing waste means recycling and reuse, not doing without material goods. Reducing the runaway consumption of open space can mean a return to small town and village patterns of development, as well as enhancing the appeal of cities. Using fewer pesticides is turning out to be a way to more profitability for more and more farmers. They hire "scouts" who track insect populations and tell them when they need to spray (and when not), saving substantial money in most years.

The power of individual impacts is often hard for a single person to visualize, but when we multiply any action by millions it becomes impressive. The recent change in home laundry detergents brought about by phosphate bans in all three states, for example, was painless and virtually without cost to consumers. Yet almost overnight it accounted for a 30 to 50 percent reduction in a major pollutant of Chesapeake Bay (phosphorus from sewage plants). Achieving the same reductions through technological changes to the plants would have cost hundreds of millions of dollars and taken years for construction.

And just as increasing individual consumption has ripple effects far beyond the direct impact, so does reducing it send out beneficial ripples. Thus channeling growth into more compact population centers not only saves open space, but it makes mass transit viable,

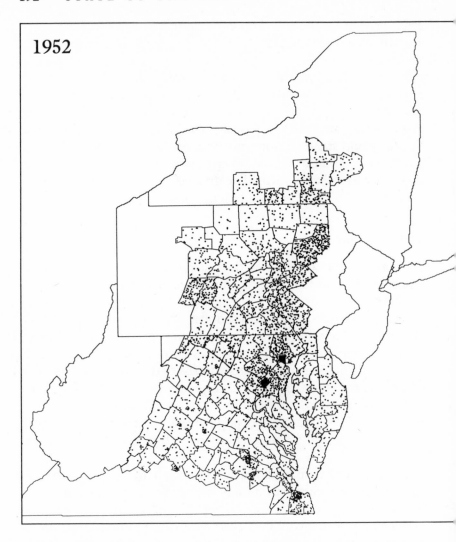

FIGURE 5.1. SOLID WASTE PRODUCTION TRENDS IN THE CHESAPEAKE WATERSHED: 1952–1986 *Solid waste production in the watershed not only increased dramatically in absolute terms, but the production of waste* per capita *rose from about 2 pounds per day to 3.3. Note: Each dot = 2 tons/day.* [By S. Tennenbaum and R. Costanza, Chesapeake Biological Laboratory, University of Maryland]

1986

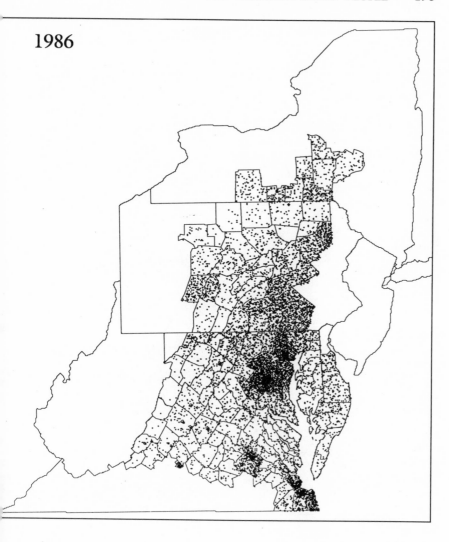

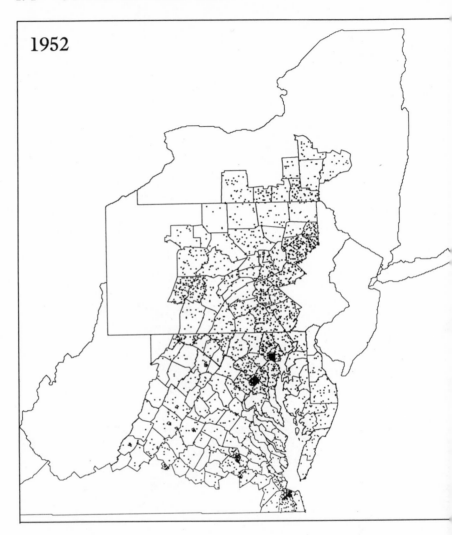

FIGURE 5.2. ENERGY CONSUMPTION TRENDS IN THE CHESAPEAKE
WATERSHED: 1952–1986   *As population grew in the watershed by about 50
percent, energy consumption grew by more than 100 percent. Note: Each dot =
500 million BTU* [By S. Tennenbaum and R. Costanza, Chesapeake Biological Laboratory, University of Maryland]

1986

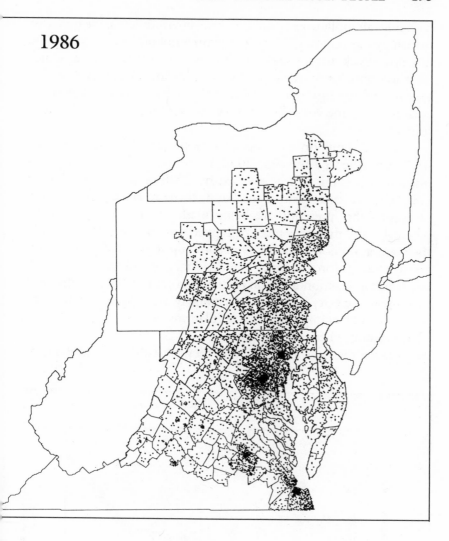

reducing air pollution from cars and environmental degradation from highway building. Recycling plastics not only saves energy, but it helps attack the problem of throwaway plastic waste, which now accounts for more than 60 percent of the 14 billion pounds a year of garbage humans throw into the world's oceans (where sea creatures become entangled in it or eat it, clogging their digestive tracts).

At least 2.6 million more persons are projected to move into the bay's watershed by the year 2020, a number that many planning officials now think will be reached by 2005 or 2010. (See Figure 5.3.) The choice is clear, if the bay is to be restored. The impacts per capita that presently are being made on the system must be reduced—and then they must be capped so that, to the bay, it is as if the coming millions did not even show up. One need not wait on government to force changes in individual patterns of consumption and waste generation to begin reducing impacts on the bay (see the accompanying box), although it is unlikely the reductions will come fast or broadly enough without regulations.

In guiding where such regulation will be most effective, a few overarching themes stand out. First, they must attack the fundamen-

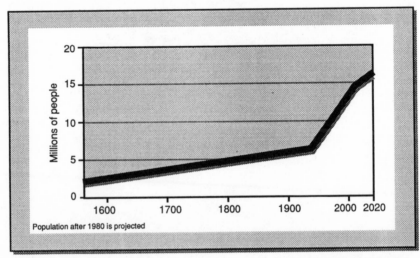

FIGURE 5.3. POPULATION TRENDS IN THE CHESAPEAKE WATER-SHED.   [Adapted by Joseph Hutchinson from state and federal census data]

tal sources of pollution and degradation. There is nothing wrong with continuing to rely on "fixes" in the interim such as more benign pesticides, cleaner automobile exhausts, and new sewage treatment technologies. But these must increasingly be seen as means to an end (less automobile use, for example) rather than as ends in themselves. Second, some of the most notable environmental successes have resulted from outright banning of the polluting substance or activity rather than regulating it or developing technologies to lessen its impact. Examples include getting the lead out of gasoline, ridding the environment of the DDT that was killing our eagles and ospreys, outlawing production of PCBs, and switching to nonphosphate detergents throughout the watershed.

The Need for Limits

Reducing individual impacts can go far to reconcile environmental progress with more people moving into the watershed; but it is quite conceivable that it will not go far enough unless we also move to limit the total number of people in the watershed. It is not too early to begin facing the need for such limits. The economic and environmental policies, as well as the physical infrastructure such as roads and sewers and bridges, that we lay down in the next decade or two will go far to determine population movements and growth well into the next century.

One of the fastest-growing portions of the watershed, Washington, D.C., and suburbs, is perhaps the most immediately susceptible to growth control. The federal government should consider decentralizing some of its apparently endless increase in jobs and agencies to outside the watershed. Few people seriously think we should simply post "keep out" signs around the region; but we can move to eliminate current subsidies to new growth in government taxing and spending policies and start to calculate the real costs of growth. To the extent that high growth rates can be uncoupled from economic prosperity, we may be able to rationally discuss limits to growth.

This will take a new kind of economics. The current economics counts actions such as clear-cutting an old-growth forest as a pure "plus" for GNP, never including the costs of losing wildlife along with a prime filter for air and water pollution. The growing

What Can I Do?

Each of us, in our everyday lives, has the ability to help the Chesapeake Bay and its counterparts all over the country. Here is just the barest sampling of ways everyone can start today being part of the solution:

Energy

- Lower your home or business thermostat in winter; turn it up in summer. Just a couple degrees can save substantial amounts of energy, thereby reducing costs, pollution from power plants, and the need to construct more plants.
- Check the energy efficiency of your appliances. When replacing them, get the most efficient ones available.
- Use fluorescent lights to replace incandescent ones. Many are now available without the harsh light normally associated with fluorescents. They cost more, but last ten times as long, using far less energy and paying back their cost in a year or so.
- Use a clothesline rather than the dryer whenever possible.
- Plant deciduous trees to block the summer sun and keep your house cooler all summer while letting the sun in all winter.
- Don't keep the refrigerator any colder than necessary.
- Turn your hot water heater down a few degrees. You will never notice the difference.

Water

- When replacing or installing toilets, install water-saving, low-flow units. Retrofit old ones with a toilet dam.
- Install low-flow shower heads. They're cheap and they save hot water heating bills.
- Fix leaky faucets.
- Plant species of shrub and grass that are native to your local environment and require little watering.

Waste/Recycling

- Recycle all glass, metal cans, aluminum, corrugated cardboard, and motor oil. Lobby your local government for better recycling facilities, such as curbside pickup.

- Don't debate whether paper is better than plastic for supermarket bags—bring your own washable canvas or string bags and reuse them for years.
- Take a mug instead of buying coffee in styrofoam or plastic cups.
- Avoid purchasing disposable, nonrecyclable items—razors, cameras, plates, for example.

Yard and Garden

- Stop using chemical herbicides and insecticides. Choose plants that won't need fertilizer. Investigate organic growing methods.
- Compost leaves in the fall instead of burning them, and never bag them for landfill disposal.

Toxics

- Stop pouring solvents, paints, preservatives, and such down drains or toilets. Never dispose of used oil or antifreeze down residential drains or storm drains (or on the ground).
- Use natural pest control products for insects.

Transportation

- Reduce your driving. Bike, walk, or use mass transit whenever possible.
- Buy the most fuel-efficient car you can. Aim for 35 miles per gallon.
- Try to live near where you work. Car pool if you don't.
- Urge your elected officials to support statewide land use management programs to reduce suburban sprawl.

Streams

- Join a local group to monitor the health of a neighborhood stream. (The Chesapeake Bay Foundation can help you contact the local chapter of Save Our Streams, a hands-on environmental group.)

Septic System

- Find out if your toilet flushes to a wastewater treatment plant or a septic tank (buried somewhere in your yard). Keep it maintained by calling a septic tank service at least every few years.

discipline of *ecological economics*, which specializes in valuing the products of the natural world as well as manufacturing output, is one place to begin.

It may well take some preaching, too. Our churches have for the most part been slow to address the moral and spiritual aspects of restoring Chesapeake Bay and caring for the lands of its watershed. They could play a powerful role in interpreting what the biblical "dominion" over the earth given to man in Genesis should mean in our modern-day era of environmental crisis—certainly it should not be taken as a license for the kind of ownership that sees only private property rights unencumbered by responsibility for the impacts of private land use on the commonwealth.

CONCLUSIONS

☐ We have already exceeded the bay's capacity to sustain a healthy environment, given current population numbers and the per capita impacts of that population.

☐ Only by reducing the environmental impacts and demands on natural resources of every person in the watershed can we support more people and restore the bay.

☐ A continued high standard of living is not incompatible with a reduction in individual impacts on the environment.

☐ There has been a tendency to control the by-products of polluting technologies rather than fundamentally rethinking the technologies themselves. With a growing population, this approach has severe limits.

☐ Population growth is the fundamental source of pollution. And at some point it will overtake and offset even the substantial gains to be had by reducing the individual environmental impacts of people.

THE LAND INDUSTRY

One of the few human rights that aren't officially guaranteed in this country is an agreement that the place you grow up caring about will be there for you when you're ready to start a family of your own.

—ROBERT YARO, Center for Rural Massachusetts

Arguably, the industry with greatest environmental impact across the bay's watershed is neither manufacturing, nor agriculture, nor chemicals. It is what might be called the land industry: the development, sale, resale, surveying, landscaping, homebuilding, subdividing, speculating, zoning, planning, rezoning, and other activities that all relate to turning open space into where we live and work. It is an industry whose raw materials are nothing mined from distant caverns like coal or oil, nor chemicals delivered in tank trucks and rail cars. The feedstock of the land industry is our natural environment, our forest and fields, our views and vistas and wildlife, and the communities where we were born.

In recent decades the land industry has been as wasteful of its basic resource as the automobile industry was of petroleum in the heyday of the 400-horsepower gas guzzler—and just as polluting. Our exploitation of land now is in a phase comparable to our exploitation of oysters during the unsustainable heights of harvest in the 1870s. With oysters we realized over a century later that we had destroyed more than an economic resource—we had destroyed a major part of the bay's bottom habitat and capacity to filter and clarify the water. With the profligate conversion of open space to developed land we are likewise degrading the watershed's capacities to buffer the bay against pollution washing off the land.

But the damage from our modern land industry goes well beyond what can be measured in added pollutants or acreage of open space lost. We are frittering away the heritage of the places we live—the character of our traditional landscapes, the community of our small towns, the vitality of our urban areas.

A Growing Appetite for Land

Human population, one of the key factors driving our land industry, is growing. The increase comes as much from people moving here as from high birth rates. Maryland, for example, gained about 180,000 citizens since 1985 from births exceeding deaths; but it gained nearly 400,000 from a net movement of people into the state. Virginia in the last decade gained 480,000 from net immigration and about 403,000 from births exceeding deaths. Pennsylvania, in contrast, gained around 100,000 from births and only about 12,000 from net immigration. (These figures are for the Chesapeake Bay watershed portion of Pennsylvania only; they are statewide for

FARMS AND DEVELOPMENT

Open space, as opposed to development, generally is taken to be an unquestioned good in terms of environmental impact on Chesapeake Bay. But in preserving open space that happens to be on farms, the issue is more complicated. As discussed in the section on agriculture (Chapter 2), farms constitute a major source of pollution to the bay. Indeed, they have been among the most difficult sources to control, although the problems are not so much technical as political and financial. Developers often argue compellingly that a development with excellent controls on sediment and stormwater pollution can equal or surpass the water quality running to the bay from even the best-managed farm. Increasingly, too, modern farming techniques have destroyed the hedgerows and windbreaks and forested stream-sides that promoted wildlife. So why fight development on farmland?

One obvious argument for preserving farmland is food production. Locally grown produce and meat result in a better and more economic diet for the citizens of a state. Eating locally produced food also reduces transportation needs and thus energy use. Moreover, agriculture is still very much part of our heritage, a vital part of the "working landscape" discussed later in this section. There is more to maintaining a pleasing landscape than maximizing pollution control.

Keeping land in agriculture also keeps open options for land use in two ways. First, the nature of agriculture has gone through many changes in the last century—on Maryland's Eastern Shore it has gone from orchards to truck farming to dairying to corn and soybeans, just to give one example. The present-day intensive grain and animal cultures that dominate the watershed probably are the most polluting forms of agriculture we have experienced in this century; but there is ample historical precedent to make us think this is not a permanent state.

Maryland and Virginia.) Even within Pennsylvania, however, areas like Lancaster County, where development pressure is greatest, gained more (56 percent) from immigration than from births (44 percent).

The total population in the parts of the watershed that lie in Maryland, Virginia, and Pennsylvania will increase by at least 2.6 million people, or 20 percent, in the next thirty years. There are

Second, if it becomes necessary for preserving water quality, a farm (or parts of it) can be fairly easily taken out of production and returned to a less-polluting land use such as forest or hayfields or nontidal wetlands. Once the land becomes homes for dozens of people, however, most other options are forever precluded. If our aim is to contain sprawl development, which is harmful both economically and environmentally, most farms are the worst place to allow more housing—most of them are not near existing growth centers where we want to encourage additional development. Conversely, a farm on the edge of town might be a place that should be developed.

Development also has many impacts on the environment and the economy that extend beyond the borders of the farm it supplants. Residential areas require a multitude of new public services—road improvements, utilities, police and fire protection, schools. They also add cars, air pollution from driving and home heating, and more demand for recreational amenities. All of these impacts can be reduced with more compact development in existing centers.

There is also good reason to think that farming can be carried out with minimal pollution if we get serious about both pollution control *and* changing the way we farm to create less pollution in the first place. Such techniques, embodied in low-input sustainable agriculture (LISA) and pest management with fewer chemicals, are beginning to come into their own with the agricultural community.

Finally, working landscapes, those that contain farms and watermen's villages and towns and open space in a diverse mix, are what give each region of the bay its uniqueness and character—an essential part of what some have called the "spirit of place." For all these reasons a policy of replacing farms with development would be the most shortsighted of solutions to the bay's problems.

also close to a million people now living in counties and cities in Delaware, New York, and West Virginia—states that are not participants in the current bay cleanup programs but are partly in the watershed and contribute to pollution of the bay and its tributaries. This population, not subject to any of the Chesapeake Bay cleanup agreements, is projected to increase by 50 percent by the year 2010. In addition, there have been major movements of people within

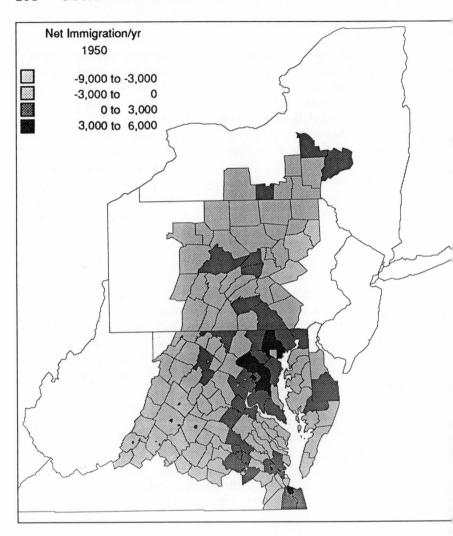

Net Immigration/yr
1950

-9,000 to -3,000
-3,000 to   0
     0 to 3,000
 3,000 to 6,000

the watershed as the cities lose residents to nearby suburbs. (See Figure 5.4.)

Simply measuring the numbers of people moving in and around the watershed, however, understates the problem with land use. Just as critical is the *efficiency*—or rather the increasing lack of it—with which they use land. Although someone arriving in the watershed today may not look much different than someone who moved here in the 1950s, the newcomers are on average much larger, hungrier

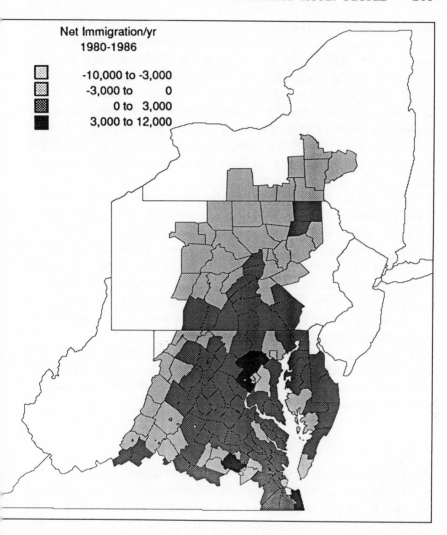

Net Immigration/yr
1980-1986

-10,000 to -3,000
-3,000 to   0
     0 to   3,000
 3,000 to 12,000

FIGURE 5.4. IMMIGRATION TRENDS IN THE CHESAPEAKE WATERSHED:
1950–1986   *The patterns show how immigration, the movement of new residents into the watershed, has been a major component of population growth,
expanding in the last decade far from existing urban centers like Baltimore,
Washington, and Norfolk.* [By S. Tennenbaum and R. Costanza, Chesapeake Biological Laboratory, University of Maryland]

animals in their appetite for land. Currently we are using 0.65 acre of land for each new person in our residential and commercial development. In the 1950s, the comparable figure was about 0.18 acre, according to the "2020 Report" on population growth issued in 1989. Averaging the trend in land use consumption gives a figure of 0.33 acre per capita over the last forty years—still double what it was during the 1950s. Put another way, the next million people moving into the bay region will use more than three times as much land as the same number moving in forty years ago, and about twice as much as the current average.

This trend is a result of shrinking family size, movement out of the more compact environments of cities and small towns, and a taste for larger homes and lots in suburbia. One county, Dorchester, on Maryland's rural Eastern Shore, actually lost population between 1980 and 1990 yet constructed hundreds of new homes, the great bulk of them on large, single-family lots—a significant consumption of open space without any growth in people. (The county's small towns nearly all lost population.) Typical patterns in the watershed show that less than a tenth of population growth, occurring on large suburban and country lots, consumed half the land developed between 1970 and 1980. And as population across the watershed increases another 20 percent by the year 2020, developed acreage is projected to increase by 60 percent.

Sprawl, the Economy, and the Environment

At first glance, such trends may not seem so threatening. The bay's watershed is a vast place, more than 40 million acres, and by 2020 it will still be 84 percent in forest and agriculture and only 16 percent developed. (Currently it is about 90 percent and 10 percent.) But for a number of reasons, it is misleading to look only at gross figures like these.

One problem is that 2020 is only the end of our current statistical projections, not the end of time. The longer sprawling development goes on, the more the whole watershed gets chopped up and becomes unfit for any use but more such development. Just a few hundred homes, scattered like pellets from a shotgun blast across thousands of acres, can effectively preclude farming and forestry and the unbroken habitat needed by wildlife. We have to ask now where we are headed in 2040, 2060, and beyond. The patterns of today are

setting the future of land use decades in advance; and unlike traditional pollutants such as the amount of nutrients in sewage, bad
development patterns are not quickly reversible. To return to our
comparison of rapacious land use with oyster overharvesting, the
bay is paying dearly right now for deeds done and patterns of
wasteful oystering set 120 years ago.

The more immediate problem is that our patterns of low-density
sprawl development, almost across the board, tend to be the most
costly and polluting. Aside from competing directly with the sizable
and economically important forestry and farming industries in the
watershed, low-density sprawl results in the following impacts according to the "2020 Report":

- Twice as much road building as more compact, higher-density
  development
- Nearly twice as much energy use for commuting and home
  heating
- Nearly twice as much driving time
- Twice as much air pollution from automobiles, one of the major
  sources of airborne pollutants falling on the bay
- About one-and-a-half times the air pollution from home heating
  fuel combustion
- Nearly twice as much sediment flowing toward waterways during construction

Economically, sprawl development amounts to the underutiliza-
tion of a state's most valuable finite resource, its land. Consider:

- The property tax yield of land in low-density (3-acre) lots is
  about one-ninth the average tax yield from the same land in
  quarter-acre lots (based on Maryland property tax rates).
- The cost of public services to low-density development usually
  makes it a net loser—that is, the taxes it brings in don't pay for
  the costs of services provided.
- Road construction costs in the next thirty years would be about
  $11 billion more for the watershed under sprawl development
  than under higher-density development ($17 billion versus $6
  billion).
- Existing urban areas that could accommodate significant population growth are ignored, even as they lose population to ever-
  expanding suburbs and "exurbs."

Such unmanaged new growth "has the potential to erase any progress made in [all other] bay improvements, overwhelming past and current efforts," concluded the 2020 Panel on population growth, a group convened by the three states, EPA, and the District of Columbia in 1988.

The Need for Models

Several counties across the watershed have had sophisticated planning and zoning for more than a decade. Some, such as Baltimore County and Montgomery County in Maryland, have had recent success in protecting large sections of prime farmland and open space. But too often such sophistication is only achieved as reaction to years of intensive and poorly planned development. Since most of the authority over land use in the watershed is at the county or township level, adjoining jurisdictions don't plan in concert—and restrictions on sprawl in one simply causes it to flood into an unprepared next-door neighbor.

Similarly, the huge bypass promoted as a solution for Washington's traffic problems (see Chapter 6) will unleash more growth pressures than many counties in its path can hope to handle. Baltimore County, for example, has successfully stopped sprawl development from destroying its agricultural northern section with a zoning that allows only one home per 50 acres; but ads for real estate just across the line in adjoining Pennsylvania tout new, low-density development: "New Freedom (PA), Baltimore's newest suburb."

Of the three principal watershed states, Pennsylvania has the most extreme problem with fragmented authority over land use. Whereas Maryland and Virginia have controls mostly at the county level, the powers lie in Pennsylvania with 2,600 municipalities. More than a third of these do not have zoning and more than half have no comprehensive plan to guide growth. Pennsylvania so far has shown little interest in pursuing specific land use strategies in response to the "2020 Report."

Maryland has an active and wide-ranging growth panel working on strategies. Virginia has begun a similar process, but Virginia too is handicapped in its ability to manage growth on the county level, where most of the action takes place with land use. It is a "Dillon Rule" state, which means counties can only do what is specifically stated in state laws. Courts in Pennsylvania and Virginia have not been friendly to many attempts at more environmentally responsible land use. This is not to say that Maryland has found the secret to excellent land use and growth management, only that it has the fewest legal and technical impediments.

Throughout the watershed it is rare to find examples of countryside that has been successfully "vaccinated" *against* low-density sprawl. Most local jurisdictions pay lip service to focused development by adopting plans that designate growth around existing centers and by extending public water and sewers from these areas. Meanwhile, virtually every acre of farm and forest outside public lands remains legal to develop, and it is usually cheaper to purchase than land closer to town. What is generally termed "agricultural" or "rural" zoning is usually nothing of the kind. It allows 1-to-5-acre lots, ensuring the worst kind of sprawl, absolutely antithetical to continued agriculture or forestry enterprises.

The result? The great majority of land developed in the watershed is *outside* designated growth centers and *outside* water and sewer areas. By essentially zoning most of our land for development we have created a target that is beyond anyone's capacity to manage rationally. In Maryland, for example, even if no more land were rezoned to allow more development, we would still have five or six times what we need to accommodate growth in the next several decades—even if existing sprawl continues. In Virginia, rural-looking counties such as Lancaster, in the Northern Neck, already are subdivided for about four times as many homes as exist now. Even if stricter land use measures are adopted in places like this, all existing subdivisions usually are exempted.

The Trouble with Zoning

Any successful reversal of the land use trends that are eroding our environmental cleanup goals and homogenizing the look and character of our watershed must take the bull by the horns and reexamine the zoning process that has been this nation's major land use regulatory tool since the 1920s. Zoning is a powerful tool—and a controversial one because of its capacity to create or diminish potential for wealth by instantly changing what can be built on a parcel of property.

American zoning from its start was flawed by failing to include two concepts of the German version from which it was adopted. In the first place, historic city limits were intended to be relatively inflexible boundary lines for growth. The "strip" zoning that has uglified roads from Norfolk, Virginia, to State College, Pennsylvania, and the endless suburbia bleeding away from every town center have come from ignoring this. Moreover, protecting the countryside was an express concern in Germany. This is only beginning to be talked about in the bay's watershed on anything other than a parcel-by-parcel basis. And the countryside, we shall see, is anything but a mere conglomeration of separate parcels of land.

American zoning not only made it too easy to develop most of the watershed; it made it too hard to achieve the innovation and high densities of housing needed to keep existing population centers vital and growing. This latter problem of concentrating growth where it would be most environmentally and economically sound has been compounded by modern subdivision ordinances that require such extravagantly overdesigned utilities—from streets to curbs to side-walks—as to frustrate innovative high-density development. A recent development in Maryland based on the classic scheme of the American small town needed exemptions from dozens of subdivision regulations.

Infrastructure: Growth Shapers Gone Awry

These flaws burst wide open after World War II with the wholesale adoption of the automobile—and rocketed further out of control with construction of the interstate highway system beginning in the 1960s. The resulting traffic congestion in many areas now threatens to choke the mobile society that spawned it. Such congestion is nowhere officially classed as a pollutant, but nationally and in many parts of the bay watershed it has come to have a larger impact on the quality of life than anything directly poisoning the air or water.

Sprawl development has pushed not only our consumption of land far faster than population growth alone, but also our driving, since its low densities make mass transit unworkable. In Fairfax County, Virginia, while population grew 31 percent in a decade (1975–1985) cars grew by 84 percent. In Virginia as a whole, the number of "vehicle miles traveled" (cars times miles each is driven) has been growing about *four times* as fast as population, according to state transportation officials. On the Capital Beltway, as noted in Chapter 6, the average driving speed in recent years has dipped from

47 mph to about 23 mph; and the *Washington Post* has added a weekly column, "Write Dr. Gridlock," to answer the questions of overwrought commuters. The District now has a noon rush hour that is larger than its morning and evening rush hours.

Traditional efforts to deal with these crises continue to involve raising gasoline taxes for embarking on yet another round of road building—a type of tax that falls most heavily on the poor, especially in rural areas where mass transit is nonexistent. Yet even the proposed $3 billion project to bypass the Capital Beltway would at best raise average driving speeds on the area's roads by about 0.8 mph, traffic experts say, because more roads tend to result in more driving—a vicious cycle.

Highways are an example of what commonly is lumped under "infrastructure," along with other large public works like sewers and schools. They are powerful shapers of future growth patterns— indeed, as important as zoning. (The land rush in New Freedom, Pennsylvania, was directly made possible by the construction years ago of Interstate 83, bringing areas as far away as Harrisburg, Pennsylvania, within commuting distance of the Baltimore–Washington megalopolis.)

Decisions or promises being made now to build, at public expense, new schools for areas where high growth was not planned are similarly not in the best interests of either the economy or the environment. Extending sewers or building new sewage treatment capacity at public expense in areas where development, not planning, picks the location is another infrastructure mistake. As indicated by Figure 5.5, a good deal of extra sewage capacity to accommodate new growth already exists in much of the bay region. To the extent that new infrastructure contradicts more compact patterns of development, growth management will be all but impossible.

Visions vs. Wishes

Arresting sprawl and its impacts on the environment cannot work without specific visions—and ultimately real-life demonstrations— of development alternatives that promise a high quality of life. These are glaringly absent at present. Too many citizens carry now an almost despairing acceptance that the "American Dream" of home ownership dictates the kind of sprawling development that uses whole farms for a dozen or so homes—treatment of land as

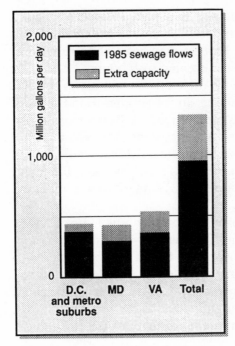

FIGURE 5.5. EXCESS SEWAGE CAPACITY *Sewage treatment capacity already exists sufficient to accommodate decades of population growth around existing centers of growth and development.* [Adapted by Joseph Hutchinson from EPA, Chesapeake Bay Liaison Office, Point Source Atlas, 1989]

almost a disposable commodity. An urban planner, looking at our decades of attention to water quality and air quality, but not to land use, once said: "Any visitors from outer space would immediately ask each other, 'Are these creatures really terrestrial beings?'" Even the most ardent bay lovers spend most of their lives on the land around it.

Recognition that sprawl is bad is just the first step into an exciting era of much more sophistication about land use. For example, a new generation of landscape planners is showing how we can accommodate high levels of population in an area while preserving the vistas and diversity and all other features of the landscape that are important to us. (See Figure 5.6.) One form of the concept centers around "working landscapes." The idea here is to preserve not just a given acreage of trees or undefined "open space" but also to keep all the features—working farms, old barns, a stretch of rural road shaded by big walnut trees, uninterrupted views down the green hush of a valley, village centers—that lend the landscape its character.

The concept presumes that for the most part, "natural" landscapes do not mean places from which humans are forbidden; nor should they be places where human influences dominate. It holds a vision of

(a) Site Before Development

(b) Site After Conventional Development

FIGURE 5.6. DEVELOPING LAND WITHOUT DESTROYING THE LANDSCAPE *These three illustrations show that growth need not be synonymous with destroying the characteristics of the natural landscape. Traditional suburban sprawl often occurs just where open space should remain to preserve the integrity of the landscape. By clustering development, the same amount of growth is achieved, but the scene retains its natural beauty.* [Reprinted from *New England Manual of Design*, Center for Rural Massachusetts]

(c) Site After Creative Development

humans as part of—not apart from—the integrity of the landscape. Once the essential characteristics of landscapes are identified, development can be fitted around them. This is one example of what we may call true vision, as opposed to the warm, fuzzy variety that currently passes for it such as "keep the Eastern Shore from looking like the western shore" or "we in (insert your favorite county here) favor balanced land use and controlled growth."

Fulfilling this true vision will absolutely require planning and zoning on a regional or state basis, as well as locally, because landscapes and their unique qualities may cross county or city borders. It further requires zoning that is innovative enough to allow high densities and nonstandard street widths, tree placements, and the like, while simultaneously placing large tracts off-limits to any development. This concept of "clustering" development, often misunderstood to mean herding everyone into brick rowhouses surrounded by asphalt, links higher-density living and views of unchanging open space like two sides of a coin. Neither can work well without the other. Clustering can also mean single-family homes, or duplexes, or mixes of several varieties of housing in densities from high to moderate.

It is perhaps ironic that our society may find it easier to preserve open space than to complement it with compact dwelling patterns elsewhere. In a notably insightful editorial, "We can't build only single homes and save open space," the Lancaster *New Era* recently said that twice in one month local politicians had bowed to community objections to dense development clustered around golf courses. "Residents in both communities have legitimate concerns about development density," the paper acknowledged, "but the question is, where do we draw the line and put multi-family dwellings? Officials must zone sections of each municipality for dense development and then make that zoning stick . . . or pay the price of not having land preservation goals and methods in sync."

Underlying the need to contain sprawl on economic and pollution grounds is an appreciation—perhaps it is new, perhaps we just lost it for awhile—that our mental and spiritual connectedness to the landscape is as important a component of the environment as clean air and clean water. Complementing the preservation of working landscapes is the revitalization of small and large urban centers on one end of the spectrum and, on the other end, the preservation of wholly natural areas. (See the accompanying box.) Stopping sprawl development will help achieve all three aims: channeling pressure away from undeveloped areas, retaining the essential nature of working landscapes through compact development patterns, and making the urban centers, with infrastructure such as roads, sewers, and mass transit already in place, the focus of renewed development interest and public spending.

Realistically, the watershed's larger urban areas have problems bigger than any solutions to be afforded by mere changes in zoning and infrastructure investment. But to the extent that the aims of the traditional environmental movement can embrace the struggling environments of the cities, it will broaden and ultimately strengthen its agendas. Preserving the environment cannot afford to be just about maintaining a diverse and pleasant natural world for the wealthy and the middle-class suburbanite in the bay's watershed. There is every reason for linking preservation of the landscape in Virginia's Northern Neck, or farmland for Lancaster County's Amish, with a better life for the less privileged inhabitants of Richmond and Harrisburg and Baltimore. There is every reason to preserve working farms and forests, and watermen's villages, as well as old-growth forest and picturesque anchorages for yachtsmen.

A "Designer Bay"?

And if that smacks too much of trying to engineer the shape of our society, then consider that we have already moved beyond the point of return. Human impacts in the watershed have grown to the point where, one way or another, we are inevitably creating what might be called a "designer bay." The question is no longer whether or not we should actively determine the future shape of the region. The question now is whether we should continue to abandon it to the unthinking forces of supply and demand for land and to piecemeal, tunnel-vision projects—or whether we should develop a true vision for melding economically sound growth with preservation of what is most attractive about living here.

CONCLUSIONS

☐ When we ride or hike through the lands of the bay region we still see a great deal of farm and field and forest. But if we could overlay these in our minds with the subdivision and freewheeling zoning already in place on much of that land, we would be sobered by this

PRESERVING OPEN SPACE

Any large-scale vision for better land use must be based on changes in state and county zoning and in regional growth policies. But meanwhile there are a number of other important tools.

Open Space Programs

The most direct way to preserve parts of the watershed from development is to buy them. Maryland from the late 1960s until 1984 had an excellent open space program that was tied directly to the pace of development. It received land acquisition money from a percentage of the state transfer tax exacted on every transaction where land is sold. The faster land was being chewed up by development, the faster funds built to preserve land from development.

In 1984, Maryland's Program Open Space was capped by the legislature so that after money reached a certain level it reverted to other uses. The cap caused the state to forgo more than a quarter of a billion dollars in open space funds until it was removed by a major environmental lobbying effort in 1989 (although a full return to normal funding won't be phased in for five years). Currently Maryland has fallen behind its open space needs by a wide gap. When Program Open Space began, it was projected that Maryland would be 10 percent developed by 1990 and that the program would have preserved an equal amount of land. But the actual numbers in 1990 were about 14.5 percent developed and 9 percent preserved, a gap of nearly 350,000 acres.

Neither Virginia nor Pennsylvania has an acquisition program comparable to Maryland's Program Open Space, although Pennsylvania's "Clean and Green" program provides tax breaks for landowners who agree to keep open space, forests, or farms intact for a minimum of seven years. This program has enrolled more than 3 million acres statewide so far. In addition, the Pennsylvania Game Commission has purchased about 241,000 acres of wildlife lands since 1970.

Virginia has a voluntary income tax checkoff to let taxpayers contribute to a state open space and recreation fund. Attempts in Virginia to use the real estate transfer tax, the funding source for Maryland's open space program, were defeated by the real estate industry in 1988. The Virginia Outdoors Foundation does, however, hold permanent conservation easements on about 65,000 acres of forest, farms, and other open space in the Chesapeake Bay watershed.

Land Trusts

Another land preservation tool that has enjoyed modest and growing success is land trusts. In Maryland since the 1950s, a variety of public and private trusts have secured permanent conservation status for nearly 75,000 acres of land. In Pennsylvania, twenty-five land conservancies have protected 152,000 acres, much of it outside the bay watershed. Legal impediments drastically restricted land trusts from operating in Virginia until 1988, but interest is now beginning to grow in this approach.

Trusts will always remain a complement rather than a substitute for effective state and national open space programs, but they are more critical than the gross acreage figures might suggest. Trusts, especially local ones (more than twenty-six have been incorporated in Maryland in just the last few years), are adept at preserving the small features that lend the landscape its character. The short stretch of tree-shaded byroad, the pretty little pond scarcely large enough for a boat, the corner where the huge old oak grows—these places are difficult for big open space programs to preserve. Yet they lend a quality to the local landscape that far exceeds the sum of their acreage.

Ag Preserves

Attempts to preserve open space specifically in the form of agriculture have also gained momentum in recent years. Pennsylvania has a $100 million farmland trust set up by a state bond issue. So far about 2,000 acres are enrolled on eleven farms.

Maryland's agricultural preservation program, which pays farmers the difference between the farm and development price for agreeing not to develop, has spent more than $100 million since 1977 to buy easements on more than 100,000 acres.

Although Virginia has no such program directly targeted at agriculture, the state has recently made a breakthrough in allowing counties to assess agricultural land at its farm value, rather than its development value. This measure has particular importance in preserving farmland that includes highly desirable shorefront along the bay and its rivers. Not every county, however, has chosen to take advantage of this mechanism.

new vision of how it will soon look. And if we were able to envision another overlay—the prevailing attitudes toward private property rights versus the common good—the future of the landscape would look even more bleak. Land use and development in the bay's watershed are overwhelmingly and fundamentally shortsighted and destructive—economically, environmentally, and culturally. We continue to use open space and unique parts of our natural heritage with the same wastefulness we have historically shown for other nonrenewable resources like coal and oil.

□ Comprehensive and enforceable visions of what kind of places we want to live in a generation from now are for the most part nonexistent. Virtually no working models of good land use have been executed on a regional scale. The specific zoning and subdivision codes that guide and shape growth are flawed and biased in favor of sprawl development and land speculation. Our placement of infrastructure, such as roads and sewers, often abets the problem.

□ Zoning, the basis for land use in the watershed, neither protects large areas of open space nor does it mandate dense growth patterns where growth is desirable. The ability to do both is critical to growth management and good land use. It is also critical if the traditional environmental agenda is to extend to the revitalization of our troubled urban areas. Dense growth, or clustering, does not mean the end of the single-family home. It means a range of densities—from high rises to townhomes and duplexes to compactly located single-family housing on individual lots. It must be accompanied by adequate infrastructure, such as sewers and roads, to achieve its full potential for minimizing environmental impact. Without changes in current attitudes, fostering compact growth is likely to be harder than keeping all growth out of an area.

□ Growth during the coming decades is going to use land at more than *three times* the rate it did in 1950 and nearly double the rate of the last decade or two. Smaller family size, the decline of cities and town centers, and the trend of large-lot, sprawl development are the reasons.

□ Pennsylvania alone among the principal watershed states has essentially rejected the "2020 Report," which warned that current growth trends could erode any progress we make toward restoring the environment in the bay region.

Part III

LESSONS AND RECOMMENDATIONS

CHAPTER 6

Four Key Battles

Even the most casual review of the state of the Chesapeake Bay region reveals disturbing trends. . . . These trends are not destiny.

—THE REPORT OF THE YEAR 2000 PANEL

The following case studies provide an in-depth look at four environmental issues where our success—or failure—may indicate how far we are likely to go toward saving the bay in the next few decades.

THE WASHINGTON BYPASS: THE WAY TO TRAFFIC HELL IS PAVED

Two vitally different futures for large segments of the Chesapeake Bay watershed were on the drawing boards as this decade began. Both are certain to shape the kind of place Marylanders and Virginians will inhabit and the quality of life they will enjoy well into the next century. These two scenarios are diametrically opposed and, all too typically, running along separate tracks, almost oblivious of their collision course. Together they represent one of those fundamental choices that will determine whether the next 2.6 million people (the projected increase for the watershed through the year 2020) can move there without further degrading the bay—or whether we are just kidding ourselves.

One future is represented by state commissions appointed in both Maryland and Virginia to recommend new growth management strategies for regional development. Chapter 5 discusses this issue in more detail, but essentially the commissions arose from the well-regarded "2020 Report," which in 1988 identified our current patterns of suburban sprawl development as the most destructive pattern of land use—with its greatest impacts on the Chesapeake Bay's resources. Sprawl development consumes the most forests, farmland, and other open space critical to protecting the bay from polluted runoff. It results in more paved areas, too, degrading more waterways with the disruptions in their natural watersheds. And such spread-out development absolutely ensures ever-greater use of automobiles, with the result of more pollution to both air and bay. With population continuing to expand, the urgent mandate to the growth commissions was to propose practical antidotes to such impacts—methods to achieve more compact development, maximizing open spaces while allowing denser growth in other areas, preserving clear boundaries between urban and rural lands.

Then there is the other future, a proposed $3 billion bypass of the congested Washington, D.C., region (Figure 6.1). Depending on the alternative chosen, its route would cover 57 to 93 miles with nine to twenty-eight major traffic interchanges through many sections that are now open space in Maryland and Virginia. More than 1 million acres now designated as open space in the growth plans of counties along the bypass routes will be at risk of developing, according to an analysis commissioned by the Chesapeake Bay Foundation.

Traditionally, the response to such risks by highway builders has been akin to the "just say no" credo of some antidrug campaigns. The growth impacts of highways are, in other words, assumed to be properly handled by affected localities. But the Bay Foundation's analysis concludes that approach simply hasn't worked—and won't work—given the magnitude and rapid buildup of growth pressure and land speculation caused by such mega-projects. Local planning, especially in the many rural areas affected, is almost always overwhelmed. Moreover, commercial development at the bypass's many interchanges would foster a new wave of spread-out commercial and industrial centers, drawing investment from struggling cities and towns both inside and outside the D.C. metro area.

The natural question that arises, of course, is "what choice do we have?" The metropolitan D.C. region is the bay watershed's version of traffic hell. Cars on the Capital Beltway, the area's original bypass

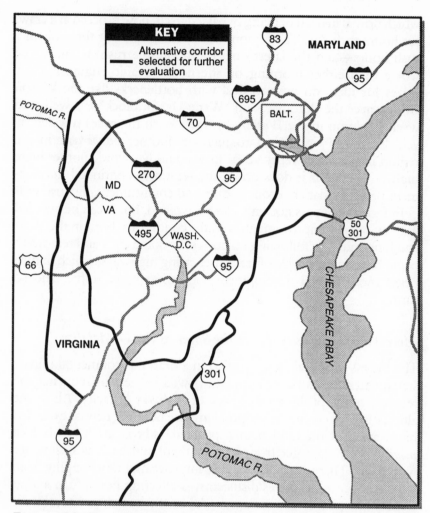

FIGURE 6.1. PROPOSED ROUTES FOR THE WASHINGTON BYPASS *Depending on the alternative chosen (either an eastern or western alignment), more than a million acres of land in Maryland and Virginia would be at risk of development—mostly without proper growth management in place to cope with its adverse economic and environmental impacts.* [Joseph Hutchinson, from Draft Environmental Impact Statement, Washington Bypass, Federal Highway Administration]

which now is in need of being bypassed itself, now proceed at a crawl for hours each day. The region now has not two but three distinct rush hours—and the latest one, the noontime rush, is said to be worse than either morning or afternoon. Traffic engineers offer prizes for ideas on how to deal with bottlenecks like the Wilson Bridge over the Potomac, and "Write Dr. Gridlock" is a well-read weekly column in the *Washington Post*. With the miles traveled by vehicles (VMT) projected to increase another *68 percent* in the region in the next twenty years, how could we avoid another huge highway—even if it does doom the region to continued development patterns that are economically and environmentally unsound?

In fact, the bypass not only can be avoided, but it can be avoided with an overall improvement in traffic conditions, both in the short and long run. The following sections offer some ways and reasons to begin breaking the cycle of traffic begetting highways, which in turn beget more sprawl development, begetting more traffic, and so forth.

More Traffic Capacity Is Not the Same as Better Mobility

The bypass proposal, as embodied in a draft environmental impact statement, follows the traditional, flawed process of reducing the region's traffic problems to a lack of highway capacity. All of the alternatives set out in the proposal involve building new or extended highways. But the fundamental problem is broader. It is a lack of *mobility*—we can't get from here to there and back as well as we would like. There are many ways to improve mobility, ranging from mass transit to incentives/disincentives affecting how much and at what hours people use their cars. All of these ideas get summarily dismissed by the bypass proposal's narrow focus on highways as the problem. In fact, highway congestion is less the disease than its symptom. The disease, of course, is perpetually increasing numbers of automobiles driven increasingly more miles each year.

More Highways Breed More Traffic

The impact statement for the bypass does not hold out the slightest hope that such a road will deliver the region from the deepening cycle of congestion and sprawl that is suffocating metropolitan areas in many parts of the country. That cycle, call it the "Los Angeles Syndrome," consists of new highway construction followed by more sprawling development, which causes more congestion on both the new and old highways and leads to a demand to build more new highways that will trigger more sprawl.

Vehicle miles traveled in the region would actually *increase* 39 to 43 percent over and above the projected 68 percent already forecast for the next twenty years, according to the bypass supporters' own draft environmental impact statement. Nor will all this increase be carried by the new bypass. Part will be imposed on other highways that are already projected to be overloaded *without* the bypass. Traffic would increase from 14 to 468 percent on various roads in the region if the bypass is built. The great bulk of through-traffic would continue to use existing routes, not the bypass. Thus it is not surprising that the bypass impact statement reveals that average speeds on area roads, if the bypass is built, would climb only from 32.2 mph to 33 mph—a gain of 0.8 mph at the price of $3 billion.

More Traffic Is Not Inevitable

The specter of having to make the best of a projected 70 percent increase in vehicle miles traveled in the next twenty years has an air of immutability about it; but in fact those forecasts are based on little more than an assumption that present trends will continue. A useful analogy here is the energy-demand projections published as gospel for the bay watershed during the 1960s by the Army Corps of Engineers. In 1965, by extrapolating from what was a period of frantic growth in energy consumption, the Corps forecast a *25-fold* increase in power generating needs by the beginning of the next century. The prediction raised shocking visions of a bay ringed with huge power plants like Calvert Cliffs.

In fact, due largely to energy conservation, the 25-fold increase has so far been less than a fivefold increase. Nor has it meant the end to our comfortable lifestyles—a fate that would surely have been prophesied had someone argued for a lowered rate of energy consumption in 1965. So it is that huge increases in traffic volumes do not represent the inevitable—only the consequence of doing nothing different in our present habits of growth and development and automobile use.

Profiting from Congestion

Just as mega-roads like the bypass are less than a solution to traffic, they have powerful economic attractions that have little to do with congestion and mobility. Traditionally, such roadways have been of more benefit to land speculators, to developers, and, in a short-term sense, to regional economies. The Greater Washington Board of Trade has boasted of its success in encouraging the development of the city (and now the region) on a grand scale by promoting new bridges and highways for the last sixty years. It also takes credit for creating the current pro-bypass coalition, DO IT–NOW (Develop Outer Interstate Throughways). But this is an exceptionally clumsy approach to economic development. And the galloping ruin of open space and degradation of the bay and its watershed make it an intolerable means of stimulating development.

Economically, too, the bypass is a boon only in the shortest of terms and narrowest of senses. The cost estimates—$1.4 to $3.4 billion, depending on the route—probably are low given the history of highway cost overruns. Nor do these estimates reflect the possibility that the additional traffic it encourages on U.S. Route 50 will require expansion of the Chesapeake Bay bridges (as well as upgrading dozens of existing highway links, secondary roads, and access roads). And the traditional, lavish 90 percent federal funding for interstate highways will most likely not be available for the bypass, since the authorization for that funding expires in 1991 and will probably be redrawn at a considerably lower level.

Finally, just as some areas of the country now forbid utilities to spend billions on new power plants if they can do better putting the same billions into reducing power demand through conservation, so must we look at what else might be done with $3 billion for a bypass that will only minimally improve mobility. For example, expansions are also being considered to the Capital Beltway ($1 billion), the Wilson Bridge over the Potomac ($750 million), the completion of Route 66 outside the Beltway ($620 million), and the completion of the D.C. subway ($2.7 billion). Virginia's Fairfax County in suburban D.C. is reported to have a $10 billion backlog in transportation projects it is not able to fund.

The Need for Reform

The bypass proposal highlights the need for three crucial reforms in transportation planning. First, the goal of transportation planning must be to achieve *mobility*, not just increase road capacity. Alternatives include bicycle paths, bus lanes, carpooling lanes, light rail, and heavy rail. In addition, alternatives should consider ways to reduce the *demand* for travel, particularly for single-occupancy vehicle use of roadways. Much traffic congestion, for example, is as much timing as anything. Strategies to even out and reduce peak flows of traffic—like "flextime" by employers and a break on bridge tolls during "off-peak hours"—can alleviate congestion without major new construction.

Second, land use planning and transportation planning must be integrated. The two are profoundly linked. Highways can trigger sprawl that crushes local land use plans; and sprawl development in turn forecloses options for mass transit and ensures more traffic that overloads new highways. Mass transit can never work economically unless growth management strategies can provide higher-density patterns of development. (Seven housing units per acre is about minimum to support a bus every thirty minutes in an area; twelve units per acre is needed for rapid transit like Washington's Metro.) Mixed-use communities with offices and residences grouped together can eliminate the need for commuting entirely.

And third, land use and transportation problems must be addressed on a regional basis. This means Washington, D.C., Maryland, and Virginia must develop a regional planning process and planning institutions. Even the most sophisticated counties, such as Montgomery, in the Maryland suburbs of Washington, cannot plan to protect themselves from being overwhelmed by traffic congestion pouring through their highways as a result of irresponsible growth in neighboring jurisdictions.

In a sense, the bypass proposal presents the bay region with an unusual opportunity. Because it is so big and has such far-reaching implications, it may help us avoid the type of incremental degradation by which the environment of so many areas gradually succumbs to unplanned growth and development. The bypass may force us to look at our future on a broad scale, much as the giant jetport proposed in the New Jersey Pine Barrens thirty years ago stimulated a far-reaching land use plan to preserve that state's unique natural heritage.

The bypass proposal represents a fork in the road. If we decide to commit $3 billion to this "solution," there will be no turning back for large segments of the watershed from the sprawl and congestion it will perpetuate. But dealing constructively and in concert with both the regional mobility crisis and the imperative to restore Chesapeake Bay could launch us into a new era of growth and environmental health.

CRABS: COULD THEY CRASH?

The blue crab, *Callinectes sapidus* ("most savory beautiful swimmer"), is the last great fishery of Chesapeake Bay. Since the early years of this century, when commercial crabbing began in earnest, the bay's waters have consistently yielded catches of 50 to 90 million pounds annually. Indeed, the bay produces more than half the nation's catch of blue crabs, and in 1983 the blue crab surpassed the oyster in Maryland for the first time as the state's most valuable seafood harvest.

As pollution, overfishing, and mismanagement have diminished the rockfish, oysters, and shad, the bay's entire seafood economy has grown more dependent on a single species—the crab—than at any time in history. Twenty years ago a crash in crab populations would have been a blow, but other fisheries would have taken up much of the slack. Today no such safety net remains.

Underlying the still rosy catch statistics on crabs are growing concerns that fishing pressure, both commercial and recreational, has burgeoned out of control in the last half of the 1980s. "Could we have a crash? Absolutely, no question about it," says Jack Travelstead, assistant commissioner for fishery management at Virginia's Marine Resources Commission. "We can no longer assume otherwise," agrees his counterpart in Maryland, William P. Jensen, of the Maryland Department of Natural Resources.

Diesels, Dredges, and High-Tech Tactics

It is in wintertime, at the bay's mouth near Cape Charles, that the reason for such concern is most visible. This is where, every autumn, the bay's "sooks," or mature female crabs, concentrate by the millions, drawn from as far away as Havre de Grace and Baltimore Harbor by the powerful urge to reproduce. The great hatching and nursery grounds around the Virginia capes are of such overwhelming importance to the species that Virginia since 1940 has proclaimed a 130-square-mile area there a sanctuary—off limits to any crabbing from June through mid-September, when spawning is in progress.

But each December, just as the sooks have burrowed down in the mud and sand bottom in semihibernation to let their "sponges" or egg masses develop, the gates of the sanctuary are rudely thrown open. It begins with an almost ritual gathering of crab boats around the center of the bridge-tunnel that crosses from Cape Charles to Virginia Beach. Big diesels rev and roar as the boats jockey for position. Heavy chain rockets through steel pulleys as each boat lowers twin dredges of heavy iron with rows of knifelike teeth 4 to 7 inches long. Then, en masse, often running so close to one another they cannot turn without warning the rest of the fleet on the marine radio, the crabbers begin plowing a swath through the sook-laden bottom like a giant combine through a wheat field. Before the season ends in March, millions of female crabs will be boarded, each the potential bearer of millions of eggs.

The best proof that dredging is not harmful, defenders say, is simply that it has been going on for decades and catches of crabs have not declined during that time. But catch figures by themselves, for crabs or any other bay species, are often misleading. A truer indication of the health status of crabs is something scientists call *catch per unit effort*. Simply stated it means that if you are catching the same number of crabs you did ten years ago but are using twice as many dredges or working twice as many hours to do it, then there are not as many crabs as there used to be.

In 1976 William Warner, author of the classic *Beautiful Swimmers*, described the winter dredge fleet as a fishery that had changed little in decades: "a select operation involving a fleet of no more than 70 vessels, and [because the work is so hard] the Virginia Marine Resources Commission is not deluged with applications [for licenses]." At that time the boats dragged two dredges measuring about 5.5 feet each. In recent winters the dredge fleet gathered in December numbered well over three hundred boats, ranging from a huge coastal trawler from Ocean City that was temporarily rigged for crabs to many boats barely large enough to handle the heavy work. The boats now sported twin dredges as large as 8 feet apiece, and special "diver" plates were added to make the dredges bite deeper into the bottom. There were three sinkings in one winter (including a head-on ramming) due mostly to inexperienced captains. Another winter claimed three lives, apparently the result of inexperience and an inadequate boat. The whole scene has increasingly had the look and feel of a goldrush, in contrast to the timeless picture of the fleet portrayed in *Beautiful Swimmers*.

Virginians often feel that their winter dredge fishery, conjuring ready images of "raping the nursery," tends to be the whipping boy for what is in fact a baywide problem. The dredgers seldom account for more than 9 million pounds a year, about 10 percent of the bay's recent annual commercial catches of crabs. Crab potters in both Maryland and Virginia catch the bulk of the commercial harvest. Recreational crabbers—you and I and our kids with those cheap, collapsible traps and chicken wings attached to strings—are estimated to catch between 5 and 20 million pounds a year in Maryland and perhaps half as much in Virginia.

How do we catch the crab? Let us count the ever-expanding ways. In the late 1930s a Virginian invented a device that would revolutionize crabbing. It was the crab pot, a 2-foot cube of wire mesh with bait in the center and funnels that allow hungry crabs to enter but not to exit. Before this, most crabbing had been restricted to shallow-water techniques like dipnetting and trotlining (baiting a long line stretched between two floats). Crab pots, usually fished on the bottom and marked by a cork on the surface attached to a line, meant that the entire bay, any depth, was now open for hunting.

During the next four decades "potting" became the method by which both Virginia and Maryland commercial watermen now catch as much as three-quarters of all crabs. The number of crab pot licenses issued annually on the bay and its rivers rose to about 2,800—then it nearly doubled, to about 5,100, at the beginning of the 1980s. More ominously, the number of pots each crabber used had begun to skyrocket. First it was 75 to 100, then 150; by the mid-1980s, 400 pots were common and 800 not unusual. Boats began to appear in Maryland with crews of three and four men (two is the usual complement) fishing as many as 1,500 pots.

With skill, endurance, and a crew of three, a captain can pull up to his pot, hook it by the cork, pull it up, empty it, rebait it, put it back overboard, sort the catch by size into bushel baskets, and hook the next pot—all in forty seconds. One such captain, Don Pierce of Rock Hall, Maryland, says he was only a casual crabber as recently as 1984. That was the year Maryland clamped a moratorium on catching striped bass to conserve what was left of that once abundant species. As Mr. Pierce illustrates, saving the striper shifted that much more pressure onto the crab. It is estimated that during the peak of crabbing on the bay there are now around 1 million crab pots—at least a 50 percent increase in the last seven years. Just to keep them baited is estimated to take a million pounds of fish a day.

Watermen are working harder now to get the same catch. Crab potters who used to work from April through November now go mid-March until mid-December. "You used to hear how much harder they worked in the old days, but now the old-timers say they never worked this hard or this long . . . they never had the boats to work in the weather we do now," says Lonnie Moore, a top crab dredger and crab potter from Tangier Island, Virginia. "The ones of us who are out here all year know—this old bay, she's overworked . . . this crabbin's out of control," says Richard Crockett, another Tangier crabber. The decline of oysters in the Virginia bay has meant that dozens of watermen from Tangier Island who used to head elsewhere in winter have now joined the dredge fishery, Mr. Crockett says. He and many Tangiermen now pursue crabs in every month of the year but March.

Technology is tweaking the pressure yet another notch. In parts of the bay nowadays the summer night erupts with powerful spotlights as early as 3 A.M. Visitors to remote Tangier Sound have been known to think the search was on for a boat sunk with all hands aboard. But it is just local watermen, who used to start around dawn, pursuing the crab ever earlier. How do they find a tiny cork marking a pot in the pitch black, maybe as much as 20 miles from home port? They rely on *loran*, an electronic device that uses radio signals from shore-based towers all along the nation's coastline to triangulate a boat's position with constant and precise accuracy. Even Maryland's ancient, wooden skipjacks now use loran to return to choice oyster bars with deadly accuracy.

A historic lawsuit in 1982 that allowed crabbers to cross the Maryland–Virginia line has also upped the pressure on the crab resource. Marylanders now account for about 10 percent of all Virginia's crabbing licenses—"and virtually every one of those who come this far are big-time crabbers, so the increase in pressure is significant," says Jack Travelstead.

Moreover, the demand for crabs has been growing by leaps and bounds, as anyone who goes to a steamed crab establishment can attest. The price per pound paid to watermen for hard crabs has risen more than twice as fast as inflation since the mid-1980s. Finally there is the recreational catch, perhaps the largest threat to the fishery in the long run. Watermen are working harder and more efficiently, but their numbers are not likely to rise much in the future (and might even decrease as it gets harder to make a full-time living on the water). But nearly 3 million more of the rest of us will move into the bay watershed by the year 2020. Our leisure time for activities like crabbing will increase, and our appetite for crabs is not likely to diminish.

The Need for Reform

Is there any limit in sight? Except for a two-year waiting period to become a commercial waterman in Maryland—and a generous 75-bushel-a-day limit on Virginia's crab dredgers—"there are no laws or regulations in effect which limit the total amount of gear that can be fished and none which regulate the total harvest." That is how a recent document on crab management from Maryland's Department of Natural Resources sums it up.

Both Maryland and Virginia recently have embarked on an unprecedented effort to prevent the crab from repeating the sad history of all too many other bay fisheries. Under bay cleanup agreements reached in 1987, the two states pledged to implement by 1991 formal plans to jointly manage crabs and other bay species. Crab management is seen as perhaps the most important of all the plans because the seafood industry is so dependent on it. "The blue crab is our test species for effective fisheries management," says Dr. L. Eugene Cronin, retired director of the University of Maryland's Chesapeake Bay research laboratories and an authority on crabs. "It spends its entire life in the bay (unlike many fish that migrate through the waters of the ocean and other states), it ranges the entire bay, it is of exceptional value, and every aspect of harvesting it is susceptible to our management—if we fall short of good management for this species, it is difficult to imagine real success for any species in the bay," Dr. Cronin observes.

Historically, "management" in both Maryland and Virginia has pretty much consisted of parceling out whatever was there, dividing crabbing areas up between potters and soft-crabbers, or between dredgers and potters, reserving certain waters for trotlines, and so forth. Both states set policy independently—as if crabs took heed of the invisible political line that separates the two states, crossing the bay at Smith Island. Thus Marylanders from Smith and Virginians from neighboring Tangier Island may crab within talking distance of one another but are bound by different rules on the size and sex of crabs they take home and the type of equipment they use to catch them.

A true management plan would be radically different. It would set flexible harvest quotas each year—higher if the crabs had enjoyed good spawning success, lower if they hadn't. The quotas would ensure that enough crabs were left to produce a healthy harvest in succeeding years. Managers could close a fishing season on short notice if quotas were being exceeded. A good plan would factor in economics too: Could watermen make more money under certain market conditions if they restricted their catch even more than the biologists required? Would catching fewer hard crabs result in catching more soft crabs, which have much higher market value? Social factors would also play a role. Although the most efficient way to take the annual harvest quotas might be to have just a few fishermen using high-tech methods, that approach might erode traditional watermen's communities and ways of life.

As of 1990, the states had met the bare technical stipulations for developing a crab management plan. But that groundwork amounted to what everyone acknowledges is largely a statement of intent, just a framework for the hard decisions that must follow in 1991. "I don't yet call it a management plan," Dr. Cronin says. "It still does not treat crabs as truly a single, baywide species, without regard to [state politics], and they still don't know how many crabs can safely be taken."

Ironically, the very nature of the blue crab, the qualities and circumstances that make it such a successful adaptation to Chesapeake Bay, are an obstacle to better management. The blue crab ranges from Nova Scotia to Argentina and has recently established itself in the Mediterranean and Japan. It thrives even in Baltimore's polluted harbor and in Norfolk's Elizabeth River, the bay's major hotspots for toxic chemicals. In fact, Baltimoreans catch them off the Patapsco sewage treatment plant and the Hanover Street bridge.

Pursued throughout the bay in every month of the year; torn from their winter beds, ripped asunder in the very act of mating; taken by pot, trotline, bank trap, dipnet, chicken neck, dredge, scrape, and weir; caught hard and caught soft—the crab yet endures. It has a lot going for it, scientists will tell you: It eats anything (just ask someone who has recovered summer drowning victims from the bay); it is pollution tolerant, salinity tolerant, temperature tolerant, and . . . "well, it just has a pissy attitude . . . it's the only thing we catch in the bay that will try to bite us back," one biologist says.

A critical question right now with the crab—one that has plagued attempts to manage other species in the past—is how many crabs must we leave to ensure healthy reproduction? It is clear that natural environmental factors, mostly beyond our control, are the key to good and bad crab years in the bay. The baby crabs that all hatch near the bay's mouth, for example, depend on the right combination of currents and winds to keep them from drifting off into the ocean. If those critical conditions fail, as they do sometimes, crab catches fall drastically a year later. In addition, since a single female crab produces millions of eggs, it takes only a handful of females, at least in theory, to produce enough eggs to repopulate the whole bay from year to year with as many crabs as we are currently harvesting (around 200 million a year).

Thus a dangerously simplistic argument is sometimes made: Since normal environmental factors overwhelm human influences in determining crab survival, as long as a relatively tiny number of crabs survive to release their eggs each year we should be okay. "We know that with zero stock [that is, adults spawning] you get zero recruits [offspring]—the question is at what point does the decline in stock begin to have an impact on recruits? With crabs there's nobody in the whole world who can say exactly where that point is," says Cluney Stagg, a researcher who has worked extensively with crab population studies in the Chesapeake. But he and other scientists all note that the same argument—a few adults can repopulate the whole bay—has been heard before with other species such as striped bass and shad. And while we argued the scientific points, these species were fished to such low levels that reproduction suffered and populations plummeted.

Capping: Prescription for Chaos?

Fishery managers say that for starters they want to cap baywide catches of crabs at current levels. Outside experts say that simply getting Maryland and Virginia in accord on the same plan represents major progress; but a simple cap doesn't go far enough, even for starters. Current harvest levels, they note, have seldom been higher. "One problem with just capping the harvest pressure where it is now is there have been, historically, tremendous natural swings (downward) in abundance—in the 20s, in the 40s, in the 60s," Dr. Cronin says. "If we have a natural decline again, and we surely will, when we have the present extreme level of dependence on crabbing, it's a prescription for chaos."

Another major obstacle is that, despite all the goals of managing crabs and other fisheries on a baywide basis, harvesting the bay always has been a tremendously fragmented affair. Dredging, for example, is mostly a Virginia fishery, and it would cost Maryland little to restrict the take of egg-bearing females. Virginians, on the other hand, note that Maryland potters catch large numbers of pregnant female crabs in the fall as they make their way to the dredging grounds to spawn. Certain areas of the mid-bay, both Maryland and Virginia, absolutely depend on catching the crabs when they are shedding their shells. Other areas of the bay depend almost wholly on hard crabs. In sum, it will prove difficult for state agencies to transcend local and factional politics when it comes down to setting specific regulations to meet overall goals.

Likely proposals to limit crab harvests will include a wide range of options: catch quotas; gear restrictions (limiting the size of crab dredges to 6 feet, for example); and limited entry (allowing no additional watermen on the bay unless they purchase the license of an existing waterman). Virginia appears likely to succeed in reducing dredge sizes, and both states seem serious about limiting entry. But there is another potentially explosive option the states have yet to grapple with: whether to restrict part-time crabbers and recreational crabbers, whose catches are now a substantial portion of the total harvest. This raises the fundamental question of whether a region with several million sport crabbers will continue to share the wealth with a few thousand commercial crabbers.

Ultimately the issue of whether the states are willing to set limits on crabbing is part of a larger question: Can we limit the whole range of human activity that increasingly is overwhelming the natural resources of Chesapeake Bay and its drainage basin? The new era of restrictions facing watermen is not unique to them. If the bay is to be restored, we are *all* going to have to face more limits on our behavior, as more and more of us enter the watershed.

As for crabs, the way we manage them in the 1990s will be a good test case for the whole new generation of fishery management plans upon which Maryland and Virginia are hanging their hopes of restoring the bay's seafood bounty and diversity. It is perhaps harder to install conservative management while a fishery is relatively healthy, as is the case with crabs. If we succeed, it will represent the first time it has happened before a species fell upon hard times.

It seems likely that in a few years we will know significantly more than we do now about the relationship between one year's crab spawning success and the next year's abundance of adult crabs. Until we do, catches of crabs, both sport and commercial, should be capped at a level thought to be sustainable. To the extent that knowledge is imperfect for determining such a level, a conservative figure ought to be used. If we follow past behavior, we will wait until the crabs signal us in no uncertain terms that we have pushed them too far. But too much is riding on *Callinectes*, too many watermen are too dependent on this one species, to take such an enormous risk.

CENTRE COUNTY: A FARMER'S WORK IS NEVER DONE

With the cold March wind whipping down the upper Penns Valley here in Centre County, Pennsylvania, the warmth in Ralph Rimmey's sunny farmhouse kitchen feels good. Mr. Rimmey, cutting you a thick slice of fresh bread, spreading it thick with butter, proffering a steaming mug of tea, does not seem much like an enemy of Chesapeake Bay. He's a lean, affable man of fifty-six, steel-gray hair, easy smile. He loves bay oysters and has read every page of Michener's *Chesapeake*. He thinks the animal rights activists who have been zeroing in on farms like his of late "have some good points . . . I never have liked the way they use a big whip to make animals run around for buyers at auctions."

It is hard, and uncomfortable, to reconcile the images: earnest, likable farmer versus water polluter; producer of foamy, pure milk emerging immaculately from glass and stainless steel facilities versus producer for years and years of ugly, manure-laden water oozing directly (until recent improvements) into nearby Sinking Creek. Mr. Rimmey and his son farm a few hundred acres and milk seventy cows; and they do it on lands smack in the middle of the drainage basin of the Susquehanna River—source of half the Chesapeake's fresh water and a substantial amount of the bay's pollution. (See Figure 6.2.) Enough fertilizers and animal manure from operations just like Mr. Rimmey's make it downstream to the bay these days that it does not seem possible for Maryland and Virginia to restore the estuary's health without dramatic reductions in these pollutants from places like Centre County.

A centerpiece of recent, stepped-up efforts to control agricultural

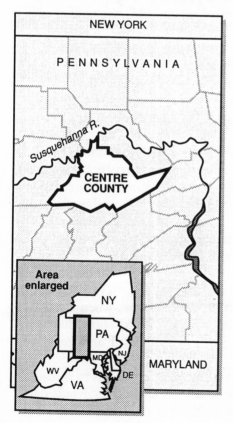

FIGURE 6.2. CENTRE COUNTY, PENNSYLVANIA. [Joseph Hutchinson]

pollution here and in the rest of the bay watershed is the Chesapeake Bay Financial Assistance Funding Program, which combines federal and state money with farmers' money (usually 80 percent government and 20 percent farmer) to reduce pollution. The goal is to reduce by 40 percent in the next ten years the polluting nitrogen and phosphorus—ingredients in fertilizer and manure—that now run into the water from farms, as well as from lawns, golf courses, and city streets. (In the Susquehanna, agriculture appears to be the principal source of such runoff, although the impacts of airborne pollutants may turn out to be substantial also.)

Looking for Signs of Progress

This case study looks at how the cleanup program is working in one county, selected by asking agriculture and water quality officials and environmentalists to recommend a jurisdiction that was neither a showcase nor a horror story, a place representing the kind of progress that is being made.

Mr. Rimmey heard of the new program by word of mouth. He signed a contract to capture and store the tons of manure his cows produce each week behind concrete barriers to keep it from running off to the creek. (A single dairy cow may produce 100 pounds of manure daily.) Two small streams that run through the swampy pasture adjoining Mr. Rimmey's dairy barn will be covered and enclosed in pipe to further protect against polluted runoff. Some of his better cropland will be turned into additional pasture, so manure concentrations from grazing cows will be spread out more. He has also fenced Sinking Creek to keep his cows from eroding its banks and using it as an open sewer.

Why now? "I'd say it was a matter of pride," Mr. Rimmey says. "I'm right on a road, and people ride by here and think, 'Look at that mess, and this man's selling milk.' A lot of the things the [bay cleanup program] recommended, I knew I should've been doing years before. I'd see my cows in the hot summer, when I was out baling hay, down there in Sinking Creek, and I'd know they were shitting in the water. . . . You just put things off and never get around to them."

Mr. Rimmey represents real progress, but he still has to spread all that manure on his land. And if he is typical of Pennsylvania dairy farmers, the combination is probably more nitrogen and phosphorus than the crops need, and the excess is still a problem for the bay. He is thinking of taking the next step in controlling pollution and joining Murry McJunkin's crop management association. Their techniques, many experts think, represent some of the best strategies for meeting Pennsylvania's (and the whole watershed's) agricultural pollution control goals.

Mr. McJunkin is seated in an office next to an Apple computer and the *Wall Street Journal*. He holds a graduate degree from Penn State and for twenty years ran the ag products division of U.S. Steel Corporation. He farms 600 acres of grain in partnership with a neighboring animal operation with 1,500 hogs and 130 milk cows. He owns not a single plow; he applies less fertilizer than most farmers and often does not bother to spray his crops to protect them from pests. Far from being a neglectful farmer, Mr. McJunkin epitomizes the way better management and better information increasingly must substitute for the "better safe than sorry" application—often overapplication—of farm chemicals and fertilizers.

The crop management association Mr. McJunkin has been instrumental in promoting began in 1979 with some of the region's better farmers' hiring pest experts to "scout" their crops, recommending that they apply pesticides only when concentrations of pests passed a certain threshold. Sometimes this meant more spraying than normal; but often it saved them considerably on pesticide use. Now there are about fifty members and 8,000 acres in the program, and the scouting fee of $4.75 an acre paid by each member is recouped several times over in savings on chemicals, Mr. McJunkin says. He no longer uses any insecticides on his corn. Rotating his fields between corn and other crops like alfalfa is enough to keep corn pests from building up. Rather than disturb the soil with traditional plowing, he uses "no-till" planting, reducing pollution and saving energy.

Perhaps most important for Chesapeake Bay, Mr. McJunkin and about half the association members have entered what is called a "nutrient management" program in conjunction with Penn State. This begins with a rather intimidating ten-page worksheet on which a farmer carefully tracks all the ways nutrients (that is, nitrogen and phosphorus) enter his farm—via commercial fertilizers, via purchased feeds, via nitrogen-fixing bacteria in crops such as alfalfa and soybeans—as well as all the ways nutrients leave, as in crops shipped to market, livestock sold, and manure. The bottom line is to calculate a nutrient balance. The closer a farmer comes to putting only as much nutrients on the soil as his crops need, the more money he saves on fertilizers and the less nitrogen and phosphorus are left to run off into waterways. Mr. McJunkin has cut back 35 to 40 percent on his use of commercial fertilizer. Experts all agree that nutrient management is the single most important practice the bay restoration program should encourage.

Tom Boldin, a grain and dairy farmer near Bellefont, is testament to what Dale Baker, an old-time Penn State ag professor, says: "Farming needs science, but it's really an art." Mr. Boldin, thirty-nine, is also president of the county conservation board that oversees the Chesapeake Bay funding programs. Just now he's giving a mini-seminar on the qualities of cow excrement: "Three kinds we get here: 'free stall,' which is basically slop and soup; 'manure pack,' very firm, mixed with the straw bedding; 'tie stall' (where the cows are milked), in between the other two. The point is you design your system around these differences." For example, he has devised a technique (not in any book of established conservation practices, he says) to cover bare cropland with a manure slurry that dries quickly to a crust, minimizing the need to use weed control chemicals and stopping soil erosion.

Mr. Boldin is prone to quote George Washington and Thomas Jefferson, "some of our greatest farmers," on the virtues of crop rotation. He changed seed dealers to get just the right kind of fast-growing, wide-leaf corn that comes up early and shades out weeds, thereby eliminating more chemical weed control. His crop rotations use alfalfa in a field for four years. Since alfalfa fixes its own nitrogen from the air, it eliminates the need for nitrogen fertilizer the first year he grows corn. And by carefully timing his fertilizer applications in each succeeding year, he can minimize the pollution potential greatly.

Assessing the Overall Picture

So it is that Centre County, and probably much of the bay's watershed, does not lack for examples of progress or even demonstrations of extraordinary talent and ingenuity by farmers in reducing pollution. But what of the overall picture? Is Centre County really ahead of the curve, making progress on a scale that offsets continued growth in animal numbers (and animal manure)? Is the goal of 40 percent nutrient reduction in the next decade going to happen? It does not seem likely at the current pace. While Mr. McJunkin's crop management association has fifty members with 8,000 acres (about half of whom are doing full-fledged nutrient management), the county has nearly nine hundred farms and some 93,000 acres of cropland. Across Pennsylvania's whole Susquehanna drainage, a potential acreage of more than 3 million, fewer than 71,000 acres are in crop management associations.

One perspective on progress is the map on Ted Onufrak's wall. Mr. Onufrak, manager of Centre County's Conservation District, administers the bay cleanup program for farmers. Red pins in the map represent the number of farms under contract since the program geared up in 1987; white pins show the number of applicants for contracts. There are twenty-five reds and twelve whites. "Thirty-seven farms in a county with 860," Mr. Onufrak says, gesturing at the map and its pins. "You'll never overcome the problem this way, and a big reason is money."

The money—Centre County is getting about $100,000 a year—is enough to contract with about three farms annually, Mr. Onufrak says. In other words, the pins on his map, representing about 5 percent of the county's farms, also represent about ten years of work at current levels of staffing and funding. That is not quite so dismal as it sounds because the bay program is at least attempting, with mixed success, to target the worst-polluting farms first. In addition, there are other ongoing efforts such as the Soil Conservation Service's erosion control programs. These are not primarily oriented at stopping manure and fertilizers, but they do control them to an extent. Finally, some farmers take steps to control pollution without any government assistance.

Still, the goal of 40 percent nutrient reductions presently seems beyond the reach of the bay program here. Part of the problem is that the bay program is spending most of its scarce funds on the most capital-intensive kinds of projects—primarily concrete and steel storage structures called manure pits. And these are not necessarily the most effective pollution controls, many experts say. Farmers like manure pits because they give them the ability to hold manure for weeks or months (depending on pit size) rather than having to spread it on their fields every day, including days and seasons when more of it is likely to run off into the water.

Yet they still have to spread it on their land sometime, and there is considerable doubt that just altering the timing of spreading is making a big dent in pollution reaching the bay. "We see manure storage as a neutral for the bay, or a plus, but not a big plus," says Doug Beegle, a soil fertilization specialist at Penn State. "I just question three manure pits a year is what Centre County should be using most of its money to buy."

Mr. Rimmey, who has opted for a very small version of a pit (it stores a week's worth of manure), and Mr. Boldin, who does not have one, both say they have known too many cases of pits leaking and giving way. They often tend to be built near streams, since that is where the "worst case" farms tend to have their barnyards. "Manure is highly corrosive, and these things eventually can give way . . . we're looking at building a series of time bombs along lots of trout streams," Mr. Onufrak says. More than a hundred manure pollution cases, the great bulk of them leakages or spills from manure pits, were investigated by Pennsylvania's Fish Commission between 1985 and 1988. An estimated 60,000 fish, including minnows, were killed. Fines of $55,000 were assessed.

There are advocates of pits, such as Mr. McJunkin, who say the ability to store and spread manure when a farmer desires helps greatly in an overall nutrient management strategy. But some Penn State agricultural scientists go so far as to say manure pits are "counterproductive" and "no public money should be spent on them." One as yet unmeasured problem with manure storage devices, say Penn State ag researchers, is that a considerable quantity of the nitrogen escapes to the air and "probably comes back down on the land somewhere."

Currently, state and federal officials are assuming that all manure stored in pits is, in large part, kept out of waterways forever and thus counts toward the 40 percent nutrient reduction goal. But taking anywhere near "full credit" for that manure, which still gets spread on the land, is bogus accounting, most independent observers agree. In some areas of the watershed, too, considerable public funds and farmers' money are being spent on liquefying and storing manure in tanks. This makes handling and spreading more convenient, but it can also literally inject large quantities of nitrogen quickly into groundwater with no chance for it to be broken down and recycled from the soil to crops. The groundwater in turn carries the nutrient to waterways in subsurface flows.

The debate over manure pits highlights a more serious flaw in the bay funding program. Although it is obvious, talking to farmers here, that they feel under much more public pressure to "clean up our act or be regulated," virtually all programs, including the bay funding, remain purely voluntary. The voluntary approach makes it impossible to target the worst farms or to emphasize the best pollution control practices.

"We discourage manure pits, we'd like to stay away from them," Mr. Onufrak says, "but that's what the farmers want. And without it, we can't get them to join the cost-sharing program or sell them on additional [pollution control] practices. . . . It's all a negotiation. You can't even make a farmer fence his cattle away from crapping in a trout stream if he doesn't want to." This also means that although the bay funding program has attracted some of the county's most polluting farms, you can still ride the back roads and pick out the places that have chosen not to participate—even though they have hogs wallowing in waterways and are polar opposites of Mr. Boldin and Mr. McJunkin.

Picking the Best Tactics

And how would the experts spend the bay program money if they could tell the farmers what to do? Several items would have priority:

- Practicing nutrient management of the type Mr. McJunkin is involved in. This approach aims at putting no more nutrients on the land than the crops can use, thus reducing pollution in runoff.
- Fencing livestock from streams. This practice not only keeps manure and urine out but prevents erosion of the banks that causes siltation, deadly to trout eggs and larvae.
- Planting cover crops such as winter wheat or rye or similar vegetation. Cover crops hold soil in place during the winter and also remove nutrients left over in the soil after the primary crop was harvested.
- Establishing buffer strips of forest between farms and all waterways. The forest stops runoff of nutrients and soil, shades streams so they don't get too hot for fish, and provides wildlife habitat to boot.

For the most part, the bay funding program will share costs on all of these practices, Mr. Onufrak says, "but farmers aren't used to doing them, and . . . many of them just don't."

Mr. Onufrak and farmers around Centre County also say there are a number of other problems that need to be corrected for the bay funding program to be effective:

- The time for implementing cleanup plans on a farm has been condensed from five years to two—too fast for many farmers to come up with their share of the money.
- The steps required from initial contact with a farmer through implementation of his cleanup are a bureaucratic nightmare of multilevel approvals and other red tape, which puts many people off. "You look at what we have to go through with one farmer, multiply it by the whole state, and try to get it done in two years . . . it's pathetic," Mr. Onufrak says.
- Farmers say there is so much turnover in staff of the bay funding program that they never get comfortable with one person. (Nor do the personnel get expert on the local situation.) Salaries for technicians in the program are set by county governments. Less than half of these positions in Pennsylvania are now allotted the full salary permissible. Average salaries range between $14,000 and $16,000. (Within a few months after he was interviewed for this book, Mr. Onufrak left his position.)
- An innovative voluntary program administered by the state game commission to help farmers fence their streams away from livestock has made a good deal of progress. But more farmers who might join say they don't like the requirement that farms be opened to hunting. "It should be a water quality program, not a hunting program," said one farmer who refused the free fencing.

Mr. Boldin, who is chairman of the local board that oversees the bay funding program, says that with money and staffing you could get 600 of the county's 850 or so farms signed up for pollution control programs easily. "But," he adds, "you need someone who can really sell it at the grass roots." Understaffing also appears to be a big problem in the federal Soil Conservation Service (SCS) in Centre County—typical of a wider problem in the watershed. It is SCS people who must actually go out with farmers and design and lay out the pollution control measures agreed to in each bay program contract.

Right now, says Larry Schardt, the county director for SCS, about a quarter of the cropland in the county has good controls on soil erosion. To double that, he says, will be the work of "years and years." It takes a forty-hour week to design a good soil conservation plan for one farm, he says. SCS staffing in Centre County has gone from five persons to three. In Pennsylvania, it has gone from about 350 to less than 250 in the last decade (recently back up to 270)— even as the workload from programs like the bay cleanup has risen dramatically.

Coping with Growth

Centre County, like all of Pennsylvania's Susquehanna basin, is more aware than ever of Chesapeake Bay and how upstream activities affect Maryland and Virginia's waters. Not surprisingly, however, local environmental concerns remain more of a rallying point there than problems manifested several hours drive from the Nittany Valley. An obvious one is growth. Pennsylvania officials frequently have said that the only environmental problem in the Susquehanna region is animal population, not human population. Governor Casey has dismissed as "draconian" the recent "2020 Report" on population growth and development, which said that unmanaged growth could wipe out all other gains in pollution control in the next thirty years.

But such rejection of the need for growth management seems shortsighted in light of the reality here in Centre County. The county's population of 125,000 already exceeds the state's twenty-year (2010) projection. Firm development proposals around the Penn State part of the county will mean a doubling of population there, and proposed expansions of sewage treatment plants will be at 80 percent capacity as soon as they are completed. Virtually all the farmland and much of the forest in the region are zoned for typical suburban sprawl development that is consumptive of open space and economically the least beneficial to the tax base.

Literally every farmer interviewed mentioned nearby farmland that had just been priced out of his reach by land speculation. Spring Creek, one of the nation's finest trout streams, is severely threatened by development of its watershed, new sewage discharges, and pumping of groundwater that feeds it. Pennsylvania's ability to control growth is fragmented among dozens of different townships and, despite a coalition of several jurisdictions in the Penn State area, remains inadequate to protect either open space or Spring Creek.

In sum, Centre County's whole environment could benefit from adopting a broader spectrum of Chesapeake Bay cleanup strategies being pursued downstream, such as growth management and stream watershed protection. It would help the bay and the county as well. In its agricultural cleanup, the county needs substantial increases in money and staffing, as well as a redirection of its current spending priorities, if it is to achieve a true 40 percent reduction of nutrients that are polluting the bay.

THE POTOMAC: A (QUALIFIED) SUCCESS STORY

In the spring of 1990 the aspiring environmental president, George Bush, placed the presidential seal of approval on the decades-long effort to clean up the Potomac River when he spent an afternoon going bass fishing on the stretch of the river below the Wilson Bridge, in sight of National Airport. This action was more than a public relations gesture. At least one national magazine, *Fishing World*, has recently described the Potomac as "arguably the best bass river in the East today." In their third annual "State of the Chesapeake Bay" report, EPA and the states of the bay region call the river "one of our nation's major success stories in water quality restoration."

While there is undeniably success and much encouragement for Chesapeake Bay to be found in the Potomac story, it is less clear whether it is a model for the rest of the bay. This case study examines the elements of our brightest achievement to date in cleaning up the Chesapeake system.

From National Disgrace to Showcase

The history of the Potomac's decline—President Johnson called it a "national disgrace" in 1965, and he was probably not the first—parallels that of most of the nation's major rivers. The nineteenth century was characterized by two trends. First, fishery harvests reached astounding heights in the Potomac. It was "not uncommon to pull 43,000 shad or 300,000 herring in one seine haul," one report said. One haul of 450 rockfish with an average weight of 60 pounds was documented. Hundreds of sturgeon were captured on a single night near the U.S. Arsenal in Washington. This was in the 1830s.

The second trend concerned pollution. As population grew to 75,000 in 1870, sewers were constructed, beginning in 1860, to convey wastes to the river. Ominous conditions began to appear. In 1894 the U.S. Public Health Service said: "At certain times of the year the river is so loaded with sediments as to be unfit for bathing as well as for drinking and cooking purposes. It contains fecal bacilli at all times." Yet as late as 1911, President Theodore Roosevelt, the French ambassador, and the American conservationist Gifford Pinchot could find evening relaxation in swimming across the Potomac.

By the 1930s conditions had further deteriorated. The population had increased nearly tenfold to about 600,000, and much of it had been connected to the ever-expanding sewer system, still discharging largely raw wastes directly to the Potomac. The river was closed to swimming and low dissolved-oxygen levels endangered the fishery resources. In 1938 President Franklin Roosevelt directed the first sewage treatment plant be built at Blue Plains, on the river's eastern bank just upstream from the Wilson Bridge. In spite of the rudimentary treatment applied to 130 million gallons of sewage per day, exploding population continued to cause declines in river quality. In 1951 thousands of fish were killed by low oxygen levels and the *Washington Post* called the river an "open sewer." A higher level of treatment was added to the huge plant in 1959, and disinfection of the wastewater began in 1968. Yet as the area's population exceeded 2 million, a 1969 conference called the river "a severe threat to anyone who comes in contact with it."

The prognosis was bleak. In addition to Blue Plains, which treated all of the waste from the District of Columbia and much of that from surrounding counties, ten other plants used the river, treating wastes from the outer suburbs in Maryland and from the rapidly growing Virginia communities of Alexandria and Arlington County. By 1970, after decades of "progress" being outstripped by population, the loads of oxygen-demanding waste, nitrogen, and phosphorus discharged to the river were greater than they had been in 1932 when there was no treatment.

For the first time, however, a clear goal had been set. "Clean water by 1975," declared President Johnson in his 1965 condemnation of the river's quality. The federal Water Pollution Control Act amendments of 1972 provided the regulatory tools and, perhaps most critical, the financial resources to achieve it. Armed with the carrot of federal funds and threatened by the stick of enforcement, state and local officials went to work at Blue Plains and the other Potomac plants.

The results have been remarkable. At Blue Plains alone, nearly $1 billion has been spent to produce a sewage treatment plant that treats over 300 million gallons a day of sewage to the highest level of any plant of comparable size in the country. The amounts of phosphorus, a key pollutant of the river and the bay, in the plant's discharge are now less than was discharged by a much smaller population prior to World War I. Indeed, there is actually more phosphorus in the "natural" water coming downriver than in the Blue Plains discharge. The amount of phosphorus put in the river from the plant has fallen in the last twenty years from more than 8 million pounds annually to about 63,000 pounds. Similar progress has been made at the other, smaller Washington area plants.

And the river around the nation's capital has responded. Dissolved oxygen levels now exceed the standard necessary to support aquatic life. Submerged aquatic vegetation, important habitat for many river species, has returned. The fishery resources appear to be rich as exemplified by the return of a modest sportfishing industry. Recreational uses of the river have proliferated. A River Raft Race began in 1978 and the Potomac RiverFest was established in 1981. The diversity of wintering waterfowl is as rich as it has been in modern times.

No Cause for Complacence

The river has been restored. But there is nothing to be complacent about. While water quality has dramatically improved, there have been unexplained symptoms of continuing problems. In 1983 one of the worst algae blooms in the river's history—a clear indicator of pollution—covered wide areas from the Wilson Bridge south to Gunston Cove. Its causes have never been completely explained other than to attribute it to a "hidden" source of nutrients somewhere in the river that was released by a combination of weather and river flow characteristics.

While the submerged grasses have returned, a large component of this comeback was an exotic species, hydrilla, introduced by accident to the river. It proved to be a boon—absorbing huge quantities of nutrients and filtering sediment from the water to where it was clean enough for native varieties of grass to come back also. Many questions remain, however, whether hydrilla, like many "invader" species in nature, may vanish as quickly as it appeared (or whether it will prove impossible for the native grasses to compete with it).

The sportfishery business is back, but this may not mean that the diversity of fisheries is as healthy as it was in earlier times. A survey at the turn of the century found eighty-four species of fish; this number had declined to seventy-eight by 1988. Two extremely important bay species, the American shad and the striped bass, have failed to show clear trends of recovery in the Potomac since their numbers crashed from overfishing and pollution in the last decade.

Finally, while water quality and natural resources have improved from Washington for several miles downstream, there is no evidence that the recovery has extended to the vast reaches of the lower Potomac. In fact, during 1985 and 1986 the dissolved oxygen levels in the river below the Route 301 bridge were worse than they had been in the prior three years. The reason for the lower river's condition is not known yet. It may be that discharges of nitrogen from the sewage plants, a pollutant that doesn't affect the freshwater portions of the upper river, are causing problems in the different chemistry of the saltier, lower river. Or it may be the influence of more polluted water pushing into the Potomac from the main bay. Controlling nitrogen from sewage to the level of technology used to control phosphorus would likely end up costing several hundred million dollars more.

A second area of concern about the Potomac comes into play if we stop focusing narrowly on water quality and examine the broader environmental picture. The history of the river for the last two centuries is one of population growth and development followed by catch-up efforts at controlling its polluting impact. It was only in the last two decades when extraordinary amounts of federal funds were available that management finally got ahead of the curve and actually "improved" the river. The massive system of waste management constructed to achieve that end, with sewers extending across an area rivaling the drainage basins of sizable rivers, has encouraged the development of an enormous population center on the banks of the Potomac. More than 10 percent of everyone living in the five-state watershed of Chesapeake Bay—an area stretching from New York nearly to North Carolina—discharge their wastes through the pipes of a single facility: Blue Plains.

While the direct pollution effects of this population have been controlled, at least in the short run, there has been far less progress in controlling the indirect polluting impacts of growth—such as destruction of natural habitat and the runoff of sediment and other pollutants from construction and the paved surfaces of developed areas. Thus the very act of controlling the simple problem of human waste may have allowed for the creation of an urban and suburban complex that has within it the seeds for long-term degradation of the environment within parts of the Potomac watershed. Partly because we have been able to maintain legal water quality in a stretch of the Potomac, we have felt free to accept continued explosive growth of the magnet of economic activity that is the Washington metropolitan area.

As growth continues, there is serious question whether either technology—Blue Plains removes phosphorus from sewage to the limits of technology—or finances can provide the continued treatment of wastes necessary to maintain the progress of the last two decades. (For example, plans are under way to expand the capacity of the Blue Plains plant from 309 million to 370 million gallons. With current technological limits this expansion may actually produce an increase in phosphorus discharge.) And federal funds to manage sewage wastes have all but disappeared. This funding was central to the region's success in restoring the river. It is also virtually certain that no other area of the bay—or the nation—can expect again to receive money for sewage treatment on the billion-dollar level of Blue Plains and surrounding treatment plants.

The cleanup of the Potomac is a success if we look narrowly at the upstream, fresher-water parts of the tidal river, where phosphorus removal is the key. It is also a success if we ignore certain elements of the larger environment (some of the country's worst traffic gridlock, for example, and a rapid loss of open spaces). But there is no guarantee that the river has truly escaped its history of population growth outstripping technology and overwhelming water quality. The 1987 Chesapeake Bay cleanup agreement, which includes the District of Columbia, is a laudable but untested attempt to ensure this does not happen again. It commits the states to a 40 percent reduction in phosphorus and nitrogen by the year 2000. These levels, once achieved, are meant to be "caps," never allowing pollution to rise, even as population increases.

Finally, there is the problem of ever larger volumes of sludge—the semisolid residue from treating sewage—that results from higher levels of treatment and growing volumes of waste. While sludge is currently handled through composting and through land application on farms, there are limits to how much can economically be disposed of this way in a given region. The alternative solution—incinerating the sludge—poses problems in a region already concerned about its air quality.

Sewage treatment, no matter how technologically impressive, must be integrated into an overall system of growth management and land use controls if we are to ensure the long-term viability of the bay's watershed and make sure that another cycle of deterioration in the river does not set in. This will mean limiting the amount of growth to a level in keeping with much more than just the ability of technology to remove certain water pollutants like phosphorus. Additional considerations range from the amount of pollution control money that is available in a region to the amount of open space needed for future generations. Growth and development planning should not work backward from the end of the discharge pipe, no matter how well engineered that pipe may be. Matched against this vision, Blue Plains and the Potomac cleanup indeed represent a success story, but certainly not a panacea.

CHAPTER 7

Recommendations

To: the integrity of the Chesapeake ... and the constant prayer that somehow we might change our course and focus 100 percent on the preservation of that integrity, instead of our present focus on using the hell out of it.

—INTRODUCTORY NOTES TO THE RECORD ALBUM
CHESAPEAKE BORN BY TOM WISNER

At the beginning of the book we set out how we must measure our cleanup and restoration of the troubled Chesapeake to date: If we measure progress by the money and effort expended on bay restoration, and by the increasing sophistication of our environmental regulations and scientific knowledge, then we have been making progress fairly steadily since the first Earth Day in 1970. But if we measure it by the responses we see to date in the bay's water quality, in its fisheries, and in its resilience, then progress is more muddled.

We put the challenge facing us in this perspective: We must not only reduce the present level of human impacts enough to restore the bay; we must also reduce those impacts enough to offset another 2.6 million people (a very conservative figure) who are projected to move into the watershed by the year 2020. This challenge, as the preceding chapters have made clear, is not being met now. And despite many notable efforts and some successes, there are many areas where it does not have much likelihood of being met unless we change tactics. Too often with restoration of Chesapeake Bay, we still are winning battles but not the war. We find this unacceptable—environmentally, economically, and morally.

252

It does not have to be this way. There is no reason to accept the often-voiced vision of our environmental future—that the best we can hope for is to slow the inevitable decline or hold the line at some semidegraded level. The brighter vision articulated in this chapter will not happen without fundamental change, however, including more limits on individual behavior in using the bay and its watershed: 15 million of us simply cannot go on behaving as if there were still only a few million of us. But the endpoint of such restraint can be a higher quality of life for all. The opposite of a mob's disjointed shouting need not be enforced silence; it can be the vibrant harmonies of a choir. We seek more than a renewed commitment to fighting the environmental wars. We want to redefine the nature of battle.

WHAT KIND OF BAY DO WE WANT?

Before setting out detailed recommendations based on the issues and conclusions presented throughout the book, let us articulate where it is we want to head. How will we know success when we see it? What kind of bay do we want?

A Clearer Bay

We want a *cleaner* bay too, of course, but defining "clean" ties us into knots over water quality standards. Clean enough for what— shipping? Swimming? Fishing? Drinking? Clean enough for fish? For what kind of fish? Carp or trout? On the other hand, *clear* water is easy to comprehend, easy to measure; and in the bay's case, clearer water means we are licking two of our biggest pollution problems: sediment and nutrients. And that in turn will mean we are improving conditions for the return of underwater grasses and improving oxygen in the water.

How clear is clear enough? We cannot be precise but, based on abundant anecdotal information, clear enough that we can see bottom 4 feet down where now we can see it only in 2 feet. Clear enough that places 12 to 15 feet deep at Smith Island, where old-timers recall spying crabs off the bottom in summer and catching them with a dipnet, are visible again. And clear enough for Bernie Fowler to see his toes in the Patuxent River some fine June day soon.

Bernie is a Maryland legislator who led the fight to clean up his native Patuxent, which drains central and southern Maryland. His story of wading out, shoulder deep, as a youth forty years ago chasing soft crabs and looking down and seeing his feet on the bottom has become a local legend. Every second Sunday in June, on Bernie Fowler Day, the senator and supporters of the major cleanup now in progress on the river dress up in their best and wade out to look for their toes. (They are still looking, but still hopeful, and having a ball in this annual renewal of faith in the river.)

The point of this is that science alone will never be able to give us all the standards we need for judging success or failure in maintaining Chesapeake Bay and its watershed. Knowledge of the bay can never substitute fully for respect for its natural integrity. All citizens of the watershed, whether they live by a river, a forest, a marsh, or a tiny creek, should feel encouraged and supported to set their own personal standards, or ones gathered from their elders, to help scientists and regulators judge whether or not we are doing right by Nature. Judge with your head, most certainly, but also with your heart (and your toes).

A Resilient Bay

Chapter 1 showed how estuaries like Chesapeake Bay are, by nature, among the most variable, dynamic, and disorderly of environments, as the flow of forty-seven rivers collides with the intruding ocean in the mixing bowl that is the estuary. Creatures there are well adapted to a measure of chaos. But in cutting nearly half the watershed's forests, filling more than half its marshes, polluting 90 percent of its underwater grasses to death, and destroying an estimated 99 percent of its oysters, humans have destroyed many of the natural mechanisms that acted to buffer and filter the bay against floods and drought and pollution and have disrupted the pathways by which food and energy moved through the estuary.

The watershed must not lose any more of its ability to soak up the rain, as the original forest and wetlands did across all the land. This capacity reduced floods and replenished the underground water table to maintain the flows of rivers and streams in drought. Wetlands and forest also filter pollutants from the water and clarify it before it runs downstream to the bay. Resilience aplenty also lay in the bay's bottom, where lush meadows of underwater grasses and vast shoals of oysters soaked up and filtered and evened out the pulses of nutrients and sediment that enter the bay, further enabling it to rebound from both natural and human disruptions.

Human structures, from stormwater detention ponds to agricultural manure pits, can be useful tools to supplement natural resilience; but as the preceding chapters point out, they are far from perfect substitutes, and we are putting too much faith in them now. We want, in sum, maintenance and restoration of a natural ecosystem that could take a beating and come back—a bay that could take favorable environmental conditions and turn them in a twinkling into seafood and wildlife like few other waters on the planet.

A Bay with Healthy Diversity

Nature seldom declines as much as it simply shifts; thus the total biomass of the bay's plants and fish and birds has not been so much reduced as it has been concentrated into larger numbers of fewer species—the ones that can adapt to polluted and stressful conditions. We want a bay with self-sustaining populations of the fish and fowl and other species that traditionally have lived in the watershed. A return to such natural diversity would be one indicator of a healthy system.

This diversity extends to human occupations. On the water, we want a bay with working watermen, a group whose survival is tied inextricably to maintenance of the highest water quality. Similarly, on the lands of the watershed we want to ensure the long-term health of farmers. Both watermen and farmers are implicated, as we all are, in many of the bay's problems. But it would be shortsighted and impoverishing to both food supply and our cultural heritage to think the answers to bay pollution lie with expediently forcing either group out of the picture.

A Bay with a Livable Watershed

However much we may love and enjoy the water, it is on the lands of the watershed that we live most of our lives. If we cannot preserve extensive natural green spaces, if our transportation systems are congested and our air is not fit to breathe, then all the rockfish and canvasback ducks in the world will not make this the "Land of Pleasant Living." Similarly, we want a watershed that retains its sense of regional heritage, rather than melting into a homogenized suburbia. The requirements for all forms of life, writes John A. Hostetler, the Pennsylvania scholar on the Amish, include not only soil, water, air, and sunlight but also *community*. Fifty years from now, the mention of "Eastern Shore," "Northern Neck," "Southern Maryland," and "Lancaster County" must continue to evoke rich and unique identities. The compact patterns of growth that best preserve and assist all the above will tend to be those that also maximize the natural ability of forest and wetlands and open space to reduce polluted runoff to the water.

A People's Bay Accessible to All

The day when farmers in Charlottesville, Virginia, and Lancaster County, Pennsylvania, take the afternoon to fish for ocean-born shad, and kids in the foothills of the Blue Ridge and the Appalachians dip silver sea-run herring from their home streams, need not be far off. The value in reconnecting these fishermen to a distant bay has value far in excess of what can be measured in pounds of fish.

By removing dams and other obstructions that have amputated thousands of miles of tributaries from annual fish migrations, we can also bring the bay to many citizens who cannot easily go to it. Systems of hiking and biking trails on land, canoe and kayak and small boat trails through the marshes, and public parks along the edges of every river system should ensure that no citizen of the watershed is more than an hour from water-based recreational contact with the bay or a tributary.

Our education systems must universally include "watershed education." Virtually no one in the drainage basin, from New York to Norfolk, lives more than half a mile from a creek. Connecting these local and intimate flows of water with something larger and grander downstream will aid and abet our ability to care for and enjoy the Chesapeake.

A Bay That Is Seen as a Whole

"A good doctor," Aristotle said, "treats the patient, not the disease." Environmental preservation too often has fought specific pollution and development threats while the environment as a whole deteriorated. Ecological science provides the framework for comprehending the "patient"—the bay and its watershed and the creatures therein—as an interrelated system, rather than responding to environmental problems as a series of unrelated "symptoms."

It should be a high priority of research to refine this image. We know, for example, that in altering the landscape on a wide scale we have changed dramatically how water and energy and food flow from forested mountain to the bay's bottom sediments, and from there into creatures that inhabit the system. But we don't understand much beyond that; and until we do, we are not likely to be successful environmental healers.

Just as critical is our ability to take the bay's pulse—monitor it—over long periods of time. In a system as turbulent and naturally variable as the bay, development of long-term trends is vital to knowing whether it is getting sick or well and whether nature or humans are causing a change. Such long-term comprehensive monitoring only began in the last five or six years, and in some places more recently than that. Its lack probably delayed our recognition of the bay's decline by a decade or more. Even well-meaning people could not say for sure what was human impact and what was natural cycle.

Monitoring is always an endangered program—the type that, like tree planting in cities, is most easily cut back when economies sag because in the short term no one misses it. We must never let that happen. Additionally we have to start similar monitoring of changes in the land, using satellite photography and other modern, cost-effective tools to track trends in the resilience of the watershed as well as the health of the water. Prime areas for land monitoring are forested stream buffers, wetlands, fragmentation patterns in forest, and environmentally unsound agricultural practices.

Finally, while we should always seek out and monitor good indicators of bay health, from eagles to submerged grasses, we should also recognize the limitations of our present ability to take the pulse of large, complex ecosystems like the Chesapeake. Natural systems often don't decline in neat and predictable increments; rather, they may approach a threshold without our knowing it—even seem to be coming back—then fail quickly and massively. What this means is that, in the absence of perfect understanding, we must act conservatively. If monitoring data (or knowledge of what they mean) are lacking, we must assume that adverse consequences could result, rather than waiting until they are glaringly evident.

The Need to Act Now

Changes to the bay and its watershed were generally gradual for the nearly 350 years following the start of European settlements in the region. But in the few decades since, there have been unprecedented explosions in population growth, in wasteful land use patterns and energy consumption, in the use of agricultural and industrial chemicals, and in continued and higher-tech overfishing by sportsman and waterman alike. As a result, the natural systems have been overwhelmed.

The specific recommendations that follow are keyed to the preceding chapters. They are not meant as detailed blueprints; rather they are guidelines for political, scientific, and citizen action that will vary from region to region. Some can be implemented quickly, while others are much more ambitious. All of them, however, are urgent if we are serious about saving the bay. The reason is the tremendous lag times between recognizing a problem and actually turning it around in a big, complex system like the bay and its watershed. While we are huddled on the sidelines plotting strategy, pollution and other impacts from relentless population growth take no time-outs.

Recognition of the problem with the environmentally critical underwater grasses, for example, began in the late 1960s. Reaching a strategy for their restoration benefited from an extraordinary infusion of federal research money in the mid-1970s. Now, in the early 1990s, we seem on the right track to bringing them back, but it may be the next century before that goal is achieved.

Similarly, the "2020 Report" on population growth and development in the watershed said this of the impacts of delaying action: The households established in the watershed between now and 1999 will contribute a greatly disproportionate amount of all the pollution from development during the next three decades, simply because they are the ones that will be here the longest. In other words, if we wait until halfway to 2020 to begin dealing with the impact of development, far more than half of the impact will already have occurred.

POLLUTION

This section addresses the major pathways—air, land, water, and accidental spills—by which pollutants enter the Chesapeake.

Agriculture

Problem

The runoff of nutrients—nitrogen and phosphorus—in both surface and underground water from farm fertilizers and manure is a major pollutant of the bay. So is the soil that washes from farm fields. Runoff of pesticides is an unquantified but potential threat to both surface and underground waters.

Recommendations

All farms must achieve "nutrient balance"—that is, the nitrogen and phosphorus in manure and commercial fertilizer that go on the soil must both be equaled, as closely as possible, by what is taken off each year in crops, in animals fed those crops, and so forth. Municipalities and farmers who spread sewage sludge on farmland, an excellent way of recycling nutrients from human wastes, must likewise take this balance into account. The best progress that has been made to date by the states is that which has involved simply helping farmers to reduce the fertilizer they apply in the first place.

Farmers must be given better information and techniques for controlling the runoff of nutrients. Some techniques billed as effective, such as conservation tillage, have actually worsened the problem in some areas. (The benefits of conservation tillage in saving energy and reducing soil erosion still make it a worthwhile technique—just not the whole solution.)

The largely voluntary approach to controlling farm pollution must be modified. Currently farmers choose what types of controls they will implement, even if they are not the most effective. And if they don't want to stop polluting, they don't have to.

It is neither practical nor desirable to regulate thousands of farmers as we do an industry with a single discharge pipe. Nor do all individual farmers have the financial and technical resources to solve all their problems without government help. But there is a broad middle ground between all-voluntary and all-regulatory. Some examples:

☐ Tie the wide range of government subsidies to agriculture firmly to pollution control practices.

☐ Target farms with especially poor pollution management practices for immediate mandatory cleanups (with full or partial financial assistance).

☐ Farms that have large animal concentrations should be treated as a "point of discharge," just like a polluting industry, and required to meet conditions of a discharge permit. A caveat: It has taken nearly two decades of applying such permits to industries before they were written stringently enough for real cleanup to result. We cannot afford to repeat with farms this history of writing initial multiyear permits that set pollution limits at whatever the operation was already achieving. In some heavily impacted counties, like Lancaster in Pennsylvania and Rockingham in Virginia, caps on animal numbers probably are necessary to cope with pollution reduction goals.

☐ Water quality, not cost-effectiveness, must dictate cleanup strategies and spending with agriculture just as it does with sewage and industrial pollution. Many experts say that excessive manure production on a farm or in a region cannot be transported long distances to areas that can use it because this tactic is not cost-effective. But it is not "cost-effective," strictly speaking, to treat and dispose of *most* of our wastes, from sewage to industrial chemicals. Like these wastes, manure *must* be gotten out of areas where it precludes achieving nutrient balance in soils.

☐ Techniques such as planting forest buffers between streams and fields, or planting winter cover crops, have great promise in controlling pollution from farms. Such practices must be mandated wherever they are effective.

☐ Farm animals must be fenced away from streams and rivers to keep manure out of the water and check erosion of stream banks.

☐ Current goals for stemming the runoff of soil from farms into the water are still based on maintaining soil productivity, not achieving good water quality. Considerably stricter limits are achievable— and must be required.

□ In addition to better controls on farm pollution, we need better farming. Changing the process that causes pollution is almost always preferable to trying to control the pollution. There is a range of innovative farming techniques known as low-input sustainable agriculture (LISA) that must be vigorously promoted by all levels of government and leaders in the agricultural community and related industries.

These LISA methods emphasize reducing inputs of commercial fertilizers and chemicals to farmland, relying instead on natural processes and biological interactions to grow and protect crops. Rotating crops to avoid buildup of crop-specific pests and to restore soil fertility (by putting crops that capture their own fertilizer from the air in the rotation some years) is a simple example. Other techniques involve substituting information for chemicals—as in hiring scouts to check whether insect infestations really justify spraying pesticides in a given field. LISA at the federal level has been zero-budgeted for years by the Reagan and Bush administrations. Its share of the federal research dollar currently is about a tenth the cost of testing, researching, and approving one new agricultural chemical for market.

Susquehanna River

Problem

Source of half the bay's fresh water, the Susquehanna, whose degraded water quality is most influenced by Pennsylvania, in turn influences much of the water quality downstream in Maryland and Virginia.

Recommendations

□ Federal agencies involved with the bay's restoration should be acting as if the entire watershed were one state, not several, and asking: Where in this "state" would they then put their pollution control efforts to be most cost-effective? The states would also do well to follow the federal example by looking at the source of their problems broadly.

The most obvious reapportionment of pollution control effort and money such "watershed" thinking may dictate would be for EPA and other federal agencies, and possibly Maryland, to put more resources upstream in Pennsylvania. Even Virginia is affected by the

Susquehanna's influence on dissolved oxygen off the mouth of the Rappahannock. A possible precedent for this approach already exists in the Susquehanna River Basin Compact—a legal, binding arrangement involving Maryland, Pennsylvania, New York, and the federal government that works to ensure that too much fresh water is not withdrawn from that river by upstream users.

□ Pennsylvania's obligations to downstream neighbors aren't being fulfilled yet, as trends in Susquehanna water quality are not much changed from a decade ago. Pennsylvania can and must do more than it is—or be held responsible for blunting a great deal of Maryland's bay cleanup efforts and, to a lesser extent, Virginia's. At the same time, Pennsylvania is entitled to ask this of its downstream neighbors: Are they making maximum progress to conservatively manage the bay's fisheries? Are they vigorously and effectively managing the intense population growth that is occurring in their parts of the watershed? Just as bay cleanup downstream will be doomed by a dirty Susquehanna, no amount of Susquehanna cleanup by Pennsylvania will produce the kind of bay we desire if Maryland and Virginia do not take care of their end better than they have to date.

□ All three states should insist that any expenditures of federal resources on bay cleanup are dispensed rigorously from the standpoint of what is best for the whole watershed.

Sewage

Problem

Nutrients—nitrogen and phosphorus—in discharges of sewage to the bay are a major factor in the decline of underwater grasses and low oxygen levels in the water.

Recommendations

□ Discharging our wastes, including sewage, to the water is not an appropriate long-range strategy. There are both technological and financial limits to the levels of treatment; already, population growth beyond the year 2005 is projected to outstrip current reductions in phosphorus levels entering the bay from sewage. The costs of nitrogen removal, a strategy in which we have barely scratched the surface, will likely cost billions. In addition, no plant ever operates for long at 100 percent effectiveness. Lapses because of accident or shoddy maintenance are translated instantly and irretrievably to the very water we are trying to protect.

□ Land disposal of sewage—spraying it on land ranging from golf courses to forests after it has received a moderate level of treatment—should be explored along with alternatives like composting that do not discharge waste to the water at all. Other techniques such as reuse and recycling of treated sewage wastewater should also receive a high priority. Continuing to hook more and more people into traditional water discharge of sewage without much better planning for where it may be beneficial (and where it is not) will increasingly preclude alternatives. For example, population densities in areas like Baltimore and Washington already make significant land spraying of sewage an impossibility.

□ In the foreseeable future, we cannot expect to dispense entirely with traditional sewage discharges to the water. But new treatment plants, both public and private, should be built only where needed to concentrate growth in accordance with a new generation of growth management planning. Currently there is more than enough capacity in existing sewage treatment plants (Figure 5.5) in the watershed to accommodate growth through 2020 and beyond. (The flaw in this reasoning, of course, is that growth is not necessarily occurring only where sewage capacity exists; but it should be a goal of growth management to channel it to such places.)

□ As a short-term goal, the current watershed-wide commitment to reducing nitrogen and phosphorus in sewage discharges by 40 percent is a good one. Virginia should get on with removing nitrogen. Pennsylvania should stop resting on its laurels for having taken the lead in sewage treatment two decades ago—the levels of treatment that once were exemplary have become distinctly average.

The 40 percent goal is no magic number and may need to be changed. What is most critical to remember and enforce is that the reduction is intended to be a *cap*—that is, once we achieve these reductions we cannot let the level of nutrients rise again, no matter how much the population increases. This sort of thinking needs to apply with the broader range of all human impacts on the environment if we are to increase population while restoring the bay's health.

□ Given the greater-than-expected difficulties in controlling nitrogen and phosphorus from land-based runoff (farms, urban pavements, suburban developments), it is worth reconsidering the increase of nutrient removal from sewage plants in the watershed to the limits of technology. This course is expensive, but so is controlling land-based sources if we do it right. Nor do we recommend ceasing efforts to clean up land runoff; but sewage controls have the great advantage of proven technology and giving precisely quantifiable reductions. Newer techniques of reducing nitrogen in sewage, now being evaluated in Virginia and in the District of Columbia, show promise to make it substantially cheaper.

□ Federal facilities must stop setting a bad example by lagging in cleaning up their own sewage discharges and other environmental pollution. Instead they should set the pace—not only in cleanup compliance but in developing innovative waste-handling techniques.

□ Septic tanks are the other major way we treat human wastes in the watershed. They rely on filtering wastes through the soil, but can result in significant quantities of nutrients entering waterways via underground flows. At a minimum, septic tank pollution of groundwater must be calculated in the 40 percent nutrient reductions we are committed to achieving as part of our bay cleanup strategies. Otherwise, there will be a tendency to simply steer more development to use septic tanks as a way around conflicts between new growth and firm limits on nutrients from sewage treatment plants.

□ Further development using septic tanks must be limited only to soils and installations that will produce no increase in nutrients reaching the bay or its tributaries through underground flows. Nutrient pollution of groundwater by septic tanks should be a legitimate reason for rejecting or scaling down development even where no human health threat from bacterial pollution exists.

□ To the extent that we remove pollutants from sewage discharges to the water, we increase the amounts of sludge, the semisolid residues from sewage treatment, that must be disposed of somewhere. Plans to incinerate sludge as a means of disposal in some areas should be rejected. This practice wastes energy, contributes to air pollution, and runs counter to the concept that sludge, which is rich in nutrients, is a valuable resource.

□ Farmland is a good place to spread sludge, so long as it does not contain unacceptable levels of toxic chemicals and metals. But farms should never be pushed out of "nutrient balance" by the application of sewage sludge, as some of our current spreading is doing. The disposal of Philadelphia's sewage sludge in Lancaster County, Pennsylvania, the part of the bay's watershed that already suffers from the grossest excesses of farm fertilizers and manure in the United States, should be stopped. If there are soils there that can accept sludge without going out of balance for either phosphorus or nitrogen, then first priority should be to use them for the huge amounts of excess manure generated in other parts of the county.

Toxics

Problem

The bay in recent decades has become subject to a range of widespread toxic impacts—from acid rain to organic chemicals and industrial metals—that are contaminating its bottom sediments and turning up in its aquatic life.

Recommendations

□ Our long-term goal must be the elimination of toxics in discharges to the bay—particularly those that persist in the environment. One place to start would be a freeze on the introduction or expansion of any additional persistent toxic chemicals in industrial discharges. This step must be complemented by an emphasis, which ultimately must come also at the national level, to change our very manufacturing processes to produce fewer toxics in the first place. There are already concepts in the federal Clean Water Act upon which to base such a freeze, and such actions are now being seriously considered for control of toxic pollution on the Great Lakes.

□ We must focus much more sharply on the toxics threat to the bay from airborne sources, both inside and outside the watershed. In the short term, vigorous enforcement of air quality regulations and applications of cleanup technology can lessen the impact. In the longer term, just as industry must change its toxic processes of production, so must society change habits like driving automobiles in ever-increasing numbers and distances—a habit that already produces a large portion of airborne pollutants in the watershed.

☐ Agriculture has finally begun to be more forthcoming with an accounting of its pesticide use in the bay watershed. Such uses exploded between 1950 and 1980, but they appear to have leveled off. Comprehensive and readily accessible tracking of pesticide use is critical. Such chemicals, carried to the bay in rainfall and in groundwater, are not thought to be causing the current declines in underwater grasses, but traces of some pesticides routinely are found in the water and they may well be having localized impacts. As more and more evidence comes to light nationally about unusual cancer rates in farmers, a more thorough analysis of agriculture's chemical use should be of benefit to farmers' health as well as the environment.

☐ Similar data and analysis are needed for the fast-growing industry of chemical lawn treatment services and for the runoff from pesticide applications by homeowners throughout the watershed. Lawns in the watershed now equal or surpass corn acreage, and a quarter of all pesticide use as of 1985 was nonagricultural. While a weed-free and insect-free lawn may look pretty to many people, it provides no particular benefit to society. Consequently any risk from it to the environment is unreasonable and uses of chemical pesticides for lawn care should be severely restricted.

☐ Linking cause and effect with toxic chemicals, because of their subtle, often chronic effects in amounts as small as parts per trillion, promises to be more question mark than certainty for a long time. The answer is not hand wringing or waiting on research to pin down precise cause and effect. The answer is to place the burden of proof firmly on the pollutant—to prove itself innocent or be eliminated—rather than burdening the environment to show damage or continue to be subjected to the toxic.

☐ Many of our most dangerous toxic impacts on the environment have come not through waste discharges, which are what we tend to regulate, but through deliberate, widespread introduction of toxics—lead in gasoline, DDT for pest control, TBT for boat antifouling paint. In coming decades, similar threats could ensue, not from chemicals, but from products of genetic engineering released unwisely into the environment. With Maryland gearing up to be a leader in biotechnology, now is the time to ensure that the products of biotechnology are rigorously analyzed for unintended impacts on the Chesapeake system.

Oil Spills

Problem

The bay is extremely vulnerable to oil spills. Regulation of oil transport and oil drilling is inadequate, and there is little reason to think a large spill could be cleaned up adequately.

Recommendations

□ Stricter safety standards for the construction, inspection, and equipping of oil transport vessels must be implemented—especially for barges, in which the bulk of petroleum products are carried on the bay.

□ Better traffic control systems and tracking of oil vessels on the bay are needed, particularly around the Norfolk, Hampton Roads, area.

□ The risks of oil drilling in and around the bay's coastline, and the impact of related onshore development, so far outweigh the benefits that it should be banned.

□ The Coast Guard must be given the resources and the mandate to carry out its job of ensuring marine safety with regard to oil transport on the bay.

Sediment and Stormwater Runoff

Problem

Current approaches to controlling sediment and other pollutants that run off in rainfall from paved areas and construction sites are inadequate.

Recommendations

□ We need to rethink our approach to sediment and stormwater control. The present systems obviously need more and better application and enforcement. But the present array of structural controls— silt fences, sediment catch ponds, infiltration devices—will never do the job well enough to allow projected large development increases in the watershed without added degradation of the water. The goal of both sediment and stormwater control must be to ensure that water leaves the site with the same quantity, timing, and quality as it did before development began, if the site was in forest or other natural vegetation. If it was in agriculture or older development, then a substantial reduction in preexisting impacts must be the goal.

□ To achieve that, or even come close, we must get away from the "end of the pipe" approach to controlling pollutants after they are already washing toward waterways. Better versions of existing structural controls exist and should be used, but only as part of a far more comprehensive system. This will include retaining natural buffers, such as forested or heavily vegetated buffers between development sites and waterways. Development on extremely steep slopes should be prohibited; large setbacks from streams should be required; no development should be allowed in floodplains. Large projects such as highway cuts cannot be allowed to expose as much soil to erosion at any one time as they presently do. The simple expedient of stabilizing cleared slopes, even temporarily, with vegetation would greatly boost sediment control in all three states.

□ An upper limit must be set on the amount of a stream's watershed that can ever be made impervious by development. Impervious surfaces such as driveways, house roofs, and patios disrupt the natural flows and quality of water to streams. They show a measurable degradation of the environment of streams by the time imperviousness reaches about 12 percent of the total watershed area (equivalent to developing the whole watershed in 2-acre suburban homes). A broader way to approach the same goal is to tie additional development in a polluted watershed to no degradation, or even enhancement, of water quality and flows in affected waterways.

□ We must ensure regular, long-term maintenance of the thousands of stormwater control ponds that are being installed across the watershed. These can fill with sediment and lose their effectiveness—and unless someone is clearly responsible for monitoring and maintenance, there is a good chance our initial expenditures of money will be wasted.

□ The individual lot exemptions that are the rule for sediment control must end. It was never intended that contractors and developers of individual lots be able to totally ignore all sediment control; but observations in some parts of the watershed, particularly rural areas, indicate that this is happening.

☐ Existing urban areas must be put on a systematic program of "retrofit" to reduce the impacts of runoff every time it rains. Installing fairly simple devices such as rain barrels beneath drain spouts, for example, can knock off the initial peak of runoff from a hard rain that is so destructive when it surges into nearby streams, causing erosion and scouring. Infiltration, which includes any technique that allows rainwater to soak in rather than running off quickly, holds perhaps the most hope for retrofit. Simple pits, for example, incorporating organic materials like shredded leaves from yards, can improve the quality of runoff. Similarly, techniques to capture the "first flush," the initial half-inch or so of rain, and divert it to sewage treatment plants have merit. Most of the pollutants are washed off in the first flush of stormwater. Allowing the rest to run off without diversion to treatment plants might avoid the current overloading of plants that can cause them to release both raw sewage and untreated stormwater. Where capacity exists at sewage treatment plants, the first flush should be diverted for treatment.

☐ Governments must make street sweeping a regular procedure, taking pollutants up before rain washes them into waterways.

☐ Cleaning up our air can reduce a major source of toxics and nutrients that run off in rainfall from impervious surfaces, as pollutants settle on them from the air.

☐ Applications of fertilizers and pesticides on lawns, golf courses, cemeteries, and other turfgrass acreage should be severely restricted.

☐ Now that EPA has issued regulations allowing states to issue permits for stormwater discharges (like storm drains), localities should move rapidly to implement this new system of controls over the quality of those discharges.

Air

Problem

Airborne pollutants that settle out across the bay and its watershed are a substantial source of pollution, though their quantities and sources are not well defined.

Recommendations

☐ Airborne nutrients should be immediately included in the 40 percent nutrient reduction goals that now apply to sewage discharges and runoff from farms and other land-based sources.

☐ Rapid implementation of the new revisions to the federal Clean Air Act must begin as soon as possible.

☐ Reducing and eventually reversing the growth of automobile use through mass transit and through more compact and efficient patterns of development must be a primary goal of all state and local growth management and air quality strategies.

☐ This goal must be complemented by a national energy policy that ties the reduction of burning gasoline and all fossil fuels not only to conservation but to air quality and to reducing the rise in global warming (the greenhouse effect).

☐ Research to quantify the impacts and sources of airborne pollution on the bay should be a priority. This research should apply to both nutrients and toxic chemicals.

Boats

Problem

Recreational boat use, one of the fastest-growing sectors of bay use, has a potential for impacts that range from habitat destruction (for marinas) to toxic pollution from bottom paints and motor oil.

Recommendations

☐ The bay and its rivers must be made an immediate "no discharge" zone for all boat toilets. Every marina must be required to have facilities or arrangements to pump out and properly dispose of such wastes. Neither the states nor the Coast Guard can be allowed any longer to shirk their responsibilities in enforcing this.

☐ Boat repair yards and marinas where boaters work on their vessels must use state-of-the-art controls on runoff that can carry toxic paints and solvents into adjacent waterways. This effort need not involve high-tech solutions. Vaccuuming or sweeping around boats after scraping the bottom paint would be an example.

HARVESTS

Pollution, mismanagement, disease, and greed all have battered the Chesapeake's seafood resources. Perhaps the marvel is how much is left—and the capacity for a comeback that remains if wise management is followed.

Fisheries

Problem

Large numbers of the bay's fish and shellfish are in decline because of overfishing, habitat destruction, and pollution.

Recommendations

☐ The management plans being developed now for each bay species must be based on the concept of catches that ensure naturally sustainable populations. They must be based on biology, not politics. They must have firm timetables for implementation and limits on total harvests (something that has never been the norm on the Chesapeake).

☐ They must also have "trigger" mechanisms, based on the up-to-date status of each species, that can kick in added conservation measures whenever needed to maintain stable stocks of fish. An example: In Maryland, whenever the average reproduction of rockfish, as measured during the most recent three-year period, falls below a certain number, the fishing season may be shut down.

☐ These plans should be set by (or at least involve the advice of) expert panels insulated from state governments and the political pressures that traditionally have confounded fishery conservation. On the other hand, parceling out the total catches set by such a panel among different fishing interests is properly the job of state agencies and legislatures. The point is that conservation and allocation must be separated.

☐ In the absence of good information—a condition that will plague us for awhile with some species—fishery management plans *must* be conservative. This may be an incentive to develop better information.

☐ Recreational fishermen must return to being just that; and commercial fishermen must be full time (within the bounds of a job that is, by nature, seasonally variable).

☐ No one but a licensed waterman should be allowed to sell catch.

☐ Recreational crabbers should be more restricted in the gear they can use to catch crabs. Abandoned or unattended recreational crab pots appear to be killing other species like diamondback terrapins.

☐ Commercial crab catches must be capped now at a level that represents a sustainable harvest. A conservative figure should be used until improved knowledge of the relations between crab spawning success and the numbers that can be sustainably harvested indicates the cap can be raised.

☐ There is a substantial problem in certain fisheries with what is known as "bycatch"—the killing of species in nets set for other species. An example: Rockfish are caught by commercial netters who are fishing primarily for shad. Perhaps the only way to eliminate such problems is to prohibit any use of fishing gear in the bay that does not capture its prey alive, so any bycatch can be freed. This measure would effectively ban only one kind of fishing gear, the gillnet, which drowns anything it snares.

☐ Hook and line fishing by sportsmen also kills substantial amounts of fish even though they are released. Education, some modification in fishing gear, and limits on when and where recreational fishing takes place can reduce this problem.

☐ Ocean fisheries that intercept shad on their way to spawn in the bay must be stopped in favor of traditional fisheries in the Chesapeake that can be managed according to the condition of spawning populations specific to each river system of the estuary.

☐ Limited entry must be enforced for the bay's commercial watermen. No one who has traditionally been a waterman should be denied a license; but the number should be frozen there. A new waterman could enter the fishery only by purchasing an existing license. This would give longtime watermen a retirement nest egg and a larger stake in conserving fish and improving water quality. The same procedure should apply to charter boat skippers. Such an arrangement also would give the state the option to "buy down" the number of commercial fishermen if that ever were deemed desirable.

☐ Virginia should establish a recreational fishing license (Maryland already has) for Chesapeake Bay and tidal waters. This would help in acquiring needed information about the magnitude of recreational fishing and in funding fishery conservation and management; it would also give anglers more of a personal stake in conserving fish.

Oysters

Problem

Oysters in the bay are an important pollution filter, a rich habitat for other species, and an economic resource. They have been reduced to about 1 percent of their historical abundance.

Recommendations

☐ The surest way to restore oysters to the bay is to temporarily stop harvesting them, to "give 'em a rest" as some watermen have said privately. Maryland and Virginia should do so immediately. Watermen and seafood packers should be employed in expanded programs to rebuild oyster populations and to maintain the infrastructure of the industry. During the time of closure, Maryland and Virginia should refine management plans to ensure that stable stocks and a viable fishery will be sustained upon reopening.

☐ We should not give up on the native bay oyster (*Crassostrea virginica*) just yet, despite arguments that it is finished and that importation of West Coast oysters (*Crassostrea gigas*) would be the fastest way to combat the disease problems that are killing native oysters in the bay. The native oyster is supremely well adapted to the bay—at least to the kind of bay we are trying to bring back—nor is there reason to believe imported oysters would survive widely in the bay. However, they might adversely affect the remaining native stocks by outcompeting them or interbreeding with them.

☐ Efforts to develop disease-resistant native oysters and to find out more about the oyster parasites, MSX and dermo, should be expanded. Support is in the interest of both state and federal governments, given the occurrence and importance of *C. virginica* from New England to the Gulf of Mexico.

☐ The prospects for using aquaculture to "get around" the disease problem by growing and harvesting oysters more rapidly than the diseases can affect them must be pursued more vigorously.

Private aquaculture should be encouraged as a complementary system to public fishing, and watermen should be given ample opportunity to participate in it. It may seem inefficient in this day and age to advocate keeping traditional ways of oyster harvesting which are still based on a hunter-gatherer strategy that on land largely gave way to agriculture several millennia ago. But pure aquaculture, while it might increase the oysters in the bay, would not guarantee a return to the natural condition of the bay bottom—oysters growing in patches scattered over millions of acres from Baltimore to Norfolk—that is so important for both habitat and water quality. Culturing the bivalves in rafts suspended above the bottom and concentrated near a processing facility might be more the rule with aquaculture.

Moreover, just as this book extends the notion of the bay's environment to the lands throughout its watershed, it also counts traditional fishing cultures and oyster skipjacks and Tangier Islanders working their tongs in the James River as integral parts of any "state of the bay." None of this can be preserved immutably like fossils in amber. But it should no more be swept away in the name of efficiency than all our native oak and poplar forest should be cut to establish plantations of a single fast-growing pulpwood species.

Waterfowl

Problem

Loss of habitat, particularly underwater grasses and wetlands, has greatly reduced the numbers of most of the bay's waterfowl species.

Recommendations

☐ There is an adequate framework in place under federal migratory bird laws for managing waterfowl. Within that framework, Maryland and Virginia generally (but not always) have acted conservatively in setting limits on hunting. Exceptions include the limited tundra swan hunt authorized recently in Virginia—despite a relatively small population of those waterfowl in the Virginia part of the bay—as well as what appears to be a slow reaction by the state of Maryland to reduce shooting pressure on wild geese in the face of protests by some sport hunters and by commercial sport hunting guides. A third exception is that both states continue to allow the hunting of redhead ducks, a species that is doing fairly well coast-wide but extremely poorly on the Chesapeake, since the underwater grasses they fed on have died. Swans and redheads should not be hunted in either state, and Maryland needs to allow biologists more say than legislators and hunters in setting seasons and limits on geese.

☐ Programs such as habitat enhancement, acquisition of wetlands, and conservative hunting limits to restore diversity to the state's waterfowl populations need to be pursued vigorously. The overde-pendence of hunters on one species, the Canada goose, which in turn is dependent for food on the farming of one crop, corn, may not be a stable, long-term situation.

RESILIENCE

The Chesapeake ecosystem has a significant ability to buffer and stabilize itself against both natural and human environmental insult. This resilience lies in its forests, wetlands, submerged grasses, oys-ters, and other features; but much of it has been lost. This section explains what must be done to maintain and enhance what is left—a task that is just as critical as building new sewage treatment plants and enforcing stricter cleanup standards on industries.

Forests

Problem

The watershed has lost nearly half its least polluting land use—the forest—and declines seem likely to continue, making it more diffi-cult to restore the bay's water quality and maintain its natural re-silience.

Recommendations

☐ We must mandate immediately no net losses of the forest that remains, as well as a goal of long-term net increase, particularly in certain critical areas. Prime among these critical zones are the edges of all waterways in the bay's drainage, particularly in agricultural regions.

☐ Goals should be set on a more local basis than the watershed—by river or stream basin. Adding forest to already heavily forested areas in New York state, for example, cannot adequately substitute for the need to replenish it as buffers between farms and waterways in heavily cleared Lancaster County, Pennsylvania. Complementing this step, we need better information on forest distribution and change immediately. Computerization of aerial photography and satellite overviews make this goal easily achievable. We must also expand research into how much and what types of forest work best as a water-quality filter and buffer, and translate this research quickly into field-level experiments and demonstrations.

☐ Give forest equal status with more traditional forms of pollution control. For example: Reforestation might be part of a nutrient reduction goal, each acre of additional forest earning so much "credit" toward the goal, just as if a sewage plant had been upgraded with new nutrient removal technology. Funding for various pollution controls could be made interchangeable among programs as diverse as sewage treatment processes and tree planting, depending on cost-effectiveness.

☐ Effective mechanisms, both regulatory and incentive-based, must be developed to deal with the fact that the great bulk of the forest we want to preserve is on lands owned by tens of thousands of private individuals and corporations.

☐ We need to prevent further fragmentation of existing forest, as several species of wildlife depend on unbroken blocks of forest. Again, as with distribution of forests, the total acreage is not the whole picture or even the most important aspect. Similarly, trends toward a reduction in the diversity of trees in favor of pine monoculture need to be better analyzed and policies developed to preserve natural forest diversity in every region of the watershed.

☐ All three states need to rewrite their forestry laws and policies to reflect growing recognition that the forest has an extraordinary number of values beyond serving as an economic resource or for maximizing production of white-tailed deer and wild turkey.

☐ Efforts such as Maryland's greenways program, aimed at preserving and enhancing stream corridor forest, are to be commended and emulated across the watershed.

Nontidal Wetlands

Problem

Continued declines in these wetlands seem likely—thwarting state and federal goals of no net loss and hurting the bay's natural resilience.

Recommendations

□ No net loss must mean just that. It should not have footnotes attached that say, in fine print, "farmers who want to sell to developers are exempted" from identifying nontidal wetlands and getting permits to regulate development of them. Despite recent federal decisions not to classify farmed wetlands for protection, identification of potential and actual nontidal wetlands on farms should continue. That way, a future developer or the current farmer would at least have the option to protect them voluntarily.

□ Maryland, which has gone further in nontidal wetlands protection than the other two states, must tighten its own law to compensate for the federal decision not to protect nontidal wetlands on agricultural lands. This would not affect farmers who wanted to farm or to sell to another farmer.

□ Virginia and Pennsylvania must move quickly toward comprehensive nontidal wetlands laws that will put meaning in their stated goals of no net loss under the bay cleanup strategy.

□ The federal government must staff its Army Corps of Engineers and other services adequately to do their job in regulating wetlands. Otherwise, federal claims of a no-net-loss policy are hollow.

□ The advertised path to no net loss is "mitigation"—which means avoidance of impacts to nontidal wetlands and, in unavoidable cases, creation of new wetlands. This last part of mitigation should be made truly a last resort until we understand the long-term performance and stability of created wetlands versus the natural ones they replace. For example, the states should stop allowing agencies such as highway administrations to build up "IOUs" for which wetlands have been destroyed and creation of new ones still is not completed. Rather, the burden should shift to the highway department to demonstrate that it has first created new wetlands in the amount it must destroy.

☐ Creating wetlands should require a bond to be posted against their failure to function as natural wetlands, and the developer or state agency should carry the burden of maintaining them for several years.

☐ No state or federal aid should go to agriculture and forestry projects that directly or indirectly (such as through drainage ditches) degrade nontidal wetlands.

☐ Efforts to protect nontidal wetlands through acquisition should be expanded. Since many of these wetlands may be small and widely scattered across the watershed, it would seem a perfect role for local land trusts.

Tidal Wetlands

Problem

Despite protective laws, goals of no net loss are not being achieved yet, and natural losses from factors like sea level rise are probably accelerating.

Recommendations

☐ As with nontidal wetlands, no net loss must mean just that. As a start, no new bulkheading for erosion control should be allowed unless an existing structure is threatened or an existing water-dependent business or community (like a watermen's village) needs protection. Creation of new marsh for erosion control is, however, to be strongly encouraged.

☐ Virginia must put its records of permits for tidal wetlands destruction in order so that the effectiveness of its protections can be evaluated. Further, the state should publish its losses annually as Maryland does.

☐ Both states must do a better analysis of the effectiveness of mitigation (see the recommendations for nontidal wetlands) to include long-term evaluations of whether created marshes are fully replacing the values of marshes that are lost.

☐ Sea level rise will be an increasingly important fact of life around low-lying areas of the bay during the coming decades, claiming thousands of acres of precious tidal wetlands perhaps within a few decades. The only way we can compensate for such losses is to ensure that upland "buffer" zones are left intact and undeveloped behind all existing marshes. With sea level rising, that upland fringe is a poor place to locate development and infrastructure like roads and sewers anyhow. It will become our "new" marsh as sea level advances—a necessary sacrifice to the sea much like the dunes we are building to sacrifice sand to hurricanes in order to protect existing development along our ocean coasts.

☐ Activities that create open water in tidal marshes, such as mosquito control ditching projects, should be discontinued if there is any chance they may worsen the marsh's susceptibility to rising sea level.

Virginia's Chesapeake Bay Preservation Act

Problem

Population pressure is often heaviest along the shoreline in Virginia; but the shoreline and adjacent shallows are often where the richest natural resources lie.

Recommendations

☐ Heavy reliance on local political will and resources must be augmented immediately by state performance standards for development and zoning.

☐ Continue and expand funding and technical support to local governments to implement the act fully and speedily. The assurance of long-term support is crucial.

☐ Only by complementing the act with strong growth management plans that apply on a regional or statewide basis can the goals of protecting the bay's shoreline and other sensitive lands in Virginia be realized in the long term. These plans do not exist now.

☐ Eliminate regulatory exemptions for development, forestry, and agriculture within the 100-foot buffer of vegetation required along the water's edge. Also require that the buffer be forest, unless another type of natural vegetation can be conclusively demonstrated to have better pollution control benefits.

☐ Make periodic monitoring and public reporting on progress of the act mandatory.

Maryland's Critical Area Act

Problem

As in Virginia, population pressure is often heaviest along the shoreline in Maryland, but this is often where the richest natural resources lie.

Recommendations

□ Pressure to expand the areas allotted for high growth in the critical zone must be resisted. Counties that maximize development densities within the present allotment system will have, in most cases, plenty of ability to accommodate future growth along the shoreline.

□ Begin a comprehensive review of how each county is complying with the act. The aim is to make corrections to strengthen it, as well as to give citizens of each jurisdiction an idea of whether their government is meeting the spirit and letter of the act.

□ Eliminate all regulatory exemptions for development, forestry, and agriculture within the 100-foot buffer of vegetation required along the water's edge. Also require that the buffer be forest, unless another type of natural vegetation can be conclusively demonstrated to have better pollution control benefits.

□ Make periodic monitoring and public reporting on progress of the act mandatory.

□ Expand the concepts of the Critical Area Act to the rest of the state, including Maryland's ocean coasts and adjoining bays.

Submerged Aquatic Vegetation

Problem

Pollution from sewage and land runoff has killed as much as 90 percent of the underwater grasses that were a critical part of the bay's functioning.

Recommendations

□ The underwater grasses should be adopted as the *primary* indicator of success or failure in reaching adequate water quality throughout much of the tidal Chesapeake and its rivers. (A caveat: They are not a particularly good indicator for many kinds of toxics.)

Water quality standards specific to each portion of the bay, based on conditions needed for good, modest, and poor growth of vegetation, are well on their way to being developed. This step will have the advantage of addressing pollution in each section of the bay—as opposed to the present blanket reductions in pollutants, which in some cases can be achieved by cleaning up a single major sewage plant on one river. If the grasses were to return to their historic habitat in the bay—and return in their native diversity of more than a dozen species—then to a large extent we will be achieving the level of water quality we desire for most bay uses.

□ We must press on with our present strategy of reducing nutrients and sediment as the ways to restore the bay's underwater grasses.

□ Redefine our restoration goals for the submerged grasses. Historic habitat for the bay's grasses has been defined by EPA at around 600,000 acres, nearly ten times the extent of the grasses in 1989. But that figure only takes into account bay bottom in water less than about 6.5 feet. There are too many anecdotal accounts of grasses growing in water 10 to 15 feet deep not to consider setting our goals higher.

□ Restrict activities such as dredging and clamming on parts of the bay bottom that seem likely to have been historic habitat for the grasses.

Benthos

Problem

Parts of the bay's bottom-dwelling communities are in decline or under stress. They are poorly monitored in some parts of the estuary.

Recommendations

□ The bottom-dwelling communities of shellfish, worms, and other creatures are, like the underwater grasses, both good habitat for fish and crabs and good indicators of changes in water quality. They should be closely monitored for changes in quantity and diversity.

□ Oysters, the best known of the bay's bottom-dwellers, should be given credit for their ability to filter large quantities of bay water.

Restoring healthy oyster populations is not only critical for seafood production, but for pollution control, and accordingly should be given high priority. (For more on oysters, see the recommendations in the Harvests section.)

Flows

Problem

In addition to water quality, both the quantity of freshwater flows and obstructions to flows such as dams have important environmental consequences for the bay.

Recommendations

☐ The current baywide goal of reopening thousands of miles of streams and rivers blocked to spawning fish by dams and other obstructions is an excellent one. It needs a timetable and it needs a commitment of money on a long-term basis; without these it is likely to languish.

☐ We are using fresh water in the bay watershed on an unsustainable basis—a practice that eventually is going to shift the bay's salinity in ways that will harm more creatures than it will benefit. Already on the Susquehanna River we are at the point where a severe drought would cause water withdrawals to exceed flow in the river, with potentially dire consequences for fish habitat below the dam at Conowingo. We need a permanent cap on consumptive losses of fresh water from the bay watershed. Water conservation and energy conservation must go hand in hand toward this goal, since power plants are a major source of consumptive water loss.

☐ Any widening and deepening of the C&D Canal at the head of the bay should be thoroughly evaluated to make sure it does not increase the net loss of fresh water from Chesapeake Bay to Delaware Bay.

THE ULTIMATE ISSUE: PEOPLE

Land use is tied closely to environmental quality in a number of ways. More water and air pollution results from converting open space to other uses. The character of the landscape and regional cultures are destroyed by sprawl development, as well as industries such as agriculture and forestry. This section tells what we must do on the land if our cleanup of the water in the bay is not to be eroded.

Individual Impacts

Problem

The way people live around the bay—the pollution their lifestyles cause and the demands they make on natural resources—are as important as *how many* of them are here. The current population is too great, given current per capita environmental impacts; and it is increasing.

Recommendations

☐ We need a stronger and more comprehensive effort to identify and reduce the impacts individuals are having on the environment of Chesapeake Bay. This will require both education and regulation.

☐ Pollution control strategies must aim more at the root causes of pollution rather than just control of the polluting by-products of this or that technology or pollution source. Both types of control strategies are needed.

☐ The most fundamental source of pollution is population growth. Reducing per capita impacts on the environment can take us a long way toward a cleaner bay, but ultimately there must also be a limit to how many people can live around the bay and sustain the natural environment there. It is past time to confront this fact in a meaningful way, given the lengthy lag times inherent in policies to limit population.

☐ Much of the bay's population growth comes from the nationwide trend of people moving nearer to the coastlines, not from high birth rates in the watershed. It is past time to debate strategies to limit this trend in many parts of the bay's watershed.

The Land Industry

Problem

Sprawl development, reflecting lack of planning for growth, is harmful environmentally and economically to the bay.

Recommendations

☐ The heart of any meaningful growth control must be plans and zoning that virtually exclude development from large areas of the landscape while mandating that a high level of development be concentrated in other, complementary areas. Large-scale, clearly articulated visions of what we want our lands and communities to be must accompany this measure. At a minimum such visions should include a whole county—and preferably an entire geographic or cultural region.

☐ At the level of specific developments, subdivision regulations must be rethought to allow much higher density of development and to allow the innovative techniques that will make such compact development attractive to buyers.

☐ Zoning, which sets the patterns for how we develop, must follow our comprehensive planning, not overrule it where the two conflict as is now usually the case.

☐ We urgently need model developments demonstrating the compatibility of dense development that preserves the character of the landscape and is attractive to live in.

☐ The economics of sprawling residential development—almost always a net loss for a jurisdiction—must be incorporated publicly and clearly in planning and zoning proceedings.

☐ Local and state governments need to examine economic scenarios for lower and slower growth rates in order to dispel the idea that boom development is always an economic plus.

☐ Open space acquisition in the bay watershed must be stepped up at all levels: local, state, and federal. Maryland's Program Open Space is one excellent example of how acquisition of natural lands may be tied directly to the rate of land development through a real estate transfer tax.

☐ The preservation of agriculture in the watershed—and also communities dependent on the water for a living—should have high priority as part of all growth and development planning.

☐ Firm goals and timetables need to be set immediately for expanding public access to the bay—ranging from riverfront parks in Virginia's Northern Neck to a trail the length of the Susquehanna

River. At a minimum, we should provide a wide range of water-related recreational opportunities within a short drive of every resident of the watershed, as well as multiple-use public access to every one of the forty-seven or so significant tributaries of Chesapeake Bay. Extensive and high-quality access to the bay and tributaries is integral to building and maintaining a constituency for its restoration.

☐ Any growth management planning must incorporate the infrastructure needed, whether mass transit or sewage treatment capacity, to support denser development without environmental degradation. Resource protection also must accompany any opening of more parts of the bay's sensitive shoreline to public access, which can degrade natural resources in heavily used areas as surely as a housing development.

TOWARD AN ENVIRONMENTAL ETHIC

What must we do, then, to save the bay and fulfill the recommendations set out in the preceding pages? We must learn to see the bay whole, as water and watershed, inseparably linked—as a system whose forests and oysters and underwater grasses and marshes are every bit as much components of pollution control and environmental health as sewage treatment plants, automotive catalytic converters, and sediment control fences. We easily accept spending $50 million or more on sewage treatment, but the filtering, cleansing forest may not be allowed to stand because it is "uneconomic" not to develop it. Likewise we will haul sewage sludge to Haiti and beyond for environmentally sound disposal; but to haul excess farm manure halfway across Lancaster County to soils that can use it is "not cost-effective." These differences must change.

We must similarly restructure our approach to environmental protection to be more than corrective of piecemeal problems as they arise. Rather, we must define and enforce limits on all of society's environmental impacts. And wherever those limits are ill-defined, the burden of proof must be on us to show no harm, not on the bay to demonstrate degradation.

Lifestyle changes alone, at least in the voluntary sense, will not occur fast enough or widely enough to sufficiently reduce our impacts on the Chesapeake environment. Nor can government simply make it all happen by fiat. It must happen as a partnership—people pushing government to push them to do what is right. That will take the highest quality of leadership, both in government and in the environmental community. The extraordinary federal/state/environmentalist partnerships that fostered our current Chesapeake Bay cleanup programs nearly a decade ago are a model for what must become the norm.

We must articulate and demonstrate visions to replace the myths of "grow or die," "economics versus environment," and "pollution is the price of progress" that underlie current development of the watershed. What is needed to save the bay must be linked wherever possible to a better quality of life, not simply to sacrifice. Saving open space while revitalizing downtowns is an example; protecting forests for water quality also benefits hunters and hikers and reduces air pollution.

Just as introducing a pollutant may have unforetold domino effects that reverberate throughout the environment, so can introducing one environmentally sound practice have "multiplier effects" for the good. Driving less to cut air pollution means, ultimately, fewer oil spills and less toxic rainwater running from parking lots and driveways. Cleansing the water enough for some of the bay grasses to rebound will, in turn, cleanse the water more, bringing back more grasses—a vicious cycle in reverse. The bay, damaged though it is, remains a system capable of enormous and rapid comebacks, once we reverse our current polluting behavior. Given a chance, it will no doubt amaze us with the bounty it can produce.

But there are also deeper reasons for cleaning up our act here in the watershed of the Chesapeake. Everywhere in the world, environmental pressures are growing most severe along the edges of land and water so exemplified by the bay. About half of all the people on earth live on about 5 percent of its land, and much of that 5 percent is around coastal edges and estuaries. The problems here are also happening globally, undoubtedly. (See Figure 7.1.) There are vital lessons everyone can learn from environmental success on the Chesapeake. They range from the technical to the spiritual.

Love for Chesapeake Bay is the closest we come in this region of the world to having an environmental ethic. Something about it stirs us instinctively, apart from the pounds and the succulence of seafood that can be derived. This love can be built on and extended to the watershed as a whole. If you love the bird, then you must learn to love and keep the forest in which it lives—and perhaps learn to love logging and clearing a bit less.

The environmental crisis is also a moral crisis. Squandering natural riches which are collectively inherited, not one iota earned, seems particularly irresponsible. We cannot justify continuing to take thus from future generations. Instead we must choose stewardship, the care of what we have, rather than a philosophy built overmuch on the acquisition of ever more material goods and the treatment of natural resources as disposable commodities.

Although we cannot preserve Chesapeake Bay for future generations without laws and regulations, all the legislation we could imagine will not be enough without an ethic that defines an enduring and nurturing relationship between humans and their environment. Nor are we likely to get to such a point without a massive commitment to education—that is, education in the sense that Jacques Cousteau once distinguished it from instruction: "Education has nothing to do with learning how to compress acetylene without an explosion or how to make an atom bomb. That's instruc-

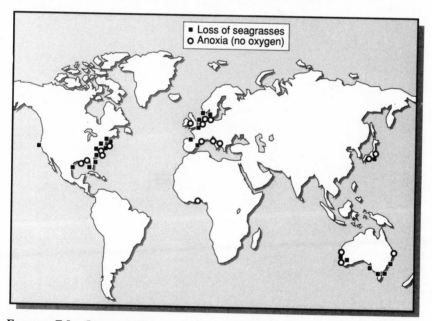

FIGURE 7.1. GLOBAL DISTRIBUTION OF COASTAL POLLUTION: 1978–1988. [Compiled by W. M. Kemp, University of Maryland, Horn Point Environmental Laboratory]

tion. A person is well educated when they know how to act or to behave in difficult situations."

Indeed, we who would save our environment are in difficult times. We need to learn how to behave, and quickly. We have already ensured that nearly a generation will grow up in parts of the watershed without the ability to catch shad and rockfish; ensured that a generation or two will never wade as children in grassy, clear shallows in pursuit of softshell crabs; and risked that many generations to come will take congested highways and strip development and sprawling suburbia as their normal environment.

We are not far from consigning a coming generation of children to seeing oyster skipjacks only in museums and books; to traveling ever farther for a glimpse of natural landscape; to only savoring the regional uniqueness attached to so many parts of the bay watershed from books and pictures or the reminiscences of their elders.

It is our tragedy that this is happening now. That it need not continue is our hope.

APPENDIX A

Report Card for the Bay

(Changes from 1991 to 1994 shown in italic type.)

Issue	Status	Trend	Comments
WATER QUALITY			
Nitrogen	Excessive	Worse	Linked to low dissolved oxygen and SAV decline
		None[a]	*Loadings may have leveled off*
Phosphorus	Excessive	Better	Linked to low dissolved oxygen and SAV decline
Dissolved oxygen	Too low	None[a]	Quite variable year to year
Toxics	Excessive	None[a]	Impacts poorly understood *New research shows widespread effects*
Sediments	Excessive	None[a]	From farms, construction sites, developed areas, erosion
HABITAT/RESILIENCE			
Forests	40% lost	Worse	Least polluting land use
Tidal wetlands	>50% lost	Worse	Losses slowed since 1970s
Nontidal wetlands	Large losses	Worse	Valuable as filter, flood control, habitat
Underwater grasses	90% lost	None[a]	Baywide water quality indicator
	87% lost	*Better*	*Still a long way to go*

289

Issue	Status	Trend	Comments
SELECTED SPECIES			
Blue crabs	Healthy	None[a]	Possibly overfishing crabs now
	Stressed	*None*[a]	*PROBABLY overfishing crabs now*
Rockfish	Threatened	Better	Harvests severely restricted
	Healthy—a success story	*Better*	*Continued harvest controls*
American shad	Threatened	Better	Maryland harvest ban 1980
	Severely depleted	*Worse*	*Virginia ban 1994; habitat also key to recovery*
Oysters	Historic low	Worse	Jobs and food; filters nutrients; prime habitat
	Another historic low	*Worse*	*Further declines annually*
Waterfowl	Less diverse	None[a]	Geese healthy, most ducks not
			New concerns about geese
Eagles	Endangered	Better	DDT ban key to comeback
	Threatened		
Ospreys	Healthy	None[a]	DDT ban key to comeback

[a] "None" can mean no trend documented—not that the situation is stable.

APPENDIX B

Chesapeake Bay Timeline

Chesapeake Bay Timeline

Nature Line		Governance Line	
1000 B.C.	Chesapeake Bay achieves its approximate modern configuration.		
A.D. 1572	Brother Carrera, a Spanish priest, says of the Chesapeake: "It is called the Bay of the Mother God, and in it there are many deep water ports, each better than the next."		
1608	Captain John Smith describes the bay: "A faire bay compassed but for the mouth with fruitful and delightsome land [where] heaven and earth never agreed better to frame a place for man's habitation."	1632	Virginia enacts legislation restricting the planting of tobacco, both to conserve soil resources and to assure an adequate supply of other agricultural products to the settlers of the colony.
1660	European settlers in the bay region reach a population of 60,000.	1680s	William Penn directs that for every 4 acres of land cleared for farming, one must be kept in woodland.
1683	William Penn notes: "Of shellfish we have oysters, crabs, cockles, conchs and mussels; some oysters six inches long and one sort of cockles as big as the stewing oyster; they make a rich broth."		
1700	Port Tobacco, in Maryland, becomes so silted that it is closed to oceangoing vessels. The forests of the watershed are being cut for growing tobacco and other farming, resulting in increased sediment loads to the bay.	1776	Baltimore enacts an "Act to Remove a Nuisance in Baltimore Town" destroying what was described as a large miry marsh giving off noxious vapors and putrid effluvia.

1785   George Washington intervenes to resolve conflicts in oystering between Virginia and Maryland. This meeting eventually results in the Constitutional Convention in Philadelphia in 1787, giving rise to the U.S. Constitution.

1850   Over 50 percent of the forest land of the watershed has been lost to farming and timbering.

1905   Pennsylvania enacts a statute to protect water quality for human consumption.

1913   The first modern sewage treatment plant in the nation is constructed at Baltimore to protect oyster beds of the upper bay from human waste contamination.

1850   The ports of Georgetown and Bladensburg are closed due to siltation. By now perhaps as much as 50 percent of the forested land of the watershed has been lost to farming and timbering.

1876   The shad harvest is at 4 million pounds— gigantic by today's standards but a "worrisome" decline by standards of the time.

1884   Oyster harvest reaches its historic peak of around 20 million bushels.

1894   Referring to the Potomac, the U.S. Public Health Service notes that "at certain times of the year the river is so loaded with sediments as to be unfit for bathing as well as for drinking and cooking purposes."

1919   The Commissioners of Fisheries of Virginia note: "One of the greatest questions for the future is that of pollution. The pollution of sewage of our ever increasing population and the waste from our rapidly growing industries is affecting the entire fish and oyster industry in and around Hampton Roads."

NATURE LINE		GOVERNANCE LINE	
		1927	The Chesapeake Biological Laboratory is founded at Solomons, Maryland, to investigate the conditions of resources in the bay.
1928	Conowingo Dam, most downstream dam on the Susquehanna River, is completed—totally blocking migratory fish passage to the greatest of the bay's tributaries.		
		1938	A sewage treatment plant is constructed at Blue Plains, in Washington, at the direction of President Roosevelt, to improve the water quality of the Potomac River.
1940	H. L. Mencken is still moved to note that "Baltimore lay very near the immense protein factory of the Chesapeake Bay, and out of it ate divinely."		
		1948	Congress enacts the first federal Water Pollution Control Act.
		1952	First baywide cruise to conduct scientific investigations of conditions in the bay.
1957	The U.S. Public Health Service declares the Potomac unsafe for swimming.		
1961	The Virginia Fisheries Commission notes that "contamination of our natural waters by pollution of various types is one of the most pressing programs facing our Commonwealth today."		
		1967	Chesapeake Bay Foundation established.
		1968	First Chesapeake Bay water quality conference.
		1970	First Earth Day.

1972	Tropical Storm Agnes inundates the bay with volumes of fresh water not seen in historical times.
1972	Enactment of the modern federal Water Pollution Control Act, designed to achieve fishable and swimmable waters and provide substantial federal financial assistance for the construction of sewage treatment plants.
	EPA bans DDT, resulting in gradual return of the bald eagle and osprey.
1975	Kepone discharges at Hopewell, Virginia, force closing of the James River to fishing for a decade.
	Senator Charles McC. Mathias (R.–MD) urges EPA to carry out a comprehensive study of water quality and other problems of Chesapeake Bay.
1976	The bay's largest oil spill occurs at Smith Point, Virginia.
1977	Second bay water quality conference held at Patuxent Naval Air Station. Scientists raise concerns, but the overall condition of the bay is held to be fairly good.
	An upper bay phosphorus strategy is adopted, leading to a commitment to remove phosphorus from major plants in Pennsylvania and Maryland.
1978	Chesapeake Bay Commission established to bring together state legislators and officials.

NATURE LINE	GOVERNANCE LINE
	1979 — Chesapeake Bay agreement signed between Maryland and Virginia, committing them to work together on bay issues.
1980 — Maryland closes its shad fishery.	
1983 — The EPA documents the death of nearly 90 percent of the bay's underwater grasses.	1983 — EPA issues a major study on the bay's condition confirming a widespread and worsening decline. Maryland, Pennsylvania, Virginia, D.C., the federal government, and the Chesapeake Bay Commission sign an agreement making specific commitments to restore the Chesapeake's water quality and natural resources.
1984 — Maryland closes its striped bass fishery.	1984 — Maryland passes its Critical Area Act restricting zoning in an area 1,000 feet back from the shoreline and extending around the entire bay and tributaries to the head of tide.
	1985 — Maryland passes a ban on phosphates in detergents.
	1986 — D.C. passes a phosphate ban.
	1987 — Virginia passes a phosphate ban.
	Maryland, Pennsylvania, Virginia, D.C., the federal government, and the Chesapeake Bay Commission sign a new agreement to clean up the bay. The key target is a 40 percent reduction of nutrients by the year 2000.
	1988 — Pennsylvania passes a phosphate ban.

APPENDIX C

The Clean Water Act

The Clean Water Act was originally passed in 1972 with the objective of restoring and maintaining "the chemical, physical, and biological integrity of the Nation's waters." The act established as a national goal that "the discharge of pollutants into the navigable waters be eliminated by 1985." Needless to say, that goal has not been met.

Essentially the act prohibited discharges of pollutants to rivers, streams, and other water bodies without a permit; a National Pollutant Discharge Elimination System was established to allow dischargers to obtain those permits. Under this system, most of the responsibility for day-to-day administration of the permit program is delegated by the U.S. Environmental Protection Agency to the states. Thousands of permits have been issued in the bay region. The act also regulates thousands of other facilities that discharge their wastes into sewers rather than directly into water bodies. While the effect of the act has been to reduce pollutants going into the bay substantially, huge amounts of toxic chemicals and other substances are still discharged legally.

An essential part of each state's task is to set water quality standards to protect its water bodies and to identify which water bodies do not meet the standards. Amendments to the act in 1987 were aimed at improving water quality standards and the control of toxic discharges, but they have yet to be fully implemented.

Another section of the act requires permits for urban stormwater discharges, but implementation of the program has been delayed for years. Not until the end of 1990 did EPA issue the guidance necessary for permits to be issued. In the act there are also provisions to control other sources of diffuse rainwater runoff; these measures hold promise but have not yet shown many results. The act also controls sludge generated by sewage treatment plants.

The Clean Water Act contains important provisions designed to protect our nation's wetlands (Section 404), as well, but the act only prohibits the placement of fill material in wetlands and leaves unregulated many activities that can degrade or destroy this resource.

The act originally provided construction grant funds for local sewage treatment plants. Billions of dollars were spent to help localities improve their plants, resulting in improved water quality in many areas. Congress has phased out the grants, making loans available instead.

Finally, a key provision of the act encourages estuarine management and provides funding in a number of designated areas, including Chesapeake Bay.

APPENDIX D

The Clean Air Act

When enacting the Clean Air Act in 1970, Congress expressed its intent "to protect and enhance the quality of the Nation's air resources" and voiced its concern "that the growth in the amount and complexity of air pollution brought about by urbanization, industrial development, and the increasing use of motor vehicles, has resulted in mounting dangers to the public health and welfare." To address these problems, Congress established a program of national air quality standards to be implemented through state plans.

Under the scheme devised by Congress, the U.S. Environmental Protection Agency identified six specific pollutants that present major threats to air quality and issued air quality standards for each. These "criteria" pollutants are particulates, sulfur dioxide, nitrogen oxides, ozone, carbon monoxide, and lead. EPA was also instructed to identify and establish standards for hazardous air pollutants. To date the agency has accomplished this for only a handful of chemicals. The standards applied to hazardous air pollutants are more conservative than for the criteria pollutants.

Each state then has primary responsibility for carrying out the act within its borders and must submit a state implementation plan detailing the manner in which the national standards will be achieved and maintained. The states also bear primary responsibility for enforcing the act. Areas that did not attain the standards established by the act by specified dates were subject to restrictions and sanctions including the loss of highway funds. Such sanctions were rarely imposed, however. Congress was concerned that significant deterioration of air quality not be allowed where the standards had been achieved and was especially anxious to protect national parks and wild areas. Thus a tiered system was established imposing increasingly stricter requirements for more pristine areas.

Automobiles were a major focus of the act, which imposed requirements for emission limits and other controls. These measures have led to automobiles that achieve lower emissions per vehicle, but the number of vehicle miles traveled each year has essentially wiped out the gains. One success has been the elimination of leaded gasoline.

After years of debate, the act was revised in 1990; many provisions were strengthened and new ones added. Pollution control requirements will be tightened in cities that have not attained federal air quality standards, reductions in acid-rain-causing emissions of sulfur and nitrogen oxides are mandated, and all facilities with major toxic air emissions will be brought under control. In addition, stricter requirements will be placed on auto emissions. Cleaner gasoline and some clean-fueled vehicles will be mandated in the most polluted cities, and chemicals that contribute to depletion of the stratospheric ozone layer will be phased out. The timetables for achieving these changes are lengthy, however, sometimes as much as twenty years. Enforcement should be improved, since operating permits will be required for major emitters of air pollution.

Glossary

The definitions presented here are not meant to be exhaustive or to split scientific hairs but to reinforce the meanings of certain words within the context of this book.

acid rain   Rain or other precipitation whose pH (a measure of acidity) is substantially more acid than normal. Acid rain has become a major pollutant of streams and lakes throughout much of the industrialized world in recent decades.

airshed   An area within which air pollutants are transported and deposited on land and water surfaces; boundaries may vary with weather conditions, but for Chesapeake Bay the airshed may include pollution sources as far away as the Ohio River Valley.

algae   Generally, any of a large class of plant life in the bay, either floating freely or growing in filamentous form on the bottom or as a coating formed on other plants like the submerged, rooted aquatic vegetation; used here as distinct from the floating plant life of the bay (see *plankton*).

anadromous   Migrating upstream from the sea, usually to reproduce.

anoxic   Without oxygen.

aquatic   Living in the water.

benthos   Bottom-dwelling creatures; examples are oysters, clams, burrowing worms.

best management practices (BMP)   A wide variety of agricultural techniques aimed at increasing soil productivity and reducing pollution; examples include plowing along the land's natural contours (rather than straight up and down slopes) to reduce erosion from rainfall, planting winter grasses to reduce wind erosion, and storing manure to keep it out of streams.

biotechnology   A range of techniques used to manipulate life in the bay in order to raise its production of seafood; can range from simple aquaculture (such as growing oysters in rafts to avoid losses to predators) to genetic engineering of organisms to make them grow faster or more uniformly.

buffer strip   A strip of varying width, left in forest or other permanent vegetation between waterways and land uses like agriculture or development, to intercept and filter out pollution before it runs off into the bay or its tributaries.

catadromous   Migrating downstream in the direction of the sea, usually to reproduce.

catch per unit effort (CPUE)   The number of fish or other species harvested per standard measure of fishing effort (such as per crab pot, per mile of net, or per man-hour of fishing time); considered a truer measure of trends in a species' abundance than simply looking at pounds caught.

discharge permit   Legal contract negotiated between federal and state regulators and an industry or sewage treatment plant that sets limits on many water pollutants or polluting effects from the discharges of its pipes to public waters.

dissolved oxygen   Level of oxygen in the water; more than 5 parts oxygen per million parts of water is considered healthy; below 3 is generally stressful.

ecosystem   Interrelated and interdependent parts of a biological system; sometimes popularly expressed as "everything is connected to everything."

estuary   A coastal water body where fresh water from rivers mixes with salt water from the ocean.

eutrophic   Overenriched or overfertilized.

fishery   The commercial or sport catch of a given fish species.

groundwater   Subsurface collection of rainwater that percolates through the earth rather than running immediately off into waterways; ranges from water a few inches deep to aquifers far below the surface; a significant source of water to the bay.

homeostasis   The mechanism whereby organisms, or even whole ecosystems, maintain stability and orderly functioning (example: sweating cools an overheated body back down to its normal state by evaporation).

hypoxic   A deficiency of oxygen; in the bay, the term is usually applied when there is less than 2 parts oxygen per million parts of water.

isohaline   The lines of constant salinity running laterally across the bay.

landings   Catches (as "landings of fish are up this year").

larvae   An early life stage or stages often following the egg stage; a period of high vulnerability for most organisms.

metals   Materials like cadmium, lead, arsenic, mercury, and copper that enter the bay from both human and natural sources; in high enough amounts they may be extremely toxic to biological life and may accumulate from low levels in the water to dangerous levels in the flesh of organisms high in the food web.

nitrogen   One of two principal nutrients in human sewage and farm fertilizers that is polluting Chesapeake Bay.

nutrient   A basic food essential for the growth of plankton in the waters of the bay; in the Chesapeake, usually either nitrogen or phosphorus.

phosphorus   One of two principal nutrients in human sewage and farm fertilizers that is polluting Chesapeake Bay.

phytoplankton   Floating plant life.

plankton   Floating plant and animal life.

pretreatment   The removal of certain wastes from sewage before it is discharged to a sewage treatment plant; usually applied to industrial toxics and heavy metals.

primary production   Plant life (in the water, algae or plankton); the organisms that first convert sunlight into food and are then consumed by higher organisms; the base of the food web.

priority pollutant   Chemical designated by the EPA as having high priority for control or removal from waste discharges because of its toxicity or potential to cause cancer or mutations.

progging   Exploring; often applied to someone who loves to hunt, fish, and trap the marshes of the Chesapeake and roam them for sheer entertainment, gathering all manner of items from wild asparagus to soft-shelled clams and Indian arrowheads.

resilience   The natural ability of the Chesapeake ecosystem to counter natural and human stresses such as pollution, floods, and drought.

runoff   The movement of pollutants from the land via water from rainfall.

salinity   The amount of salt, by weight, in the water; a salinity of 10 means there is 10 ounces of salt for every 1,000 ounces of water; fresh water has a salinity of zero; the ocean is about 33 parts salt per thousand parts of water.

scrape   A type of dredge, 3 to 4 feet across at its mouth, used by soft-crabbers; dragged through grass beds, it scoops crabs into its mesh bag; instead of teeth the scrape has a smooth bar so it does not bite deeply into the bottom, destroying the grass beds.

sediment   The soil from farms or construction sites that runs into the water in rainstorms; it can be a significant pollutant.

sludge   The semisolid residue formed from removing wastes from sewage or industrial discharges.

spat   The microscopic, free-floating larval form of the oyster; it must attach and begin forming its shell soon after hatching or die.

spawning   Reproduction in fish.

stormwater   Rainwater that runs off the land (usually paved or compacted surfaces in urban and suburban areas); it can be a significant source of pollution.

stratification   In the Chesapeake, stratification occurs when there is little mixing between the lighter fresh water sliding down the bay near its surface and the heavier ocean water moving up the bay near its bottom; this can lead to oxygen declines in the deeper waters of the bay.

submerged aquatic vegetation (SAV)   Vegetation rooted in the bottom of the bay's shallows (usually no deeper than 10 feet); important in controlling water quality and as food and habitat for wildlife; more than a dozen varieties are found in the Chesapeake.

watershed   Drainage basin; lands that slope toward a particular water body, channeling all the rain that falls on them toward that body of water.

wetlands   Vegetation that is periodically flooded or saturated by water; may range from coastal salt marsh, inundated on every high tide, to nontidal wetlands far inland that are dry most of the time; wetlands have great value for wildlife and water quality.

zoea   A larval stage of the blue crab during its early weeks of life, a stage in which the crab is quite vulnerable to environmental stresses.

References

Chapter 1: Rethinking the Bay

Blond, Georges. *The Great Migrations of Animals.* New York: Collier Press, 1962.

Boynton, W. R., Kemp, W. M., and Keefe, C. W. *A Comparative Analysis of Nutrients and Other Factors Influencing Estuarine Phytoplankton Production.* New York: Academic Press, 1982.

Gerritsen, J., Ranasinghe, J. A., and Holland A. F. *Comparison of Three Strategies to Improve Water Quality in the Maryland Portion of Chesapeake Bay.* Columbia: Versar Inc., ESM Operations, 1988.

Horton, Tom. *Bay Country.* Baltimore: Johns Hopkins University Press, 1987.

Nixon, Scott W. "Chesapeake Bay Nutrient Budgets—a Reassessment." *Biogeochemistry* 4 (1987):77–90.

U.S. Environmental Protection Agency. *Chesapeake Bay: Introduction to an Ecosystem.* Washington, 1989.

Wolfe, Douglas A. *Estuarine Variability.* New York: Academic Press, 1985.

Chapter 2: Pollution

Bechtold, William A., Brown, Mark J., and Tansey, John B. "Forest Inventory and Analysis." *Virginia's Forests.* Resource Bulletin SE-95 (1986): v.

Boicourt, W. C. *The Influences of Circulation Processes on Dissolved Oxygen in Chesapeake Bay.* Cambridge: University of Maryland Systems Center for Environmental and Estuarine Studies, 1990.

Broutman, Marlene A., Harkness, Kristen E., and Leonard, Dorothy L. *The Quality of Shellfish Growing Waters on the East Coast of the United States.* Rockville: National Oceanic and Atmospheric Administration, 1989.

Bureau of the Census. *1987 Census of Agriculture.* Vol. 1: *Geographic Area Series.* P. 38: *Pennsylvania State and County Data.* Washington, 1988.

Cameron, Diane. *NRDC's Poison Runoff Index for the Washington Metropolitan Region*. Washington: Natural Resources Defense Council, 1989.

Casman, Elizabeth. *Parameters and Concepts for Modeling: Tillage Practices, Animal Waste Management Systems, and Vegetated Filter Strips*. Baltimore: Interstate Commission on the Potomac River Basin in cooperation with Maryland Department of the Environment, 1989.

Chesapeake Bay Foundation. *Industrial Pretreatment in the Chesapeake Bay Watershed: The Untapped Potential for Reducing Toxics*. Annapolis, 1989.

Chesapeake Bay Foundation. *Oil and Gas Drilling and Transport in the Chesapeake Bay Region*. Annapolis, 1990.

Chesapeake Bay Foundation. *At Work on Our Bay: A Strategy for a "Toxics Free" Bay*. Annapolis, 1990.

Commonwealth of Pennsylvania, Department of Environmental Resources. *1989 Nonpoint Source Assessment*. Harrisburg: Nonpoint Task Force, 1989.

Commonwealth of Pennsylvania, Department of Environmental Resources. *1990 Water Quality Assessment*. (305(b)Report.) Harrisburg, 1990.

Correll, David L. *Contaminant Problems and Management of Living Chesapeake Bay Resources*. Chap. 14: "Nutrients in Chesapeake Bay." Edgewater: Smithsonian Environmental Research Center, 1987.

Correll, David L., and Peterjohn, William T. *Nutrient Dynamics in an Agricultural Watershed: Observations on the Role of a Riparian Forest*. Edgewater: Smithsonian Environmental Research Center, 1983.

Correll, David L., and Weller, Donald E. *Factors Limiting Processes in Freshwater Wetlands: An Agricultural Primary Stream Riparian Forest*. Edgewater: Smithsonian Environmental Research Center, 1990.

Domotor, Diana K., Haire, Michael S., Panday, Narandra N., and Summers, Robert M. *Patuxent Estuary Water Quality Assessment: Special Emphasis 1983–1987*. Baltimore: Maryland Department of the Environment, 1989.

Garreis, Mary Jo, and Murphy, Deirdre L. *Survey of Organochlorine Pesticide and Metal Concentrations in Chesapeake Bay Finfish*. Baltimore: Maryland Department of the Environment, Water Management Administration, 1983.

Garreis, Mary Jo, and Murphy, Deirdre L. *Inner Harbor Crab Survey: Heavy Metal and Chlorinated Hydrocarbon Levels in Callinectes sapidus in the Chesapeake Bay*. Baltimore: Maryland Department of the Environment, Division of Standards and Certification, Water Management Administration, 1986.

Hamilton, P. A., Shedlock, R. J., and Phillips, P. J. *Ground-Water-Quality Assessment of the Delmarva Peninsula: Delaware, Maryland, and Virginia—Analysis of Available Water-Quality Data Through 1987.* Denver: U.S. Geological Survey, 1989.

Heistand, Gerald M. *Detailed Analysis Report of Manure Excesses and Deficits for the Townships of Lancaster County.* Lancaster, 1989.

Heltz, George R., and Huggett, Robert J. *Contaminant Problems and Management of Living Chesapeake Bay Resources.* Chap. 13: "Contaminants in Chesapeake Bay: The Regional Perspective." College Park and Gloucester Point: University of Maryland and Virginia Institute of Marine Sciences, 1987.

Kearney, Michael, and Marcus, Andrew. *Sediment Sources and Human Impacts on Sediment Loads in a Chesapeake Bay Tributary.* College Park: University of Maryland, Department of Geography, 1989.

Klein, Richard. *An Integrated Watershed Management Policy.* Annapolis: Maryland Wildlife Administration, Department of Natural Resources, 1980.

Klein, Richard. *A Survey of the Quality of Erosion and Sediment Control and Stormwater Management in the Chesapeake Bay Watershed.* Maryland Line: Community and Environmental Defense Associates, 1990.

Lanyon, L. E. *Perspectives for Sustainable Agriculture from Nutrient Management Experiences in Pennsylvania.* University Park: Pennsylvania State University, Department of Agronomy, 1990.

Lanyon, L. E., Partenheimer, E. J., and Westphal, P. J. *Plant Nutrient Management Strategy Implications for Optimal Herd Size and Performance of a Simulated Dairy Farm.* University Park: Agricultural Systems, 1989.

Lugbill, Jon. *Potomac River Basin Nutrient Inventory.* Washington: Metropolitan Washington Council of Governments, 1990.

Malone, Thomas C. *Effects of Water Column Processes on Dissolved Oxygen: Nutrients, Phytoplankton and Zooplankton.* Cambridge: Center for Environmental and Estuarine Studies, 1990.

Maryland Department of Health and Mental Hygiene. *Monitoring for Management Actions: Chesapeake Bay Water Quality Monitoring Program—First Biennial Report.* Baltimore, 1987.

Maryland Department of Natural Resources, Chesapeake Bay Research and Monitoring Division. *Sources of Acidity in Maryland Coastal Plain Streams.* Annapolis, 1990.

Murphy, Deirdre. *Analysis of Basic Water Monitoring Program Fish Tissue Network.* Baltimore: Maryland Department of the Environment, Water Management Administration, 1988.

Murphy, Deirdre. *Contaminant Levels in Oysters and Clams from the Chesapeake Bay 1981–1985.* Baltimore: Maryland Department of the Environment, Water Administration, Water Quality Programs, 1990.

Singewald, Joseph T., Jr. *Shore Erosion in Tidewater Maryland.* Baltimore: Maryland Board of Natural Resources, 1949.

U.S. Army Corps of Engineers (Baltimore and Norfolk Districts) with the State of Maryland and the Commonwealth of Virginia. *Chesapeake Bay Shoreline Erosion Study: Draft Feasibility Report.* Baltimore and Norfolk, 1990.

U.S. Department of Agriculture. *Statistical Summary 1988–1989 and Pennsylvania Department of Agriculture Annual Report 1988.* Washington, 1989.

U.S. Environmental Protection Agency. *Point Source Atlas.* Washington: Chesapeake Bay Program, 1988.

U.S. Environmental Protection Agency. *Chesapeake Bay Nonpoint Source Programs, Region 3.* Annapolis: Chesapeake Bay Liaison Office, 1988.

U.S. Environmental Protection Agency. *Report of Internal and Management Audit: Report of Audit on the Management of the Chesapeake Bay Program Point Source Pollution Program.* Audit Report E1H98-03-0208-9100467. Washington, 1989.

U.S. Environmental Protection Agency. *Baywide Nutrient Reduction Strategy Progress Report.* Washington: Chesapeake Bay Program, 1989.

U.S. Environmental Protection Agency. *The State of the Chesapeake Bay.* Third Biennial Monitoring Report. Washington, 1989.

Virginia Department of Conservation and Historic Resources. *Virginia Nonpoint Source Pollution Assessment Report.* Richmond, 1988.

Virginia Polytechnic Institute and State University. *Watershed/Water Quality Monitoring for Evaluating Animal Waste BMP Effectiveness.* Blacksburg: Agricultural Engineering Department, 1988.

Virginia State Water Control Board. *Virginia Water Quality Assessment 1990.* Vol. 1. Information Bulletin 579. Richmond, 1990.

Chapter 3: Harvests

Atlantic States Marine Fisheries Commission. *Interstate Fisheries Management Plan for the Striped Bass of the Atlantic Coast from Maine to North Carolina.* Washington: Versar, Inc., 1990.

Broutman, Marlene A., Harkness, Kristen E., and Leonard, Dorothy L. *The Quality of Shellfish Growing Waters on the East Coast of the United States.* Rockville: National Oceanic and Atmospheric Administration, 1989.

Chesapeake Executive Council. *Chesapeake Bay Stock Assessment Plan: An Agreement Commitment Report.* Annapolis, 1988.

Chesapeake Executive Council. *Chesapeake Bay Blue Crab Management Plan: An Agreement Commitment Report.* Annapolis, 1989.

Maryland Department of Natural Resources. *Preliminary Review: Current Status of Maryland's Oyster Resources.* Annapolis, 1985.

Maryland Department of Natural Resources Tidewater Administration and Virginia Marine Resources Commission. *Chesapeake Bay Fisheries: Status, Trends, Priorities and Data Needs.* Annapolis and Newport News, 1988.

Norton, Smith, and Strand. *Stripers—The Economic Value of the Atlantic Coast Commercial and Recreational Striped Bass Fisheries.* College Park: Maryland Sea Grant, University of Maryland, 1984.

St. Pierre, Richard. *Historical Review of the American Shad and River Herring Fisheries of the Susquehanna River.* Harrisburg: U.S. Fish and Wildlife Service, 1979.

U.S. Environmental Protection Agency. *Strategy for Removing Impediments to Migratory Fishes in the Chesapeake Bay Watershed.* Washington: Chesapeake Bay Program, 1988.

U.S. Environmental Protection Agency. *Chesapeake Bay Alosid Management Plan.* Annapolis: Chesapeake Bay Program, 1989.

U.S. Environmental Protection Agency. *Chesapeake Bay Oyster Management Plan.* Washington: Chesapeake Bay Program, 1989.

U.S. Environmental Protection Agency. *Implementation Plan for the Submerged Aquatic Vegetation Policy.* Washington: Chesapeake Bay Program, 1990.

Virginia Sea Grant College Program. *A Plan Addressing the Restoration of the Oyster Industry.* Charlottesville, 1990.

Chapter 4: Resilience

Board of Public Works Wetlands Administrator. *Report to the Board of Public Works on Activities Under the Maryland Wetlands Act (1978 through 1987).* Annapolis, 1988.

Chesapeake Bay Executive Council. *Habitat Requirements for Chesapeake Bay Living Resources.* Washington, 1988.

Chesapeake Bay Nonpoint Source Program Evaluation Panel. *The Urban Stormwater Runoff Presentation: Selected Issues Relating to the Implementation of Nonpoint Source Control Programs.* Background paper. Annapolis, 1988.

Grace, Russell E., Kearney, Michael S., and Stevenson, J. Court. *Marsh Loss in Nanticoke Estuary, Chesapeake Bay.* Washington: American Geographical Society of New York, 1988.

Harris, Larry D. *The Fragmented Forest.* Chicago: University of Chicago Press, 1984.

Hillyer, Saunders C. *The Maryland Critical Area Program: Time to De-Mythologize and Move Forward.* Annapolis: Chesapeake Bay Foundation, 1988.

Jackson, Jerome A. "Preface." In *The Past, Present, and Future of North American Forest Ecosystems and Their Avifaunas.* Madison: University of Wisconsin Press, 1989.

Jordon, Thomas, Kearney, Michael S., Stevenson, J. Court, and Ward, Larry G. *Sedimentary Processes and Sea Level Rise in Tidal Marsh Systems of Chesapeake Bay.* Proceedings of a conference held 9–11 April 1985. Easton, 1985.

Kearney, Michael S., and Stevenson, J. Court. *Sea-Level Rise and Marsh Vertical Accretion Rates in Chesapeake Bay.* College Park and Cambridge: University of Maryland Department of Geography and Horn Point Environmental Laboratories, 1985.

Kearney, Michael S., and Stevenson, J. Court. *Sea-Level History of the Chesapeake Bay Over the Last Few Centuries.* College Park and Cambridge: University of Maryland Department of Geography and Horn Point Environmental Laboratories, 1989.

"The Last Wetlands." Special issue of *Audubon Magazine,* July 1990.

Maryland Department of State Planning. *Maryland's Land: A Portrait of Changing Uses, 1973 to 1985.* Baltimore, 1987.

Pennsylvania Forestry Association. *Pennsylvania Forests* 7 (3): 1988.

Pennsylvania Wildlife Federation. *First Environmental Quality Index.* Harrisburg, 1988.

Secretary of the Interior. *Wetland Losses in the United States: 1780's to 1980's.* Draft report to Congress. Washington, 1990.

Sullivan, Kevin. *A Summary of the Chesapeake Bay Critical Area Commission's Criteria and Program Development Activities 1984–1988.* Annapolis: Chesapeake Bay Critical Area Commission, 1989.

Teal, John, and Teal, Mildred. *Life and Death of the Salt Marsh.* New York: Audubon/Ballantine, 1975.

U.S. Army Corps of Engineers. *Chesapeake Bay Low Freshwater Inflow Study Main Report.* Baltimore, 1984.

U.S. Army Corps of Engineers. *Chesapeake Bay and Tributaries Reallocation Study.* Baltimore, 1988.

U.S. Environmental Protection Agency. *The State of the Chesapeake Bay.* Third Biennial Monitoring Report—1989. Data Analysis Workgroup of the Chesapeake Bay Program's Subcommittee. Washington, 1989.

U.S. Environmental Protection Agency. *Macrobenthic Communities of the Lower Chesapeake Bay: March 1985–June 1988.* Washington: Chesapeake Bay Program, 1989.

U.S. Environmental Protection Agency. *Chesapeake Bay Wetlands Policy Implementation Plan.* Draft report. Washington: Chesapeake Bay Program, 1990.

U.S. Environmental Protection Agency. *Implementation Plan for the Submerged Aquatic Vegetation Policy.* Washington: Chesapeake Bay Program, 1990.

U.S. Environmental Protection Agency and U.S. Fish and Wildlife Service. *Mid-Atlantic Wetlands: A Disappearing Natural Treasure.* Washington, 1985.

Virginia Institute of Marine Science. *Distribution of Submerged Aquatic Vegetation in the Chesapeake Bay.* Gloucester Point: College of William and Mary, 1989.

Chapter 5: The Ultimate Issue: People

Hillyer, Saunders. *Analysis of Land Use Effects of the Proposed Washington Bypass.* Background paper. Annapolis: Chesapeake Bay Foundation, 1990.

2020 Panel. *Population Growth and Development in the Chesapeake Bay Watershed to the Year 2020.* Annapolis, 1988.

Warner, William W. *Beautiful Swimmers.* Westford: Murray, 1978.

Chapter 6: Four Key Battles

Chesapeake Research Consortium. *The Bi-state Conference on Chesapeake Bay.* Annapolis, 1977.

Hostetler, John A. "Toward Responsible Growth and Stewardship of Lancaster County's Landscape." *Pennsylvania Mennonite Heritage.* 1989.

Maryland Department of State Planning. *Maryland's Land: A Portrait of Changing Uses, 1973 to 1985.* Baltimore, 1987.

Woodlief, Ann. *In River Time: The Way of the James.* Chapel Hill: Algonquin, 1985.

Chapter 7: Recommendations

Chesapeake Bay Foundation. *The Chesapeake Crisis: Turning the Tide.* Annapolis, 1990.

Chesapeake Research Consortium. *Perspectives on the Chesapeake Bay, 1990: Advances in Estuarine Sciences.* Gloucester Point, 1990.

Costanza, Robert, and Daly, Herman E. *Toward an Ecological Economics.* Baton Rouge: Coastal Ecology Institute, Center for Wetland Resources, and the Department of Economics, Louisiana State University, 1987.

"Costing the Earth." *Economist,* 2 September 1989.

Morris, Ian. "The Future of the Chesapeake Bay and Its Resources." Speech. Cambridge, 1986.

"Reflections: Encountering the Countryside—1." *New Yorker,* August 1989.

"Reflections: Encountering the Countryside—2." *New Yorker,* September 1989.

U.S. Environmental Protection Agency. *Chesapeake Bay Program Technical Studies: A Synthesis.* Washington, 1982.

U.S. Environmental Protection Agency. *Chesapeake Bay: A Profile of Environmental Change.* Washington, 1983.

U.S. Environmental Protection Agency. *The State of the Chesapeake Bay.* Third Biennial Monitoring Report—1989. Data Analysis Workgroup of the Chesapeake Bay Program's Subcommittee. Annapolis, 1989.

Westinghouse Ocean Research and Engineering Center. *Proceedings of the Governor's Conference on Chesapeake Bay.* Annapolis, 1968.

Index

Acknowledgments

Writing prescriptions for the health of the environment is as much art as science, as dependent on developing a feel for the mesh of humans and their environment as on the results of water-quality tests. No author can do that alone. This book represents a collaborative effort that involved hundreds of people who willingly gave time and energy to the authors. Below are a few of them.

Will Baker, listed elsewhere as Chesapeake Bay Foundation president, was also full-time editor of this book. He was invaluable, both for his guidance and advice, and for his rare ability to know when not to give it. Jane Shorall and Ann Marie Helms at CBF took on duties too numerous to mention, without which this book would have emerged sometime next century.

The scientific advisory board for the book often went beyond the technical nature of its job by providing insight and inspiration. Thanks to Bob Biggs, Les Lanyon, Karl Hirschner, Walt Boynton, Bill Richkus, and Bob Huggett; to CBF Trustee Gene Cronin, who at the authors' request commented on technical and scientific portions of the book; and to Tom Wisner, bay singer and educator, who added his unique and cosmic insights.

Bill Boicourt, Mike Kemp, and Court Stevenson of the University of Maryland, and Charles Spooner and his staff at EPA's Chesapeake Bay Liaison Office frequently illuminated our views of the Chesapeake ecosystem.

The support given coauthor Bill Eichbaum by his employer, World Wildlife Fund and The Conservation Foundation, was critical to the timely completion of the whole effort.

Among the CBF staff, some were especially involved in shaping this book: Joe Maroon, Jean Watts, Jolene Chinchilli, Roy Hoagland, Lamonte Garber, Tom Sexton, Anne Powers, Mike Hirshfield, Rupert Friday, Sandy Hillyer, Bill Goldsborough, Mike Heller, and Patrick Gardner. Steve Fletcher did yeoman work in sorting through fifty years of manure statistics for many animals.

Richard Klein of Community and Environmental Defense Associates traversed much of the bay's watershed for the data and provided keen observations that underlay our sediment and stormwater section.

Finally, thanks to the editors at Island Press for believing in the project from the start, and to Sita Culman of the Abell Foundation for her thoughtful questions during the drafting of the text.

Tom Horton,
Bill Eichbaum
March, 1991

About the Authors

TOM HORTON was born and raised on the Eastern Shore of Maryland; he grew up hunting, fishing, and consorting with watermen. As a reporter on Chesapeake Bay for the *Baltimore Sun* (1972–1987), he has won numerous local and national awards, including the National Wildlife Federation's Conservation Communicator of the Year, the Scripps-Howard Meeman award for best conservation series (on the Amazon jungle), and the Kenny Rogers national award for hunger reporting (on the Ethiopian famine). His book *Bay Country*, a series of essays on the Chesapeake environment, won both the John Burroughs Medal for the country's best natural history book of 1988 and a similar award from the Wildlife Society.

WILLIAM M. EICHBAUM is vice-president of the Environmental Quality Program of the World Wildlife Fund and The Conservation Foundation. Prior to joining WWF/CF, he served in a variety of governmental positions, including Undersecretary, Executive Office of Environmental Affairs, Commonwealth of Massachusetts, and Assistant Secretary for the Office of Environmental Programs, Department of Health and Mental Hygiene, State of Maryland. In Maryland he was instrumental in the creation and management of the Chesapeake Bay Program, including Maryland's Critical Area Commission. He has also served on several committees of the National Research Council investigating marine matters and is a board member of the Coastal Society.

Also Available from Island Press

Ancient Forests of the Pacific Northwest
By Elliott A. Norse

Balancing on the Brink of Extinction: The Endangered Species Act and Lessons for the Future
Edited by Kathryn A. Kohm

Better Trout Habitat: A Guide to Stream Restoration and Management
By Christopher J. Hunter

Beyond 40 Percent: Record-Setting Recycling and Composting Programs
The Institute for Local Self-Reliance

The Challenge of Global Warming
Edited by Dean Edwin Abrahamson

Coastal Alert: Ecosystems, Energy, and Offshore Oil Drilling
By Dwight Holing

The Complete Guide to Environmental Careers
The CEIP Fund

Economics of Protected Areas
By John A. Dixon and Paul B. Sherman

Environmental Agenda for the Future
Edited by Robert Cahn

Environmental Disputes: Community Involvement in Conflict Resolution
By James E. Crowfoot and Julia M. Wondolleck

Forests and Forestry in China: Changing Patterns of Resource Development
By S. D. Richardson

The Global Citizen
By Donella Meadows

Hazardous Waste from Small Quantity Generators
By Seymour I. Schwartz and Wendy B. Pratt

Holistic Resource Management Workbook
By Allan Savory

In Praise of Nature
Edited and with essays by Stephanie Mills

The Living Ocean: Understanding and Protecting Marine Biodiversity
By Boyce Thorne-Miller and John G. Catena

National Resources for the 21st Century
Edited by R. Neil Sampson and Dwight Hair

The New York Environment Book
By Eric A. Goldstein and Mark A. Izeman

Overtapped Oasis: Reform or Revolution for Western Water
By Marc Reisner and Sarah Bates

Permaculture: A Practical Guide for a Sustainable Future
By Bill Mollison

Plastics: America's Packaging Dilemma
By Nancy Wolf and Ellen Feldman

The Poisoned Well: New Strategies for Groundwater Protection
Edited by Eric Jorgensen

Race to Save the Tropics: Ecology and Economics for a Sustainable Future
Edited by Robert Goodland

Recycling and Incineration: Evaluating the Choices
By Richard A. Denison and John Ruston

Reforming the Forest Service
By Randal O'Toole

The Rising Tide: Global Warming and World Sea Levels
By Lynne T. Edgerton

Saving the Tropical Forests
By Judith Gradwohl and Russell Greenberg

Trees, Why Do You Wait?
By Richard Critchfield

War on Waste: Can America Win Its Battle with Garbage?
By Louis Blumberg and Robert Gottlieb

Western Water Made Simple
From *High Country News*

Wetland Creation and Restoration: The Status of the Science
Edited by Mary E. Kentula and Jon A. Kusler

Wildlife and Habitats in Managed Landscapes
Edited by Jon E. Rodiek and Eric G. Bolen

For a complete catalog of Island Press publications, please write:
Island Press, Box 7, Covelo, CA 95428, or call: 1-800-828-1302